THE BUDGET WEDDING SOURCEBOOK

Also by Madeline Barillo:

The Wedding Sourcebook
The Wedding Sourcebook Planner

The Budget Wedding Sourcebook

Madeline Barillo

LOWELL HOUSE

LOS ANGELES

NTC/Contemporary Publishing Group

Library of Congress Cataloging-in-Publication Data

Barillo, Madeline
  The budget wedding sourcebook / Madeline Barillo.
    p. cm.
  Includes index.
  ISBN 0-7373-0307-7
    1. Weddings—Planning. 2. Weddings—Costs. 3. Budgets, Personal. I. Title.

  HQ745 .B365 2000
  395.2'2—dc21

                                      99-088248

Design by Laurie Young

Published by Lowell House
A division of NTC/Contemporary Publishing Group, Inc.
4255 West Touhy Avenue, Lincolnwood, Illinois 60712, U.S.A.

Printed in the United States of America

International Standard Book Number: 0-7373-0307-7

67890 DOC DOC 019876

To Cele Lalli

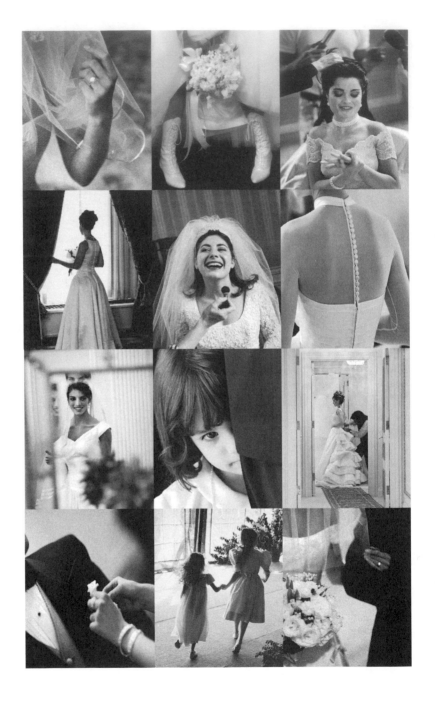

CONTENTS

ACKNOWLEDGMENTS

This book was written with the help of many people who generously shared their expertise—or kept me laughing—while I juggled many jobs and many deadlines. I would like to thank Hudson Perigo; Jama Carter; Dianne Woo; Sue Regan; my father, Joseph Barillo, who was the best research assistant a writer could hope for (he worked for free and never missed a deadline); and my husband, Gregory Flagg. Thanks also to Cele Lalli, Robbi Ernst III, Patricia Bruneau, Packy Boukis, Gerard Monaghan, Lois Pearce, Michelle Hodges, Joyce Scardina Becker, W. Donnie Brown, Charisse Min Alliegro, Lynn Dennis, Anna Marie McElroy, Lisa Michael, Sue Winner, Christine Morrissey, Gabriella Pannunzio, Beverly Ann Bonner, Linda Hiniker, Sherry Richert, Betty Jackson, Karen DeKay, the Reverend Robert Dittler, Fran Casler, Susanne Smith, Amy Connor, Janice Anthony, Ronnie Fein, Christine Hockin, Toni DeLisi, Loretta Stagen, Lisa Maronian, Christopher Semmes, David Bentley, Gunnar Sahlin, Jay Jennings, Ron Maddox, and Rev. Roger Coleman.

PREFACE

Every bride deserves a beautiful wedding, whether she is marrying into royalty or just thinks her fiancé is a prince of a guy. Every bridegroom deserves the best, too.

This book is a gift to you.

It's based on the premise that elegance and affordability need not be mutually exclusive, and that *everyone* can afford the wedding of their dreams if they know the insider secrets that consultants, bridal professionals, and recently married couples already know. Read through the pages and you'll become an expert, too.

The Budget Wedding Sourcebook contains tips and techniques I've learned after more than sixteen years of covering the wedding industry for books, newspapers, and magazines, including *Modern Bride*.

No matter how many books I write, how many lectures I give, or how many courses I teach on "The Perfect Wedding," my dear friend and former college roommate Christiana Figueres always finds it hilarious that I ended up in the wedding business.

Christiana has a great reverence for blushing brides, mind you, and has been one herself, but loves to remind me just how much I hated planning my own 1983 wedding, a formal affair at the U.S. Military Academy at West Point.

"*You* of all people, writing about this stuff!" she squeals whenever we pass a bookstore. "Imagine that!"

Christiana has a good memory. Although I've now had the pleasure of meeting hundreds of engaged couples, I was not an ecstatic bride-to-be. Instead of embracing the moment and finding joy in the journey, I fussed over details and obsessed over silly things like whether the tablecloths would be the right shade of peach or the leaves on the trees would reach their perfect autumn splendor by my October wedding date. (As if I had *any* control over the trees.) Worst of all, I worried more about what other people would think than what my fiancé and I wanted. I must have made my mother miserable.

It wasn't until I became a journalist and got my first assignment covering weddings that I realized what a rare and special time planning a wedding can be. It's a wonderful opportunity for evaluating your life's goals and how you and your future spouse will reach them together. It can be a time for romance, for quiet reflection, and for savoring love and commitment. Sadly, I had missed that point before.

My introduction to the wedding industry came while working as an editorial assistant and obituary writer for a city newspaper. I wrote obituaries from morning till night, then verified them over the phone with distraught relatives. It was not a satisfying job. One day a sympathetic editor offered me a wedding story, and I pounced on it. (Interviewing engaged couples *had* to be better than talking to grief-stricken family members.) The experience was wonderful. I never cease to be inspired by brides and bridegrooms-to-be whose joy is literally infectious. There's a saying that "everybody loves lovers." It must be because they never fail to lift the spirits of everyone around them.

Later, when I did some graduate work in marriage and family therapy, my regard for couples deepened. I learned to appreciate how fragile—and precious—relationships are and how important it is to love and be loved.

Over the years, I have written about every phase of wedding planning—from buying the rings to booking the honeymoon—and also have covered stories on business, education, dance, cooking, party planning, and consumer/legal issues. When you think about it, planning a wedding really involves *all* these things.

The idea for this book came in response to the many couples who called or wrote to me asking for help planning a beautiful wedding on a budget. Either they didn't have a fortune to spend or they simply didn't want to do so.

After reading the many tips and clever ideas contributed by consultants, couples, and wedding guests, sprinkled throughout this book, give consideration to those you would feel comfortable using. You'll laugh all the way to the bank after learning how to buy a designer gown for a song, or when to shift the reception time by a couple of hours in order to slice the bill in half. Granted, you may draw the line at renting limousines from a funeral parlor, as one expert suggested (no kidding!), but among the hundreds of cost-cutting ideas are surefire ways to save from 10 to 70 percent in every single wedding category.

Use this book to plan a personal, beautiful celebration. Congratulations! May you have the wedding of your dreams.

INTRODUCTION

So you're getting married. Congratulations!

You've found a lifetime partner, and suddenly the whole world looks different and your life is moving in a new direction. Now that you are half of a happy couple, it's no longer me and you—it's wedding plans for two.

For many couples, being engaged is one of the most euphoric times in their lives. From the marriage proposal to the first telephone call to your parents announcing the wonderful news, this is a beautiful time that you will remember your whole lives. Suddenly the littlest things—like picnics on paper plates or moonlight walks to the corner store—make life seem marvelous, if not magical. Love songs seem more mushy and sentimental, as if they were written for just you two. Go ahead, savor it.

Yet somewhere along the way, don't be surprised if the wedding journey takes a bumpy detour. A temporary detour, but a bumpy one nonetheless. Somewhere between engaged euphoria and married bliss, couples experience the "sticker shock" of wedding planning. It's a hit that rattles them to the bone.

The bewildered couple add up what it will cost to create a ceremony bower of flowers, dress the bride in a designer gown, toast their happiness with imported champagne, and fly off into the sunset on a Hawaiian honeymoon. On average, the tab is anywhere from $20,000 to $25,000 or much, much more.

First, they faint. Then, they cry.

"There goes our retirement account!" they lament. "I could sell my condo, you could sell your car." "We could try to win the lottery." "We could invite *no* guests!" They realize a wedding could easily cost them as much as a new sports car or a down payment on a house. It's an enormous sum for an event that will last only one day. And since the tradition of the bride's parents paying for the wedding has become an outmoded custom, most couples today are paying for all or part of their weddings themselves.

Relax.

Before you start rehearsing ways to ask your rich uncle for a loan, think about what professional planners have known all along: Beautiful weddings happen on any budget. It doesn't matter if that budget is mere pocket change or a king's ransom. Beautiful weddings are the result of careful planning and creative choices.

This book is all about how to have it all, without spending it all.

Forget about sacrificing or clipping coupons or feeling deprived. It's easier than you think to have a lavish wedding on a limited budget. It's not *how much* you have to spend, it's *how* you spend it that makes the difference between a wedding that leaves you feeling cheated and the wedding of your dreams.

Surprised? Don't be. Elegance doesn't have a price tag. (Take the basic black dress. It's a timeless classic. Any woman can afford one.) Think of the most memorable weddings you've attended. It's a sure bet that money didn't make or break the celebration; it was the fabulous food served or the fact that guests laughed and danced till dawn. A ceremony can be utterly romantic whether the bride wears a $6,000 gown, an heirloom hand-me-down, or a simple, elegant suit.

With a little creativity and thoughtful planning, it's easy to create unforgettable ambiance and elegance without breaking the bank. The secret is to focus on the elements that matter the most to you, and learning to make easy choices and painless substitutions that don't feel like sacrifices.

"You have to prioritize. Determine what elements are the most important to you, and when you know what they are, you can allocate your funds accordingly," says Cele Lalli, former editor in chief of *Modern Bride* magazine. "You can easily economize and still have a beautiful event! There are so many options. You don't need to cut back. Just cut some things out, and you can still have *everything*."

Over the years, I've written about marriage and wedding planning for *Modern Bride*, event-planning magazines, and the *Advocate* and *Greenwich Time* newspapers in Connecticut. I've met and interviewed hundreds of couples whose resourcefulness was inspiring. Some had very little to spend on their celebrations, but their satisfied guests never would have known it. Others had virtually unlimited resources but chose *not* to spend them on a wedding.

Jody and Scott hired one caterer to prepare the rehearsal dinner, wedding buffet, and postwedding brunch—and got a whopping discount on all three. Another groom, also named Scott, and his wife, Colleen, saved hundreds of dollars on flowers for the bride and bridesmaids just by choosing loose-arm bouquets instead of tightly wrapped clusters. Despite booking their reception on one of the most expensive dates of the year—New Year's Eve—they still brought it in under budget by doing clever things like using top hats as centerpieces and ordering wholesale favors by mail. Tomiko and Jason did away with expensive limousines and flower arrangements by having the ceremony and reception at an all-inclusive hotel site.

Some enterprising couples go to extremes. An article in *Family Circle* magazine featured a bride and groom who did a bit of creative underwriting. In exchange for publicity and promotion before and during the wedding, they got free services from more than twenty wedding "sponsors." A list of sponsors was included in the calligraphic invitation, and guests took home T-shirts with the sponsors' names listed on the back.

But you don't need to rent out ad space on your wedding veil to find easy ways to economize. It's important to realize early in the planning that all couples are on a budget of some sort. Few people have the dollars to match their dreams, and the wedding industry is, after all, built on dream making. Bridal magazines appeal to every wedding fantasy imaginable. Those colorful layouts are meant to inspire couples—and sell pricey products and services, from wedding gowns and "bridal" hosiery to place settings and tiered cakes. These publications are invaluable resources, but it's easy to get carried away by the "wedding princess for a day" fantasy and to long for more than you can reasonably afford.

Unfortunately, engaged couples are prone to making emotional purchases when planning a wedding. They get carried away by the thought of once-in-a-lifetime indulgences and are vulnerable to vendors who gush, "It's your *wedding*, dear, of course you deserve the fancier gown!" Although most service providers are ethical and not out to fleece you, many see dollar signs flashing when a bride and groom approach.

Most couples have no idea what their wedding will actually cost, notes Robbi Ernst III, a nationally renowned wedding expert and author whom *The Wall Street Journal* has named the Cecil B.

DeMille of weddings. Many of the planning articles in books and magazines don't accurately reveal "average" costs because prices vary so much nationwide, Ernst notes. For example, a wedding in the urban Northeast may cost three times as much as a comparable wedding in the rural Midwest.

"The first real difficulty with quotes that are given in magazines is that the magazines really do not want the unpleasant picture of reality," Ernst says. "Magazines still think in terms of fantasy and don't want to destroy a bride's dream. But as a wedding consultant, I have to deal with reality. And the reality is that a wedding actually costs twice the amount that the bride originally thinks it will cost."

With that in mind, you have the power to make informed choices.

This book is designed to make the planning process easier and less costly. It's full of techniques contributed by engaged couples, newlyweds, wedding consultants, and industry professionals. You'll learn commonsense tricks such as shifting the wedding date or time to save a fortune. You'll learn the difference between being cost conscious and being cheap or chintzy. Anyone can have a $1.98 wedding, but do you really want to have one?

The whole point of budget wedding planning is to become your own consumer advocate and research prices and options. You'll learn when to scrimp and when to splurge. By doing so, you'll learn to get the maximum value and quality for your money, and pocket the savings or put it into another category. ("Mary, we saved so much on the catering that we can take that trip to Fiji!")

Use this book to fine-tune your priorities. And may every day of marriage be as wonderful as your wedding day.

CHAPTER ONE

PRIORITIES AND EXPECTATIONS

C hances are you've been thinking about your wedding for a
long, long time. Without realizing it, most women have been
planning their weddings for years—long before they've even met
their fiancés, and sometimes even since childhood. So many popular fairy tales end with fairy-tale weddings, it's no surprise that
women often long for a bit of fantasy and pageantry in their own
weddings someday. Glossy wedding magazines are modern-day
wish books that perpetuate the idea of a magical wedding, perfect
in every way.

We've all been guests at weddings. Fabulous, fun weddings
and downright boring ones. Ultraextravagant blowouts and chic,
simple affairs. We've all gone home saying, "That was an unforgettable reception!" or "When I get married, I want a romantic
ceremony just like that." Or even, "I'll be sure to hire a better
orchestra than Sally and James did. It was awful!"

Whether your parents have mentioned it or not, they definitely have an idea of what they envision for your wedding. It probably began with wishful thinking when you were born ("Maybe she'll wear her mother's wedding dress, and I'll walk her down the aisle.") We are all part of a social fabric, and we all take comfort in social rituals. Weddings are both family traditions and community affairs. They connect us to the people who love us, and they celebrate a rite of passage.

Making comparisons and giving careful consideration to what you really want and don't want is OK. As a matter of fact, it's a great way to get started in wedding planning. It's sometimes easier to determine what you want by ruling out what you *don't* want. ("No assigned seating! We want people to sit wherever they choose.")

By determining what elements matter the most to you, you'll be able to make trade-offs that don't feel like sacrifices. This, in turn, makes it a breeze to plan a beautiful wedding on any budget. When a couple have a clear idea of what they really want, it's easier to focus their financial resources on those elements.

IDENTIFYING YOUR PRIORITIES

What means the most to you in a wedding? Is it a drop-dead-gorgeous gown, a reception in a romantic inn, or a veritable jungle of breathtaking flowers? For some couples, it's live music that keeps guests dancing till dawn. For others, it's a gourmet meal that would impress Martha Stewart. Some couples find it useful to begin by writing down their ideas of the "perfect wedding" and reading them aloud to each other.

If you don't know exactly what you have in mind, think about the look or style of the celebration you are going after. Formal? Chic? Understated elegance? Country? Romantic? Themed?

Casual? Family oriented? Sophisticated? Trendy? Look through wedding magazines for inspiration. Maybe you can't spend three million on a reception (or don't want to), but you can strive to achieve a certain "look" or "feel" at the event.

What Do We Want and What Can We Live Without?

Ponder this fundamental question: What are the three elements of my wedding that will mean the most to me? Think of the three essentials you can't bear to live without—things that are so important or meaningful to you, you aren't willing to compromise or scrimp on them.

My three highest priorities are:

1. _____
2. _____
3. _____

My three lowest priorities are:

1. _____
2. _____
3. _____

CLARIFYING YOUR EXPECTATIONS

If you're having difficulty isolating the basic three priorities, try this expectations exercise:

Spend some quiet time with your fiancé talking about your ideas of the perfect wedding. Ask each other, "What are weddings in *your* family like?" "Who is invited?" "What do they wear?" "What family traditions are important?"

It may be helpful for each of you to fill out the worksheet on page 5. Do it without any distractions, and don't think about what your parents or relatives would want. This is *your* wish list. Then, compare what you both have written.

You may find that your future spouse envisions a ballroom full of guests, while you assumed the guest list wouldn't top three dozen. Or, that while your family expects a five-course catered meal at a swanky reception site, his family expects a homespun reception on their back porch complete with a potluck dinner.

Couples are often surprised by how stressful wedding planning can be. Their respective families can have vastly different

ideas of what a wedding "should be." If this happens, avoid battling over which family's traditions are "better" or "right." Instead, start from scratch and decide what your *own* traditions will be as a couple: "Mom, this is how Jim and I want to do it. Our wedding will be different from yours and from his parents, but it will still be wonderful."

One of the biggest misconceptions about budget wedding planning is that couples think they are "taking advantage" of kind friends and relatives who are eager to contribute their time, talents, or financial resources. Don't feel guilty! Say "Yes, thanks!"

Planning a wedding is a joyful, infectious experience. You'd be surprised how many people truly want to help and relish getting involved.

1. What kind of wedding would make me happy? Check off all those that apply.

   ❑ Ultraformal
   ❑ Formal
   ❑ Semiformal
   ❑ Casual
   ❑ Military
   ❑ Themed
   ❑ Unusual site
   ❑ Double wedding
   ❑ Ceremony and reception at same site
   ❑ Outdoor wedding
   ❑ Other _____

   ❑ Daytime
   ❑ Evening
   ❑ Special ceremony
   ❑ Intimate
   ❑ Destination wedding
   ❑ Site with a spectacular view or special features
   ❑ Historical site
   ❑ Wedding at sea
   ❑ No children invited
   ❑ Lots of children

2. What do I *most* want other people to remember about our wedding?

   ❑ Menu
   ❑ Theme
   ❑ Setting/location
   ❑ Music/entertainment
   ❑ Favors

   ❑ Wedding cake
   ❑ Flowers/decorations
   ❑ Ceremony
   ❑ Reception
   ❑ Bride's gown or veil

   ❑ Special touches (arriving by horse and carriage or exchanging vows underwater, etc.) _____
   ❑ Other _____

3. How many guests should we include? What percentage will be bride's family? Bride's friends? Groom's family? Groom's friends?

continued on next page

4. How much we can afford to spend overall?

5. What kind of ceremony do I really want?

   ❏ Religious
   ❏ Write our own vows
   ❏ Ceremony held at reception site
   ❏ Ceremony held away from a house of worship
   ❏ Civil
   ❏ Outdoors
   ❏ Interfaith ceremony
   ❏ Candlelight
   ❏ High Mass
   ❏ Ceremony to include our children from a former marriage, or special honored guests

6. What special elements mean the most to me? What am I willing to splurge on?

7. What am I willing to cut corners on?

8. What kind of financial assistance can I reasonably expect from parents or others? From bride's parents? From groom's parents? Others (grandparents, etc.)? Be sure to clarify how and when this help will be provided:

   "Grandma, we are grateful you have offered to pay for the honeymoon! We've opened up a checking account to handle wedding expenses. Shall I deposit your check now so we can book the trip in advance?"

9. What other kinds of help or services have been volunteered from friends or loved ones?

   ❏ Baking the wedding cake
   ❏ Sewing the gown

- ❏ Addressing invitations
- ❏ Lending gown/veil/crinoline slip
- ❏ Flowers
- ❏ Calligraphy
- ❏ Lending transportation
- ❏ Lending honeymoon accommodations or luggage (condo, etc.)
- ❏ Lending utensils, linens, glassware, china, or other
- ❏ Contributing the reception site (private home, use of country club)
- ❏ Driving wedding party to church
- ❏ Making party favors
- ❏ Providing accommodations for out-of-town guests
- ❏ Making pickups or deliveries
- ❏ Researching the Internet or making phone calls for you
- ❏ Handing out wedding programs
- ❏ Catering the reception
- ❏ Creating centerpieces or decorations
- ❏ Providing entertainment
- ❏ Helping with an at-home wedding
- ❏ Other _____

10. Do I know anyone who has recently gotten married and can offer practical advice?

11. Whose wedding have I attended that most closely matches the one I envision for ourselves? What was special about it?

12. In our families, what do weddings usually entail? (Is there always a sit-down meal? Are there any special ethnic traditions? Are children included? Is the ceremony always a religious one? Are certain foods served? Are special rituals performed?)

continued on next page

THE WEDDING EXPECTATIONS WORKSHEET *CONTINUED*

---

13. For the bride: *My idea of the perfect wedding is . . .*

14. For the groom: *My idea of the perfect wedding is . . .*

15. How do these answers correspond to what others want and expect from us?

16. What possible conflicts may arise?

17. How would we deal with them?

THE WEDDING PLANNING CALENDAR

Planning a wedding is like planning a corporate takeover, only much more romantic and fun. There are endless details to consider, finances to arrange, jobs to delegate, strategic choices to make. The average engagement lasts more than thirteen months, which is comforting, considering just how long everything seems to take. Now that you've found a partner for life, it can be daunting to plan the party of a lifetime.

A wedding can be planned in a day, a week, or a decade. You don't need more than a year, although it helps, since many of the in-demand photographers and caterers and the most popular ceremony and reception sites are booked that far in advance.

Ignore all those stories of frazzled, exhausted brides or brides who lose sleep worrying their gowns weren't ordered early enough.

A wedding can be planned in any amount of time. Many couples, either by choice or by chance, don't have the luxury of a long lead time and still pull off elegant, unforgettable receptions. Remember that any product or service can be ordered in a rush—for an extra charge.

After you've made the happy announcement to both sets of parents, you should decide what type of wedding you both want. The style and level of formality dictate all the subsequent choices, including the time of the ceremony and what the bride should wear (for example, a chic suit for a civil ceremony, a long gown and train for an ultraformal affair).

Begin by concentrating your energy on the five fundamentals:

1. Calculate a realistic budget.
2. Book a date at a reception site. Once this is done, everything else falls into place.
3. Arrange for a ceremony site, date, and time that's compatible with the reception date and time.
4. Select a wedding gown and arrange for it to be delivered and altered on time.
5. Book a photographer and/or videographer. Once it's all over, the pictures or video are the only lasting record you'll have.

The good news is that wedding planning involves a flurry of concentrated activity in the early stages, followed by months of nothing to do, followed by intense activity in the final weeks before the wedding.

Some couples begin by buying a calendar and marking off important dates and deadlines right up to the wedding day. As each task is done, cross it off on the calendar. Or use the following calendar as a guideline. Your tastes and personal preferences will dictate how you allocate your time.

Twelve to Eighteen Months Before

- Select engagement ring.
- Place engagement announcement in your local newspaper.
- Have engagement photograph taken.
- Discuss wedding style, level of formality, time of day, and size of wedding with fiancé.
- Discuss with fiancé the possibility of hiring an event planner or wedding consultant.
- Meet with clergy. Reserve church or ceremony site.
- Have a meeting with fiancé and both sets of parents to openly discuss wedding expectations, costs, and responsibilities.
- Book a reception site. Find out if catering, cake, entertainment, flowers, linens, or other services are included and whether ceremony can be performed on site (if desired).
- Interview florists, photographers, videographers, musicians, caterers, and other wedding professionals. Discuss deposits and cancellation clauses. Book their services.
- Invite attendants to be in your wedding.

Nine Months Before

- Shop for wedding dress, headpiece, veil, and accessories.
- Order wedding gown and accessories.
- Register for china, linens, crystal, or other items.
- Discuss honeymoon plans and make reservations. If traveling abroad, research whether you'll need a passport, inoculations, and/or a visa. If marrying abroad, contact that country's consulate office here in the United States. Find out what the legal requirements are and what kinds of documents, waiting periods, and residency requirements are necessary.

- Meet with bridesmaids to select their attire.
- Begin to record gifts as you receive them, noting when they were received.
- Ask both families to compile preliminary guest lists, including relationship (friend, uncle, etc.), current addresses, and phone/fax numbers.

Six Months Before

- Choose and order attire for the groom and the male attendants.
- Draw up final guest list. Write each name, address, and response on a chart.
- Book site for the rehearsal dinner.
- Order bridesmaids' gowns and accessories.
- Have both mothers select their dresses. The bride's mother traditionally chooses her ensemble first. Next, the groom's mother chooses a dress similar in formality and in a complementary color.
- If desired, hire a calligrapher or arrange for computerized calligraphic services. If envelopes are available, save time by addressing them before the invitations arrive.

Four Months Before

- Select and order invitations.
- Order personal stationery for writing letters and thank-you notes.
- Reserve rooms at a hotel for out-of-town guests. Ask about discounts for wedding groups.
- Confirm that attire for bride, groom, attendants, and parents has been ordered. Confirm delivery dates. Keep the contracts on file!

- Shop for trousseau and clothing for prewedding parties.
- Order wedding rings.
- Plan rehearsal dinner menu and guest list.
- Make "tasting" session appointments with caterer and baker to sample wedding menu and wedding cake.
- Select ceremony liturgy and music.

Two Months Before

- Check requirements for medical tests and marriage license.
- Mail invitations at least four to eight weeks before wedding date.
- Plan luncheon or special party for bridesmaids.
- Choose gifts for attendants and future spouse.
- Make appointment for bridal portrait to be taken. The session should take place two to four weeks before wedding.
- Pick up wedding rings and check engraving.
- Meet with musicians or disc jockey to discuss playlist for reception.
- Meet with photographer to discuss the ratio of candid to posed shots you want included in keepsake album and any specific photographs you want taken at reception and ceremony.
- Bring fabric swatches to florist and finalize details for all flowers.
- Call bridal shop to determine when gown will arrive. Make appointment for final fitting.
- Make ceremony rehearsal arrangements.
- Arrange for wedding day transportation for important guests and bridal party.

✢ Make sure all official and civil documents are in order: baptismal, communion, and confirmation certificates, citizenship papers, proof of divorce, etc.

✢ Order party favors to give to guests.

One Month Before

✢ Make appointment with hair and makeup stylists for bride and wedding party.

✢ Have final fitting for wedding gown.

✢ Have formal bridal portrait taken.

✢ If taking your husband's name, make arrangements to change your name on Social Security card, driver's license, car registration and insurance, bank accounts, credit cards, insurance policies, school and office records, passport, voter registration, etc.

✢ Draft a new will and change insurance beneficiary, if desired.

✢ Consult lawyer about prenuptial agreement, if desired.

✢ Fill out a change of address form from the post office.

Two Weeks Before

✢ Go with fiancé to pick up marriage license.

✢ Address formal announcements so they can be mailed on the wedding day.

✢ Prepare seating chart for reception and rehearsal dinner.

✢ Make wedding day flowchart of events, hour by hour, to give to bridal party and all key vendors: caterer, florist, photographer, officiant, disc jockey.

✢ Give caterer finalized guest count.

❖ Confirm honeymoon reservations and buy traveler's checks, if desired.

❖ Break in those wedding shoes! Wrap them in plastic or plastic bags and walk around the house in them.

One Week Before

❖ Pack for honeymoon. Be sure to include money, camera, passport, clothes, comfortable shoes, and necessary medications.

❖ Give ushers instructions for seating guests, details about guests with special needs, and maps and/or programs to hand out.

❖ Arrange for your and your fiancé's transportation from reception to airport or train, hotel, etc.

❖ Remind groom and groomsmen to pick up rental attire.

❖ Double-check that rental attire has all the right pieces in the right sizes.

❖ Wrap gifts for attendants; present gifts at rehearsal dinner.

❖ Arrange for someone to collect gifts brought to reception and deliver them to your home.

❖ Confirm that your airplane or train tickets are ticketed with correct date, time, destination, etc.

❖ Give best man a check for officiant's fee to be delivered right after the ceremony.

❖ Arrange for transportation from the airport after the honeymoon.

❖ Confirm vocalist and organist.

❖ Arrange for backup transportation for you and your fiancé to church, just in case.

One Day Before

- ✤ Attend rehearsal and rehearsal dinner. Set a specific time for everyone in wedding party to meet on wedding day. Don't overindulge in alcoholic drinks or caffeine.
- ✤ Determine where and when everyone will meet for wedding day photos.
- ✤ Place honeymoon luggage in car.
- ✤ Lay out all clothes, jewelry, and accessories for the next day.
- ✤ Be sure wedding gown is stored away from heat, pets, water, young children, or an open window.
- ✤ Discuss reception-line procedure with parents and bridal party.
- ✤ If not using a professional consultant, assign someone else to run interference for you on the wedding day. That way the caterer, photographer, florist, and others know who to go to with questions.
- ✤ Get to bed early!

CHAPTER TWO

THE BUDGET BLUEPRINT

Discussing the wedding budget is about as much fun as watching nail polish dry, but it's absolutely necessary if a couple is to have a beautiful celebration without going crazy or going into debt. Besides, it's good practice for the day-to-day budgeting and long-term financial planning ahead in your new life together. Marriage is an emotional and physical partnership, but let's face it; it's a financial union, too. Even if a bride and groom choose to keep separate Swiss bank accounts, they are still fiscally entwined. Learning how to compromise and negotiate with each other over the wedding finances is invaluable experience for the future.

It's important to realize that every couple has a budget of some sort—whether it's $500 or $150,000. Even if you can afford to charter a plane to pick up Hawaiian orchids at the base of a volcano, you still need to plan for and allocate certain amounts to certain expenditures. It actually makes the whole process easier.

If you don't have as much to spend on your wedding as you'd like, don't despair. The endless hype and hoopla in wedding magazines exist to promote every bridal product imaginable. Don't be overwhelmed by those celebrity wedding television specials in which supermodels tie the knot in $10,000 gowns and honeymoon on private tropical islands to the tune of $5,000 a day.

You may not be able to spend three weeks at a premier hotel on Bali, but you may be able to spend a few *days* of unadulterated luxury there. You may not be able to pay full price for a famous designer gown, but if you time it right, you could snap one up at a 70 percent discount during the designer's annual sample sale. Call the bridal salon and ask when the next one is scheduled.

Remember, it isn't how *much* you have to spend that makes your wedding meaningful and memorable, it's how effectively you spend what you have. There are many clever and often overlooked ways to save significantly without losing any of the romance and glamour.

WILL OUR DOLLARS MATCH OUR DREAMS?

The first roadblock many couples face is in the early planning stages: How could they possibly know how much to spend on favors or an eight-piece band if they've never planned a wedding before? The second is realizing just how much it all costs—and how much it varies from one region of the country to another.

I've heard every figure from $17,000 to $39,000 for a wedding with 200 guests, fancy sit-down dinner, formal gown, and bridal party with five ushers and five bridesmaids. That's an enormous range in price, but no matter how you slice it, it's a lot of money. According to *Bride's* magazine, wedding costs have steadily inched up since 1990. The magazine's media kit notes that the average cost of a wedding (with 200 guests and 10 attendants) varies significantly by geographical region:

$29,454	New York Metro region (Connecticut, New York, New Jersey)
$18,918	West Coast (California, Arizona, Nevada)
$16,195	Midwest (Illinois, Wisconsin, Indiana, Michigan)

AVERAGE COSTS AND PERCENTAGES

What's reasonable for flowers? How much should I spend on a wedding cake?

These are difficult questions to answer if you've never planned a wedding before. Listed below are general ranges for a formal wedding with all the trimmings, for 125 to 175 guests, with a total budget of $20,000 to $25,000.

Remember, costs will vary dramatically depending on geography and what your priorities are. While one bride may be content with inexpensive daisies, another may feel positively deprived without costly orchids. That means the floral budget could swell by literally thousands of dollars. Use the figures below as a road map, but realize your priorities may take you in other directions.

Catering and reception	$7,000–$13,000 (national average: $7,800)
Flowers	$800–$3,500 (national average: $800)
Music	$800–$3,000 (national average: $900)
Photography	$1,300–$4,500 (national average: $1,300)
Videography	$400–$1,200 (national average: $500)

19

Wedding gown	$200–$5,000 (national average: $900)
Headpiece/veil	$125–$350 (national average: $160)
Mother-of-the-bride attire	$155–$350 (national average: $230)
Wedding cake	$180–$1,500, or $1–$15 slice
Invitations	$300–$500, or $1–$10 each
Bridesmaids' attire	$150–$325 per attendant (includes accessories and shoes)
Formalwear rental	$75–$150 per attendant
Engagement ring	Two months' salary (national average: $3,000)
Officiant/ house-of-worship fee	$200–$300 (national average: $240)
Limousine	$350–$450 (national average: $390)

Note: These figures are guidelines compiled by the author after evaluating many wedding statistics and ranges suggested by consultants and industry professionals.

According to the June Wedding Inc.® Association for Event Professionals' *Wedding Consultant Training Manual*, sixth edition, couples spend a little more than half of their budgets on the catering and reception (50 to 54 percent) and an additional 10 percent each on flowers and photography. Music runs anywhere from 6 to 10 percent of the budget, and a wedding consultant costs about 15 to 20 percent. The remaining money is spent on invitations, officiant fee, wedding attire, and other miscellaneous vendor expenses.

From these percentages, it's easy to see just how substantial a chunk the catering and reception costs take.

Write It Down

The only way to get a handle on expenses is to record them. Use the worksheet in this chapter to compare prices and services and to keep track of estimated versus actual expenditures. Not all of the expenses listed here are essential; some are downright frivolous. How you choose to divvy up a budget has a lot to do with your priorities and expectations—and what will make you happy as a couple.

Creative thinking doesn't hurt. Don't buy services if you can borrow or barter them. Think of easy substitutions that save money but don't feel like sacrifices. Make a list of every friend or relative who has something to donate or lend, be it a vacation condo, luggage for the honeymoon, a wedding veil, or cases of champagne for the reception.

Wherever time or talent permits, do it yourself. When I got married, I didn't care if the dinner menu was prepared by a master chef, I just wanted to wear a gown made with stunning fabric. When the silk satin gown I found was $300 more than I'd planned to spend, I couldn't bear to pass it up. I economized by making my own wedding veil (a savings of $140) and trimming the fresh fruit cup from the menu (a savings of $200). For the veil, I called the dress designer in New York and asked if I could purchase six of the white silk flowers that decorated the gown's waist and shoulders. A few days later, I received the loose flowers ($12) in the mail and purchased a few yards of white tulle, some white ribbon, and a handful of seed pearls at a craft store ($11). I wrapped a wire hairband with the ribbon and sewed the flowers and pearls across the top. Then I gathered the tulle and attached it to the underside of the band. It was a quick project—no talent required—and the tab was a mere $30.

TOTAL WEDDING BUDGET: $_____

PRODUCT OR SERVICE	ESTIMATED EXPENSE	ACTUAL EXPENSE
CEREMONY		
Officiant's fee		
Site fee		
Marriage license		
Vocalist/organist fee		
Guest book		
Wedding programs		
Tent and/or outdoor flooring		
Maps/directions		
Chair rental		
Ceremony music		
CD or tape		
musicians		
Accessories		
aisle runner		
chalice		
chuppah		
candelabra		
banners		
pew decorations		
rice		
rose petals		
butterflies		
bubbles		

PRODUCT OR SERVICE	ESTIMATED EXPENSE	ACTUAL EXPENSE
FLOWERS AND DECORATIONS		
Bridal bouquet		
Bridesmaids' bouquets		
Boutonnieres		
groom		
fathers		
ushers		
ring bearer		
Flower girl bouquet or basket		
Corsages for mothers and honored guests		
Floral hair decorations		
Altar flowers		
Pew decorations		
Flower petals to scatter or throw		
Flowers for:		
chandeliers		
archways		
doorways		
staircases		
balconies		
church door		
Chuppah flowers		
Reception flowers/ decorations		
flowers to decorate music stands		
restroom floral arrangements		

continued on next page

PRODUCT OR SERVICE	ESTIMATED EXPENSE	ACTUAL EXPENSE
FLOWERS AND DECORATIONS CONTINUED		
head-table flowers		
guest-table centerpieces		
flowers to decorate bride's and groom's chairs		
flowers for wedding cake		
Other decorations:		
candles		
mirrors		
topiaries		
lighting		
balloons		
tulle		
fabrics		
trellis		
unity candle		
family medallion		
RECEPTION/ CATERING FEES		
Catering—guest meals		
$ per person to include:		
Additional hors d'oeuvres		
$ per piece or dozen:		

PRODUCT OR SERVICE	ESTIMATED EXPENSE	ACTUAL EXPENSE
RECEPTION/		
CATERING FEES *CONTINUED*		
Meals for:		
musicians		
photographer		
wedding consultant		
videographer		
other		
Ice sculptures		
Wedding cake		
Dessert		
Sweets table		
Cake-cutting fee		
Cake knife fee		
Beverages		
champagne		
wine		
beer		
liquor		
soft drinks		
after-dinner liqueurs		
mixers		
ice		
bottled waters		
specialty drinks		
cappuccino bar		
Bartending fees		
Corkage/pouring fees		
Additional food stations		
Table linens and napkins		

continued on next page

25

PRODUCT OR SERVICE	ESTIMATED EXPENSE	ACTUAL EXPENSE
RECEPTION/ CATERING FEES *CONTINUED*		
Rental items		
chairs		
guest tables		
banquet tables		
cake table		
lighting		
plants and trees		
chafing dishes		
serving pieces		
flatware		
crystal/glasses		
centerpieces/vases		
decorative mirrors		
tent		
flooring		
fountains		
dance floor		
heaters/ air conditioning		
grills or portable cooking stations		
Music		
Parking		
Serving staff		
Site rental fee		
Overtime fees		
Setup fees		
Cleanup (breakdown) fees		
Taxes		

PRODUCT OR SERVICE	ESTIMATED EXPENSE	ACTUAL EXPENSE
RECEPTION/		
CATERING FEES *CONTINUED*		
Service charges		
Gratuities		
Party favors		
Champagne for toast		
Accessories		
printed napkins		
candles		
matchbooks		
place cards		
candies		
guest book		
decorated pen		
wedding program		
ring bearer pillow		
ATTIRE		
Bride's attire		
gown		
headpiece/veil		
shoes		
hose		
jewelry		
undergarments		
Makeup session		
Hair session		
Manicure/pedicure		
Parents' attire		
mother		
father		

continued on next page

PRODUCT OR SERVICE	ESTIMATED EXPENSE	ACTUAL EXPENSE
ATTIRE *CONTINUED*		
Alterations		
Bride's trousseau		
Groom's formalwear and accessories		
PHOTOGRAPHY AND VIDEOGRAPHY		
Engagement portrait		
Wedding portrait		
Keepsake album		
Extra albums for parents or wedding party members		
Videography		
Personal camera, film, and batteries		
Disposable cameras		
MUSIC		
Reception		
disc jockey		
live band		
quartet or combo		·
taped music		
Ceremony		
vocalist		
organist		
harpist		

PRODUCT OR SERVICE	ESTIMATED EXPENSE	ACTUAL EXPENSE
MUSIC *CONTINUED*		
choir		
taped music		
other		
rehearsal dinner music		
TRANSPORTATION		
Limousine		
Gondola or boat		
Horse and carriage		
Transportation to pick up attendants or out-of-town guests at airport		
Transportation for newlyweds to airport or honeymoon site		
HONEYMOON		
Accommodations		
Meals		
Travel expenses		
Travel or trip cancellation insurance		
Traveler's checks		
Spending money for souvenirs, sundries, etc.		
Luggage		
Transportation to and from airport		

continued on next page

29

PRODUCT OR SERVICE	ESTIMATED EXPENSE	ACTUAL EXPENSE
PREWEDDING PARTIES		
Invitations		
Catering		
Entertainment		
Engagement party		
Showers		
Rehearsal dinner		
Bachelor party		
Bridesmaids' luncheon		
LEGAL FEES		
Estate or tax planning		
Prenuptial agreement		
Will		
RINGS		
Engagement		
Wedding		
INVITATIONS AND STATIONERY		
Wedding invitations		
Place cards		
Wedding announcements		
Personal stationery		
Thank-you notes		
Reception cards		
Response cards		

PRODUCT OR SERVICE	ESTIMATED EXPENSE	ACTUAL EXPENSE
INVITATIONS AND STATIONERY *CONTINUED*		
Postage		
Save-the date cards		
Wedding programs/maps and directions sheets		
Newspaper announcement fee		
"We're Moving" stationery and announcements		
MISCELLANEOUS		
Wedding consultant fee		
Gifts for attendants		
Gifts for future spouse		
Telephone		
Fax fees		
Wedding insurance		
Thank-you gifts to parents and anyone who helped with wedding		
FEES FOR MOVING INTO NEW HOME		
Mortgage or rent		
Moving expenses		
Furniture		
Household linens		
Kitchen items		

Look What We Saved!

Imagine: If you could trim just $100 from fifteen wedding expense categories, you'd save $1,500. If you could save $200 in each, that windfall is doubled! Adopt the penny-saved-is-a-penny-earned mentality and you'll have money left over to put in the bank—or spend on a splurge!

After you've sat down with your fiancé and realistically calculated a budget you are both comfortable with, vow to stay within 10 percent of that figure. As an added incentive, give yourself a reward for saving a certain amount of money or actually having funds left over. Perhaps you could take a romantic vacation or buy dining-room furniture or season opera tickets.

Cutting costs is easier than you think. Buy a gown on sale and save up to $500. Choose a chicken entrée over lobster and truffles and pocket another $400. Or go ahead and serve lobster, but schedule the reception meal as a luncheon rather than a dinner. (The same menu may be less when served during the day, since the site is free to book an evening reception, too.) Borrow a friend's veil or make one yourself and save $100. Cut the after-dinner mints from the catering package and save another $75. These are all painless trade-offs.

As you make your choices, record them in the chart on page 33. Try to save at least something in every category. After the wedding, figure out how you will enjoy spending or saving the difference!

OUR SAVINGS GOAL

TOTAL: $_____

EXPENSE CATEGORY   AMOUNT SAVED

1. Wedding flowers (for example, "By choosing carnations over stargazer lilies, we saved $100 on the centerpieces.") $ _____

2. Photography_____ $ _____

3. Videography_____ $ _____

4. Menu_____ $ _____

5. Music for the ceremony_____ $ _____

6. Music for the reception _____ $ _____

7. Liquor and beverages_____ $ _____

8. Invitations_____ $ _____

9. Wedding gown and veil_____ $ _____

10. Formalwear for groom_____ $ _____

11. Wedding cake _____ $ _____

12. Honeymoon_____ $ _____

13. Transportation_____ $ _____

14. Favors and accessories_____ $ _____

15. Gifts for spouse and wedding party_____ $ _____

CHAPTER THREE

GETTING STARTED AND
GETTING ORGANIZED

Ready, set, save!

O nce you've given careful consideration to what you *really* want for your wedding, how much time you have to plan it all, and how much you can reasonably spend, it's easier to get started— and get organized.

Getting organized is as important as finding the right gown. Service providers love to work with couples who have a game plan and have done their homework because it makes life easier for them. They don't have to second-guess what the bride (or groom) had in mind, and the couple are less apt to agonize or waffle over every decision.

This is nothing to sneeze at. The major complaint of wedding professionals is that couples come to them asking for "something different" or "something gorgeous," yet they haven't figured out *specifically* what they want. While attending an international convention of event professionals, I remember hearing a successful consultant groan about wishy-washy clients who made her job harder. "I'm not psychic," she said. "I'm great at my job, but I'm not a mind reader!"

After vowing to get organized, decide whether you want to plan the wedding yourselves or hire a professional wedding consultant or event planner. A consultant can help plan the whole affair, from the engagement party to the honeymoon itinerary, or handle just one part, such as finding a gown restoration expert or helping you choose dependable vendors in your price category. (For more on consultants, turn to chapter 4.)

THE ORGANIZATION GAME PLAN

It's time to begin thinking like a professional event planner, consumer reporter, and military strategist all rolled into one. By doing your own research, checking out sources, weighing options, and making informed choices, you'll get full value for every dollar spent. To spend wisely, it's important to set up a record-keeping file.

Computer Files

Some couples prefer to organize their wedding budget and expenses on a computer, using one of the software programs made for wedding planning or using a file system created on their own. You can keep track of guests, gifts, acceptances, regrets, thank-you notes, addresses, measurements, and hundreds of other details. With the click of a button, you can remove people from the list or print out bridal registry choices. Or you can create spreadsheets and sophisticated charts and address lists quickly and easily.

Notebook Binder Files

Other couples aren't as comfortable using a computer. If you prefer the old hard-copy-and-file-folder way of managing data, that's fine, too. First, buy a three-hole punch and one or two three-ring notebook binders (or an oversized accordion file). Use one binder to organize vendor price lists, brochures, and menus. Insert one of those plastic pages made to hold business cards, and file every card scooped up at bridal shows or while interviewing vendors. Add tab dividers to separate the vendor pages, and keep a few blank pages for notes.

The second binder can be used to keep track of contracts, important dates and appointments, invoices, fabric swatches and ribbon samples, and other categories. Consider using tab dividers to create sections for each of the following categories:

- ❖ Planning calendar
- ❖ Flowers
- ❖ Catering and reception
- ❖ Photography and videography
- ❖ Wedding gown, headpiece, and veil
- ❖ Attire for the attendants and parents
- ❖ Music for reception and ceremony
- ❖ The ceremony
- ❖ The wedding party (names, addresses, measurements, etc.)
- ❖ Contracts and paperwork
- ❖ Important addresses, phone numbers, E-mail addresses, fax numbers, Web site addresses
- ❖ The wedding day schedule
- ❖ Guest list
- ❖ Gifts and thank-you notes
- ❖ Invitations and accessories
- ❖ Bridal registry

- Honeymoon
- Out-of-town guests
- Parties
- Rehearsal dinner
- Gifts for spouse, attendants, and parents
- Moving and planning for your new home
- Legal considerations (prenuptial agreement, name change, insurance, wills, etc.)
- Important delivery and pickup dates
- Payment schedules
- Wedding day seating chart
- Vows and ceremony readings
- Wedding favors

Index Cards

Another way to organize is to keep a box of index cards on hand in a recipe box or shoe box. Record the name of every vendor, wedding party member, and guest on a separate card. Assign a new card to every vendor you interview and use it to record prices, notes, and impressions. On each guest card, record name, address, and gift(s) sent; when thank-you notes were written; whether the guest has accepted or declined; and which table the guest has been assigned to. Use the wedding party cards to record the responsibilities of each usher or bridesmaid, as well as important information about ordering their outfits and accessories.

Once these filing systems are set up, it's easy to tote the binders, disks, or cards around in a briefcase or car and have important information organized and accessible at any time.

The next step to organized planning is to adopt a mind-set that will help you make informed choices driven by value and quality, not just cost. The whole point of budget planning is to get the most for your money and to make creative choices that will leave you feeling satisfied rather than deprived.

THE GOLDEN RULES
OF BUDGET PLANNING

Keep the following golden rules in mind while doing your wedding planning and shopping.

1. Don't shop based on price alone.
2. Guests will remember the food only if it's truly awful or there isn't enough of it.
3. If money is very tight, spend it on the wedding cake and an expert photographer, and cut corners everywhere else. The three wedding essentials are a bride, a groom, and a wedding cake. By hiring an expert photographer, you'll make sure you—and future generations—will have fabulous pictures to treasure long after the wedding is over.
4. Strive to save time, money, or both.

THE GOLDEN RULES
OF BUDGET SHOPPING

■ **NEVER SHOP WHILE YOU ARE RUSHED OR TIRED.** Otherwise, you'll be tempted to spend more than you can afford and risk making choices you might regret.

■ **DON'T SHOP ON PRICE ALONE.** A bargain isn't a bargain if it doesn't offer quality, value, or service. Cheaper isn't always better.

■ **COMPARISON SHOP—AND SHOP THE SALES.** Shopping for wedding services is like shopping for shoes or dresses—you seldom snap up the first item you see. Look for sales. Scout for bargains. Compare prices. Sure, many manufacturers have "suggested" retail prices, but that doesn't mean vendors will sell the same gown for the same price. Prices may vary as much as 70 percent. Look for seasonal sales. After the holidays is a good time to buy favors, invitations, and stationery. Even wedding gowns are seasonal. Ask the bridal salon when the next "season" is arriving and shop the between-season sales. Let's face it, you can find white wedding gowns in long or short sleeves every day of the year.

■ **REALIZE THAT EVERYTHING IS NEGOTIABLE.** This applies even to package deals that are seemingly set in stone. "Negotiate!" advises wedding consultant Charisse Min Alliegro of Princeton Event Consultants in Princeton, New Jersey. "For example, if valet parking and ladies' room attendants are not needed, ask if you can omit them. It never hurts to ask."

■ **DON'T HIRE A VENDOR OR BOOK A SERVICE SIGHT UNSEEN.** Always make an appointment to meet and interview the vendors first. Consultants advise interviewing at least three in each category. It's important to feel comfortable with the people you intend to hire. You don't have to fall in love with them; you just need to have a good, working relationship with them. View their samples. Taste the cake, sample the dinner menu, listen to the band, touch and try on the gown. Visit the florist and check out the flowers in the refrigerated case.

■ **TREAT SERVICE PROVIDERS WITH COURTESY AND FAIRNESS.** By doing so, they are more likely to do the same for you.

■ **DON'T BE AFRAID TO APPROACH VENDORS WAY OUT OF YOUR PRICE RANGE.** The honest approach is best: "I really love and admire your work, but my budget is modest. Could you possibly find a way to work within our price range?" Everyone likes to feel appreciated and valued, and a vendor who senses that you really respect her craft—whether it's cake decorating or floral design—may be willing to meet you halfway.

■ **DON'T SHOP FOR A WEDDING GOWN ON SATURDAY.** That's when every bride in the world shows up. You won't get the undivided attention of the sales staff.

■ **THINK OF YOURSELF AS A CONSUMER REPORTER.** Analyze every deal for value. Ask friends and recently married couples for advice and referrals. Before hiring a service provider, contact the local Better Business Bureau to see if any complaints have been lodged against that provider. Many state or city department of consumer affairs offices offer free publications on wedding planning and other consumer issues such as shopping by mail or avoiding fraud.

■ **USE THE INTERNET.** You can save yourself a lot of legwork by doing your research on the Internet. It's a great time-saver and an unbelievable source of immediate information. Plus, you can research limo prices or view photos of floral arrangements at three o'clock in the morning. If you don't have access to a computer, use one at a local library, high school, or community college.

Advises wedding consultant Packy Boukis of Only You in Broadview Heights, Ohio, "You can literally plan your wedding on the computer, from the hotel your guests stay at to unusual sites to have your wedding, like a submarine docked at a museum or a mansion. This cuts the bride's planning time phenomenally!" She says you can view photographs and get phone numbers right away.

■ **TAKE ADVANTAGE OF FREE INFORMATION AND COUPONS.** Go to bridal shows and stop at every vendor booth. It's an efficient way to collect price lists, learn about services, sign up for free raffle drawings, and scoop up certificates and coupons good for discounts or free services. Many bridal shows have a circuslike atmosphere—

demonstrations, tastings, and entertainment sessions are going on simultaneously—but couples who can stand the commotion can accomplish a lot of comparison shopping in a short amount of time. Even if you don't end up hiring any of the merchants you meet, you'll go home with free ideas, a better sense of what's out there, and a shopping bag full of videotapes from bands and disc jockeys. You may even win a free wedding dress or honeymoon.

Flip through the back pages of major wedding magazines and send away for every free brochure and catalog. You can get free mail-order catalogs for invitations and accessories; samples of wedding favors; travel brochures; and samples of napkins, stationery, ribbons, chocolates, seeds, and confetti. Also available are coupons and handy booklets on everything from buying a ring to qualifying for a mortgage, as well as information on purchasing gift certificates. The world is full of free information waiting to land in your mailbox. Ask and you shall receive.

Visit the library and check out travel and etiquette books, cookbooks for menu ideas, and craft books for tips on favors and accessories. It's silly to go out and purchase something like a honeymoon travel guide. Even if you intend to use it again someday, the information on accommodations and prices will be outdated by then.

Pick up free local vendor guides. These are available in most major newspapers several times a year (call the features editor and ask when the next bridal supplement appears). You also can find free guides at photography studios and jewelry stores. Granted, they are mostly advertising pages masquerading as "news" articles, but the information is helpful and will lead you to vendors.

■ **START A FILE OF TOLL-FREE NUMBERS.** Don't be charged for a single telephone call if you don't have to be! Bridal magazines are chock full of toll-free numbers for travel, registry, and wedding gown sources. Or call the national toll-free directory assistance line at 1-800-555-1212.

■ **GET A PRESS KIT FOR RECEPTION AND CATERING SITES.** A press kit, sometimes called a media kit, is the free information packet reporters request when writing a newspaper or magazine article. It includes information on the site, articles written about the facility or its chef, lots of photographs, price lists, itemized package deals, brochures, and testimonials.

■ **NEVER PAY CASH—AND NEVER PAY IN FULL BEFORE YOU HAVE TO.** If the company that sold you a gown or promised you catering suddenly shuts its doors, you may be left in the lurch. I covered the story of a woman who was jilted just weeks before her wedding. It was bad enough her fiancé had left her; the poor woman was mortified to learn that the reception she had fully paid for was absolutely nonrefundable. She had neglected to arrange for a contract with a cancellation provision. Since she had paid in cash, there was no way to withhold payment. The happy ending, though, is that she decided to hold the reception anyway as a party for local homeless people. A disc jockey who read my article about her in the newspaper donated his services, and local social service agencies provided transportation for the guests.

The moral is: Don't pay ahead of schedule, and always use a credit card!

A federal consumer law, Federal Regulation C, protects consumers by allowing them to dispute payments made to merchants who fail to deliver goods or services as promised. The credit card company will withhold full payment until you have made good-faith attempts to successfully resolve the dispute. (There are restrictions. Check with your credit card company.) If you prefer to pay by check, keep the canceled checks as proof of payment.

■ **GET IT IN WRITING.** The jilted bride could have prevented her problems by having a signed contract. Most vendors will ask you to sign a contract. If they don't, insist on getting all services and purchases in writing. You'll want to include the date the contract was signed; a detailed list of specific items and prices; the date(s) these services will be delivered; a list of payments including the initial deposit, how payment was made (check or credit card numbers), and when the balance is due; plus clauses on the cancellation policy (what happens if the wedding is called off or the vendor backs out) and price escalations. (If food prices rise dramatically between the time you signed the catering contract and the date of the wedding, is the original price quote still in effect?) Make sure you and the vendor sign the contract and that someone else signs as a witness.

■ **DON'T SHOP FOR A GOWN (OR ANYTHING ELSE) WITH THE ENTIRE BRIDAL PARTY.** It's too distracting, and everyone will have an opinion. Instead, bring along one or two honest friends whose judgment you value.

■ **EXAMINE EACH CHOICE CRITICALLY AND DON'T BUY ON IMPULSE.** Ask yourself: Can I really afford this? Do I really *need* this? Will guests really remember this? The day after the wedding, will I regret not having done this or bought this? If any of these questions are keeping you up at night, the answer is probably no.

■ **LOOK FOR "PIGGYBACK" DISCOUNTS.** Ask the caterer or reception site manager if they have discount arrangements with other vendors. For example, you may save by using the recommended "house" photographer, band, or florist.

■ **SAVE TIME AND MONEY BY FAXING AND E-MAILING INSTEAD OF MAKING LONG-DISTANCE PHONE CALLS.** Don't even think of calling a hotel in Hawaii to inquire about travel packages when you can do it on-line. Consider faxing and E-mailing whenever possible. While compiling an address and phone list of vendors, ask for their E-mail addresses and fax numbers, too. And check out your long-distance phone company's best rates for calls. If your bridesmaids live in another state and it's cheapest to call them after 8 P.M. or on weekends, call them then. Sure, you may be saving just pennies a call, but it's surprising how often brides need to contact the attendants ("What shoe size are you?" "Do you like pink?"). Calls to five bridesmaids, one matron of honor, a best man, and five ushers quickly add up.

THE TOP 50 SHORTCUTS TO SAVINGS

Couples who have set a budget, clarified their expectations, and determined their priorities are well on the way to becoming savvy, discerning consumers. The next step is to learn the best shortcuts for saving.

This chapter is a crash course in techniques for planning a wedding more quickly and economically, and squeezing value from every purchase. If you are planning a wedding in a hurry (by chance or by choice), commit this chapter to memory. The remaining chapters go into more specific details about the major spending categories.

■ **1. SHOP IN SEASON; AVOID THE EXOTIC.** In general, you'll pay more for anything that's imported, out of season, or in high demand. If the wedding's in December but your heart is set on flowers that bloom only in May, you'll pay top dollar to have them flown in from another part of the world.

■ **2. SHIFT THE DATE OR TIME OF THE WEDDING.** Most brides favor a Saturday night reception, which is the most expensive night of the week to book a reception site, caterer, band, or disc jockey. Consider a midweek, Friday, or Sunday date instead. Schedule the wedding for midmorning or midafternoon, and you may get a steep discount from the caterer, the disc jockey, the photographer, and the videographer. That's because demand is low during the daytime. The reception site manager will be able to schedule a second wedding for the evening and can get a double "turn" on the room. Bands and disc jockeys usually discount their prices for a daytime wedding by up to 40 percent (it means they can work another gig at night), and many reception facilities offer the same menu at lowered prices during the day.

■ **3. TIME IS MONEY.** It's common sense that any wedding product or service that is labor intensive or hand detailed commands a higher price than something requiring less time to produce. A wedding cake with simple piped frosting costs less than a cake with dozens of handmade, sugar-spun flowers or molded chocolate ribbons.

■ **4. LESS IS MORE.** Carry one dramatic, exotic flower tied with a beautiful ribbon instead of an expensive, hand-tied bouquet with many blooms. A gown with many, many yards of fabric costs more than a simple design requiring less yardage.

■ **5. PARE DOWN THE GUEST LIST.** More guests mean more of everything!

■ **6. TRIM THE BRIDAL PARTY.** Sure, they pay for their own attire, but every extra attendant means *two* extra places at both the reception and rehearsal dinner (for their spouses or escorts); the cost of a larger limo; and another hotel room, bouquet or boutonniere, and gift. It adds up.

■ **7. HIRE A WEDDING CONSULTANT.** No matter what the wedding budget, a good consultant has the expertise and knowledge to help you get more service and value for your money and stay within spending limits.

■ **8. AIM HIGH.** Don't be intimidated by pricey vendors. Ask for a discount or their "best possible price," or suggestions for altering the package. If you find a vendor whose work you really admire but can't afford, be sincere and tell her so. She may be flattered enough to work within your budget.

■ **9. AVOID BUYING ANYTHING "BRIDAL."** Accessories like cake knives and ring pillows suddenly cost more when called "bridal." Buy an undecorated knife and wrap a white ribbon around it yourself—you'll save up to $70! A simple white pen for signing the guest book costs $25 in "bridal" collections—or just a couple of dollars at a stationery store.

■ **10. SKIP THE INSERTS AND OVERSIZED INVITATIONS.** Forget about extra response cards, fancy paper liners, vellum covers, or oversized invitations. They cost more and translate into more postage.

■ **11. BUY STANDARD SIZES.** Choose standard-size napkins and tablecloths. Extra-large napkins and linens that drape straight to or "puddle" on the floor mean extra fabric and higher cost.

■ **12. SHORTEN THE RECEPTION.** Trim the reception from five to four hours, and you'll save a bundle. People will hardly notice, and you'll spend less on liquor, entertainment, and wait-staff charges.

■ **13. AVOID MAJOR FLOWER-GIVING HOLIDAYS.** Don't schedule your wedding for the times of year when people send flowers: Valentine's Day, Mother's Day, Christmas, Thanksgiving. Prices tend to be much higher during these times of the year, and you can't be assured of the florist's undivided attention during these busy seasons.

■ **14. ASK ABOUT MARKET BUYS.** Trust your florist? Ask him to find the best values on the market (called the "market buy") the week of your wedding. If you aren't insistent on particular blooms, you can get fabulous flowers at great prices.

■ **15. SKIP THE FOOD STATIONS.** Food stations are novel and provide an entertainment factor but heavily pad the tab. Depending on the type of food (seafood and caviar stations are the most expensive) and number of servers required, you may be charged an extra $8 to $25 per person on top of the basic per person fee.

■ **16. HOLD THE LIQUOR.** Make your reception liquor free. Yes, it's perfectly acceptable!

■ **17. SERVE THE HOUSE WINES OR LIQUORS.** The house brand is the wine or liquor served when you don't specify a particular premium brand. A catering establishment buys its house brands in large quantity, so they're invariably cheaper than a premium brand.

■ **18. SUPPLY YOUR OWN LIQUOR.** Ask if you can bring your own liquor. If so, buy it wholesale.

■ **19. SERVE A SIMPLE MEAL.** Guests don't need a choice of four entrées. Choose one. "As far as the meal is concerned, all you need is an appetizer, a salad, an entrée, and your wedding cake," says Cele Lalli, former editor in chief of *Modern Bride* magazine. "You don't need to do anything else."

■ **20. PARE DOWN THE MENU.** Trimming just one item like shrimp cocktail or a fresh fruit cup ($3 times 200 guests) can result in whopping savings.

■ **21. HOLD A HOTEL WEDDING.** One of the best bargains around is a wedding at a hotel! Have both the ceremony and reception on site, and you'll save on flowers and transportation right off the bat. Moreover, many hotels include extras in the per person or package charge, such as the wedding cake, centerpiece flowers, the band, photographer, and wedding night accommodations for the bride and groom. Some hotels offer discounted rooms for wedding guests and throw in a free anniversary dinner for the newlyweds one year later.

■ **22. AVOID THE HOLIDAYS.** Don't schedule your wedding for Christmas Day, Thanksgiving, Easter, or New Year's Day. Catering establishments charge more for these dates because it costs *them* more in holiday staff overtime.

■ **23. BORROW.** Does your aunt have a romantic condo on the beach? Ask to use it for the honeymoon. Is your former college roommate now a pastry chef? Ask her to make the wedding cake as your wedding gift. Don't be shy! You'll be surprised how many people would love to help with the wedding—be it lending a wedding veil, extra chairs, silver chafing dishes, or the use of their backyard for the ceremony.

■ **24. BARTER.** Exchange *your* services for someone else's. If you're a public relations consultant, offer to do a press kit for the photographer in exchange for more pictures. Give the florist a discount at your business if he'll discount his flowers for you.

■ **25. BUY A DEBUTANTE'S GOWN.** Debs and brides have elegant white dresses in common. Buy a debutante's gown and pocket the savings.

■ **26. BUY A BRIDESMAID'S GOWN.** These days, many bridesmaid's gowns come in white. There's a huge selection, and you'll pay half the price of a wedding gown.

■ **27. SHARE THE COST.** Ask the officiant if another couple is being married at your church on the same day; they might be willing to split the cost of wedding flowers. Is your sister or best friend getting married soon, too? Consider going halves on the wedding veil or aisle runner.

■ **28. DO IT YOURSELF.** If sewing your own wedding gown is too daunting, think about taking on smaller projects. Buy supplies at a craft or stationery store and make the favors, veil, place cards, invitations, or centerpieces yourself.

■ **29. HIRE A TALENTED AMATEUR.** Call up the local cooking school, college photography or video department, or a music academy and ask for referrals. Hire a beauty school student to do the bridal party hairstyles. Scout the local garden club for someone who's a genius with flowers. There are plenty of talented nonprofessionals looking for the experience.

■ **30. CHOOSE PACKAGE PRICING.** Nine times out of ten, you'll save money by going with a package deal.

■ **31. BOOK ONLY THE SERVICES YOU WANT.** Don't buy the entire package unless *all* of it is needed or wanted. Why pay for champagne in the limousine if you won't drink it? Negotiate, swap, or cut it out.

■ **32. AVOID A TENT WEDDING AT HOME.** It's pricey! You'll need to rent the tent and all the extras, too—flooring, lights, heating or air conditioning, portable toilets, a dance floor, tables, chairs, linens, and decorations to cover unsightly poles.

■ **33. CHOOSE BLACK OR SILVER LIMOUSINES.** They cost less to hire than white ones, since most limousine companies have more of them in their fleets.

■ **34. BOOK A LUXURY SEDAN.** They cost less than limos but still transport you in style.

■ **35. BE CAREFUL ABOUT BUFFETS.** Compare prices. A buffet is not necessarily cheaper than a sit-down meal and may actually cost more because more food is needed to keep the buffet replenished and looking attractive.

■ **36. SHOP WHERE THE VENDORS DO.** Scout for bargains at wholesale floral supply stores, wholesale food clubs, restaurant linen and supply companies, and bulk-printing operations.

■ **37. BUY OR REGISTER FOR ITEMS THAT CAN BE USED FOR THE WEDDING, OR USED AGAIN.** Decorate the reception site with a trellis, wooden pergola, candles, or potted plants that you can use later in your new home. Silk floral centerpieces can find a lasting place in your dining room. White leather pumps will go with a wedding dress and with a summer outfit later on.

■ **38. ANALYZE EVERY DEAL.** Thoroughly check out every service offered and the cost of every single item. Add them up. Are you getting value for the money? Are there extra, hidden charges to consider?

■ **39. ASK FOR VOLUME DISCOUNTS.** Formalwear shops often offer "quantity" incentives; for example, rent tuxes for the ushers and the groom's tux is free. Some bridal shops offer discounts on bridesmaids' dresses for large wedding parties. Ask the hotel reservations office if discounts or freebies are possible for booking a certain number of guest rooms.

■ **40. BOOK EARLY.** Lock in prices by booking early and insisting on a cap on future price escalations. Be sure the price escalation clause is spelled out in the contract.

■ **41. DON'T INVITE CHILDREN TO THE RECEPTION.** You'll be charged a full per person fee, even if they have only peanut butter sandwiches and milk.

■ **42. GET IT IN WRITING.** Get all goods and services recorded in a written contract. Include everything. Specify where and when services will be delivered, exactly what is being ordered ("five 10-inch bouquets to include red pansies, blue snapdragons, and white carnations"), what the fees are, when the deposit and balance are due, and provisions for cancellations and price escalations.

■ **43. SHOP THE SALES.** Scout the newspapers for blow-out sales on wedding gown samples and discontinued styles. You'll save 50 to 70 percent off retail! Buy invitations on sale, linens on sale, paper goods on sale, and so forth.

■ **44. TAKE ADVANTAGE OF EVERY COUPON AND DISCOUNT.** Look for coupons on invitations, flowers, and more in direct-mail coupon packets sent to your home. Pick up coupon booklets at your local photography studio or florist. Ask the human resource officer at your company if employees are entitled to discounts with certain airlines or hotels.

■ **45. COMPARE PRICES.** Ask if the vendor will match a competitor's prices.

■ **46. PAY BY CREDIT CARD AND GET FREQUENT FLIER MILES OR INCENTIVES.** Charge all the wedding expenses on a credit card that offers frequent flier miles or bonus points for special goods or services. After taking a course I teach on wedding planning, a mother of the bride from Connecticut called to tell me she had paid for her daughter's entire wedding on an airline credit card and earned enough miles to go to Hawaii after the wedding. The newlyweds left for the honeymoon, and the bride's parents left for their own getaway trip to recuperate!

■ **47. BECOME AN EDUCATED CONSUMER.** Collect information. Become a consumer reporter. Go to bridal shows and pick up every brochure, free video, discounted coupon, and price list offered. Look in the advertisement pages at the back of wedding magazines and call every toll-free number for free samples and catalogs. It's amazing what ends up in your mailbox: invitation samples, free favors, demo discs for computer software, and more.

■ **48. USE EXPENSIVE TOUCHES SPARINGLY.** Love exotic flowers? Use one or two as focal points in the centerpieces, surrounded by less costly flowers and greens. Heart set on luxurious linens or fabric chair covers? Rent them just for the head table.

■ **49. FORGET FAVORS.** Skip them. Most people don't remember them or keep them.

■ **50. SKIP THE CHAMPAGNE.** Few people actually drink it. It's wasted! Guests are happy to toast with whatever is on hand.

CHAPTER FOUR

THE WEDDING
CONSULTANT

Are you short on time, money, or both? Paying for the services of a professional consultant or event specialist to plan your wedding can end up being a bargain. Surprised? Couples usually are. Most of us still think of wedding consultants as those pushy, high-powered people who stage lavish parties for the rich and famous. Some consultants do specialize in celebrity events, but many more help plan weddings on any scale—even those on a shoestring budget of a couple thousand dollars.

A professional wedding consultant can help save you time and money and spare you the hassle of all or part of the wedding planning. A consultant also can help couples avoid making costly mistakes and make the most of even the tightest budgets. That's because consultants have extensive resources at their fingertips and also are skilled in the ABCs of party planning: choosing vendors, negotiating contracts, locating the perfect antique veil or table linens, booking a reception site, or finding flowers in the exact shade of peach the bride fancies. They know local price ranges for various services and how to map out a realistic budget. And they know creative ways to implement a theme or add special touches that don't cost a fortune.

"The budget is one way a consultant helps clients get organized," says wedding consultant Patricia Bruneau of L'Affaire du Temps in Milpitas, California. "By hiring a consultant, they can save time and phone calls in figuring out what they are spending. This in addition to the most important thing with everyone, and that is time—which is money! A consultant is trained and has experience with hiring professional vendors that fit a client's personality, budget, and style. This eliminates the need for them to 'Yellow Page' hunt and become frustrated."

A consultant worth his salt will know instantly how many photographers are available in your town, in your price range, in your preferred style (such as photojournalism), and how much of their services your budget will allow. He will be able to suggest ways to get more mileage from your money, such as hiring the photographer to shoot fewer hours of live coverage in exchange for more formal portraits.

"A person with limited resources will benefit greatly from hiring a wedding consultant," says consultant Packy Boukis of Only You in Broadview Heights, Ohio. She notes that couples striving to save more may actually spend more, or make disastrous decisions if they aren't careful. "Hiring a wedding consultant is a wise decision. If you search for the cheapest photographer, videographer, florist, or limousine and base your decision on price, you may be disappointed. Usually a consultant knows *why* a vendor is less expensive—perhaps a baker doesn't have a fancy shop, but bakes wedding cakes for the local upscale hotel. Now that's a find!

A consultant knows information about vendors that takes years to accumulate."

Having that inside track is like money in the bank. For example, Boukis has several bands in her database that she books directly without having to go through a middleman. The band gives her the same price as they do an agent, and she passes the savings along to the bride. "I have saved a bride as much as $2,000 when she books the band through me, and since I don't accept rebates from vendors, I pass that savings along to my client."

By hiring a consultant, you get a person who wears many hats: a creative director who has the expertise to create a theme or look; an etiquette expert who knows tricky things like where to seat divorced parents; a financial minister who works on your behalf to get the best services and quality; and a team leader who oversees all the work done by the vendors you've engaged.

In a way, every wedding has one person who ends up being the "consultant." It may be the mother of the bride who steps in and handles the emergencies, or the photographer, banquet manager, or even the bride herself. Whether you hire a professional consultant or not, decide early in the planning who will be appointed the wedding day master organizer and the keeper of the schedule. That way, if the flowers don't arrive, everyone will know who he or she should turn to.

HOW DO I FIND A CONSULTANT?

Because vendors of all kinds are often generically listed in the Yellow Pages under "Wedding Consultants," it's important to ask the consultant about her specific training and professional credentials.

Find out what she specializes in. Is it generic event planning (anniversaries, birthdays), meetings, corporate events, weddings, theme weddings, second marriages, destination weddings? Ask if there is a budget range she most commonly works with. (Is it $500 or $50,000?)

If the consultant claims he is certified by a certain organization, contact the organization to verify this. Being certified by an organization means the consultant has completed a certain level of wedding-specific business education and has made a commitment to continuing education and professional standards. Some unethical consultants claim to be certified but are not. Don't fall for this ploy.

Consultants may be hired for anywhere from one to three initial planning sessions, to coordinating the entire wedding from engagement party through honeymoon itinerary. Some specialize in wedding-day-only work, where they come on the day of the wedding to get everyone to the church on time, or troubleshoot in case the cake collapses or the photographer gets stuck in traffic. That means if you have only $5,000 to spend, you might allocate $150 to $300 to meet with a consultant for just a two- to three-hour planning session and map out a strategy for stretching those resources to your best advantage. By the end of the session, the consultant will have told you what's possible ("Have you thought about a brunch or Friday night reception?"), what's not, how to cleverly make the most of it all, and what to expect to pay for goods and services. Now that's a bargain.

Consultant fees vary widely from region to region and according to the size and complexity of the wedding. A consultant may charge an hourly or flat rate, or a percentage of the total wedding budget. Generally, fees range anywhere from 10 to 15 percent of the total wedding costs. Hourly rates can be anywhere from $75 for vendor referrals to $150 to $300 for an initial consultation. Comprehensive wedding planning services may cost several thousand dollars.

 Relatives and friends are well meaning and want to help. However, what will they do if a vendor gets a flat tire on the way to the ceremony? Will they have a cell phone? Will they have the phone number to the vendor's place of business? What if the lines are busy because it is Saturday? Will they have the [vendor's] cell phone number?

Just like every home built needs a general contractor, businesses need managers. Schools need principals and superintendents because someone has to be responsible. On the day of the wedding, someone needs to protect the bride from all the small details that go awry. I ask all vendors who have emergencies to contact me—the consultant—first. The wedding is the beginning of a marriage and the first step to your life together. You want it planned, carried out—and most of all you want to enjoy it!

—*Packy Boukis, wedding consultant*

Several major associations nationwide are devoted to training and certifying wedding consultants and event planners. These groups educate consultants on everything from etiquette and protocol to developing relationships with quality vendors and marketing business contracts. All will provide referrals to consultants in your area. Some of these associations are listed below.

The Association of Bridal Consultants
200 Chestnutland Rd.
New Milford, CT 06776-2521
(860) 355-0464
E-mail: BridalAssn@aol.com

The Association of Certified
  Professional Consultants
7791 Prestwick Circle
San Jose, CA 95135
(408) 528-9000

June Wedding Inc.®
  An Association for Event Professionals
1331 Burnham Ave.
Las Vegas, NV 89104-3658
(702) 474-9558
http://www.junewedding.com

Wedding Consultation Professional
  Development Certificate
San Francisco State University
College of Extended Learning, Downtown Center
425 Market St.
San Francisco, CA 94105-2406
(415) 904-7700

Weddings Beautiful Worldwide
3122 W. Cary St.
Richmond, VA 23221
(804) 355-6945
E-mail: 104664.3577@compuserve.com

Referrals

Sometimes "consultant" services are offered by the hotel, church, or synagogue where the couple will be married. Ask if the service is free. The consultant actually may be a party planner, catering manager, special events coordinator, or ceremony specialist. Ask what kind of specific training or expertise he has and how many weddings he has actually worked on. You may end up with the organist's wife who loves weddings and is just trying to help out (but hasn't got a clue!) or with a really savvy professional.

When asking a consultant for a reference, realize that no one ever gives the names of dissatisfied clients. The best sources for honest, reliable referrals are vendors in *related* fields. Ask a few florists, photographers, or reception site managers for the names of wedding consultants who are highly respected in your area. Chances are the same names will pop up again and again.

Commissions and Percentages

Some experts recommend being wary of the consultant who receives a commission from vendor referrals, since that might limit the consultant's resources, which is not always in the best interest of the client. Others argue that a reputable consultant will only recommend vendors who offer superior service and value to clients. Another sticky issue is payment by percentage. Some consultants charge a percentage of the total wedding budget. An unscrupulous consultant may not be as motivated to negotiate for lower prices for the couple if she is getting a percentage of the final tab. An ethical consultant, however, will work to provide the highest quality at the lowest cost. Ask for a referral from friends or relatives who have recently married. If you don't know anyone who was married recently, asking the right questions and trusting your own instincts will help you find a good consultant.

QUESTIONS TO ASK
WHEN HIRING A CONSULTANT

- How do you charge?
- Can I view your portfolio?
- Will you be able to advise us on etiquette matters?
- Will you be present on the wedding day, or do you send an associate?

- What kind of professional training or certification have you received?
- If we want to do most of the planning ourselves, will you guide us and then step back?
- Do you accept rebates or commissions from vendors?
- How long have you been in business?
- Do you have a Web site?
- Do you use a cell phone?
- If need be, can you work entirely by phone and fax with us? Have you ever done that before?
- How many weddings have you worked on?
- What is the full range of services you offer?
- What is your specialty?
- What is the average budget for the weddings you work on?
- What kind of business permits, licenses, insurance, and liability coverage do you have?
- What do you include in a contract?
- Do you prepare a wedding day schedule of events?
- How will you keep us informed of what tasks have been accomplished and when?
- How do you view your role? How will you be attired on the wedding day?
- Which weddings you have worked on are you most proud of? How do you safeguard against common pitfalls and potential disasters?
- What creative ways have you helped couples to save money or maximize a budget?

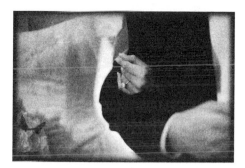

CHAPTER FIVE

THE MYTHS AND REALITIES OF WEDDING PLANNING

Florists, caterers, and other industry insiders aren't the only wedding experts out there. Friends who have recently gone through it all are an underutilized source of honest, useful advice. They're the real pros.

WHAT INSIDERS KNOW

During the planning process, call up everyone you know who has recently tied the knot and invite them to dinner. Then pick their brains. They'll tell you what they loved about it all, what they hated, and what they wished they had done differently. You'll get invaluable tips for dealing with mothers who act as if it's *their* wedding, mothers-in-law who won't shorten the guest list, or future spouses who change their minds mainstream and want to elope.

They'll also share with you the myths and realities of wedding planning that only the "initiated" have come to know.

■ **FORGET ABOUT BELIEVING THAT THIS WEDDING IS EXCLUSIVELY "YOURS."** A wedding affects family and friends. The very fact of asking loved ones to surround you on that day draws in a whole cast of characters who will have a lot of opinions on how it should proceed. (And goodness, will they voice them!) Even if you elope, they will save their opinions until you get back.

■ **EVERYTHING TAKES LONGER THAN YOU EXPECT AND COSTS MORE THAN YOU WOULD HAVE THOUGHT.** Face it, you've probably never done this before. The only people who can plan a wedding with one hand tied behind their backs are professional wedding consultants and Martha Stewart. That's because they do it every day. (Besides, it isn't *their* wedding, and they don't have *your* mother telling them what needs to be done at every step.)

■ **PRESENT A UNITED FRONT WITH YOUR FUTURE SPOUSE.** It's good practice for marriage. When the parents start arguing about whether one side has invited more guests than the other, you won't fall into the trap of taking sides.

■ **REALIZE THERE IS NO SUCH THING AS THE PERFECT WEDDING.** When I tell this to students in my wedding planning classes, the room usually gets quiet and I watch the color drain from their faces. Then I explain that having "perfection" as the ultimate goal can be a recipe for disappointment. Perfection is a stressful, if not impossible, aspiration. Instead, it may be more realistic to strive for a simply "wonderful" day; a chance to be surrounded by the people you love most. Don't allow yourself to become obsessed with the desire to make everything fairy-tale unforgettable or to become so overwhelmed with the planning that you forget to enjoy the process. It's the journey that matters, not the destination.

■ **DON'T AGONIZE OVER EVERY DECISION.** There will always be cheaper choices and more expensive choices. Just pick one and go on to the next decision.

■ **MEMORIZE THE THREE Cs: COMMUNICATE, COMPROMISE, AND BE CONSIDERATE.** Make decisions jointly with your future spouse. If he or she doesn't care about the napkin color and wants to leave it up to you, that's fine. Just offer the option of making the decision together. When you don't agree on choices, try to negotiate and come to a compromise.

■ **THE OLD ADAGE THAT YOU MARRY A FAMILY IS TRUE.** Even if your future spouse hasn't seen his parents in decades, they may still have a profound effect on him. During the wedding planning, parents' opinions suddenly count, and he may try to please them more than ever. Realize the apple doesn't fall far from the tree, and his values and beliefs were molded by his parents or the loved ones who raised him.

■ **WEDDINGS TEND TO BRING OUT THE FAIRY-TALE LONGINGS IN PEOPLE.** Blame it on the wedding industry, romance novels, and fairy tales. Even people who are downright practical get gaga over wedding stuff like tiara headpieces and a reception in a castle. If wedding planning suddenly brings out the Cinderella in you, don't sweat it. Buy a poufy dress and enjoy it. When will you get to dress like a princess or go for a moonlight ride in a horse-drawn carriage again?

■ **ETIQUETTE IS SUDDENLY IMPORTANT WHEN YOU GET ENGAGED.** Even if you've never given a thought to using the right fork, you may be suddenly protocol crazy when planning a wedding. That's because weddings are highly ritualized affairs that have long been fraught with "rules" for doing things "appropriately." Etiquette has changed a lot over the past twenty years. Don't get too caught up in doing what's "right" or "socially correct." Remember, etiquette is really about guidelines for making people feel comfortable.

■ **YOUR PARENTS WILL INVITE PEOPLE YOU'VE NEVER MET.** These strangers will show up at showers and at the wedding reception. They may be your mother's old college roommate or your father's business colleagues, and it may mean *you* have to bump a friend from the list to make your parents happy. Consider that your parents are proud and want to show you off—or that it's payback time for all the friends' weddings they've been invited to.

■ **NO MATTER WHO PAYS FOR WHAT, EVERYONE WILL HAVE AN OPINION ON WHAT YOU SHOULD DO.** Just listen, smile sweetly, and then make your own choices.

■ **PREPARING THE GUEST LIST IS *STRESSFUL!*** Border wars have been started for less. Avoid the battles by determining exactly how many guests each side can invite. It doesn't have to be split down the middle. Depending on who is paying for the wedding and whether one side simply has more relatives, you may wish to allocate more to one side. If either side won't cooperate and insists on exceeding the guest count, politely inform them what the per person fee is and that they are expected to cover it. (That is, assuming the reception hall can accommodate all those people.)

■ **DON'T ASSUME THAT A CERTAIN PERCENTAGE OF GUESTS WON'T COME.** If you are praying that a certain number will decline, they are positively guaranteed to all say yes and even ask if they can bring additional guests.

■ **THE WEDDING IS FOR THE COMFORT AND ENTERTAINMENT OF YOUR GUESTS.** Inviting people to a wedding is like inviting them to your home. Make them feel welcome, pampered, and cared about.

■ **DON'T LET YOURSELF GET INTO DEBT.** It isn't worth it to be saddled with credit card bills for months or years after the wedding. Don't do it.

■ **IT'S REALLY JUST ONE DAY (EVEN IF IT IS A BIG DAY).** Keep it in perspective.

THE MOST COMMON WEDDING MYTHS

■ **ONLY VIRGINS SHOULD WEAR A WHITE WEDDING GOWN.** White dresses became popular only after Queen Victoria wore one in the 1840s. White symbolizes different things in different cultures: joy, fertility, or virginity. Anyone can wear a white wedding gown if she chooses.

■ **THE BRIDE'S FAMILY ALWAYS PAYS FOR THE WEDDING.** Here's good news for the bride's family: Tradition once dictated that they paid for the whole enchilada, but not anymore. These days, couples are paying for all or part of the wedding themselves, and any relatives may chip in.

■ **TO KEEP COSTS DOWN, IT'S ALL RIGHT TO INVITE MARRIED COUPLES WITHOUT THEIR SPOUSES.** No, it isn't. This often comes up when inviting co-workers whose spouses you may have never met. If the couple are getting divorced, that's another matter, but if the couple live together and have a joint social life, it puts your co-worker in the uncomfortable position of leaving the spouse at home.

■ **A BRIDE MARRYING FOR THE SECOND TIME CAN'T WEAR A LONG GOWN.** Wrong! A bride can wear any gown she chooses, as long as it looks flattering and makes her feel lovely. This may be a remarriage, but unless you are marrying the same man the second time around, it's the first wedding for the two of you.

■ **GIFTS OF MONEY ARE ALWAYS CONSIDERED TACKY.** In some cultures, gifts of money are appropriate and expected. The gift is intended to help the couple get financially established.

■ **THE BRIDE AND GROOM HAVE THREE MONTHS TO WRITE THANK-YOU NOTES.** I've never figured out where this one came from. Send a note promptly, preferably within a few days to a week after receiving the gift. Givers want to be sure the receiver got the gift. And an expression of thanks is necessary and welcome—the sooner, the better.

CHAPTER SIX

REAL COUPLES, REAL BUDGETS

In this chapter you'll meet three couples who turned straw into gold. They planned amazing weddings on a budget, and you can, too. Each took modest wedding resources and utilized them to the fullest. The result for each bride and groom was a wedding that dreams are made of.

Lynn and Bob of Connecticut had a churchyard picnic. Weddings in their part of the country average a whopping $35,000 or more, but their goal was to have good food and good company in a beautiful setting. Their wedding was absolutely lovely.

Anna Marie and Glen of New Jersey knew they couldn't afford to fly in his family from one state and hers from another for a big blowout wedding, so they planned an intimate destination wedding in Jamaica. Their nuptials in a tropical paradise were the stuff movies are made of.

Finally, Lisa and Shawn of Montana wanted an outdoor wedding that could include lots of friends and family without breaking the bank. Their at-home ceremony was full of unique touches that didn't cost a fortune.

Each of these couples spent $3,000 or less. Not every bride and groom will want to do what they did, but their stories (as told by the brides) provide inspiration for personalizing a wedding and having it all when you don't have a lot to spend.

LYNN AND BOB DENNIS
DARIEN, CONNECTICUT

Total budget: $3,000
Guests: 150

When we look back at our recent wedding, it was perfect. Perfect for us the second time around. I have known Bob since I was a young girl. He lived next door to my grandparents. In fact, my grandfather showed him how to properly "hang a door," as carpenters would say. We both were married before. Bob has two children and was married for thirty-seven years. I have two children and was married for over twenty-seven years. Collectively, we have sixty-four years of marriage between us.

Once we decided to marry, we chose a small church in town that we both had been attending for a number of years. The pastor counseled us for almost a year. It was the best foundation for marriage or remarriage one could have received.

Bob and I made a list of our friends, past ones who had remained by our sides during divorce, new ones we had made as a couple, and those in our work and social circles. We had about 150 people to invite—that's a lot on limited funds. The date we chose was special for us and happened to be on Friday the 13th in September, and at high noon.

Our total budget was $3,000. To save money, we did the following.

Invitations

A simple pen-and-ink sketch of the church was drawn by the printer from a photograph (he also drove by the church to take a closer look). A shadow of this print was the backdrop for our wedding invitation. It was printed on simple parchment-color note-size cards. The copy was created by me on the computer and given to the printer to overlay onto the card. A matching card, a little smaller, was created for the response card.

Program

Using my home computer, I created and printed the program. It listed our extended family members' names (the wedding party), their relationship to the bride and groom, and a mini-map for directions to the park where the reception was to be held. These were handed out by two grandnephews at the front door of the church as the guests arrived.

Wedding party

Three of our four children participated in the wedding party, as well as two step-grandchildren. The girls wore simple, long navy blue dresses. No jewelry. The men wore banker's gray slacks, white shirts, navy jackets, and matching ties that I purchased for them at a clearance sale. My bridal attire was an off-white, two-piece dress with a long skirt with a slit to the knee on one side, and a long-sleeved button-front jacket trimmed in satin. It was purchased on sale, in part with a gift certificate I had received from a fund-raising contest held at work. Flowers were simple white daisies, blue bachelor's buttons, ivy, and white French silk ribbons, with a few pink roses for additional color.

Music
The pastor's son played the traditional wedding march on the piano in church during the ceremony. For the preservice music, we chose the selections, including a song from *The Phantom of the Opera*. Our pastor sang the Lord's Prayer during our wedding service.

Reception
Our plan was to have an accordionist lead the procession of wedding party members and guests on a short walk from the church to the local park, where rented tables and chairs would be waiting for a picnic reception. Due to last-minute rain, the reception was held in the basement of the church. The centerpieces consisted of cut-glass salad bowls (rented for $3 each). To keep the picnic-in-the-park theme, the salad bowls were filled with goldfish (10 cents each) and floating dahlia flower tops clipped from a friend's garden (colorful and fun!). Mini-flags, written in calligraphy by the pastor's wife, said: NO FISHING!

Food
A friend of ours who owned a local deli made us delicious chicken with honey Dijon sauce box lunches (homemade food!) that were served in foil tins tied with bridal tulle ribbon. Drinks were cold sodas and bottled water. The three-tiered wedding cake was made by my future daughter-in-law. It had rolled fondant icing, bridal tulle around the base of each layer, and fresh flowers for decoration.

Entertainment
Music was provided in the form of a sing-along with a strolling accordionist.

Photography
We hired a retired professional photographer. We used the 4 × 6 prints he shot and made our own wedding album. A photo of our entire wedding party was used as our Christmas card a few months later.

Rings

Through a friend, we purchased matching gold bands with an old-fashioned coin edge. We had them engraved on the inside.

Honeymoon

My husband's boss gave us a week at his summer cottage on Long Island. It was absolutely charming and beautiful, complete with fireplace, deck, and *peace!* In fact, as an ongoing gift, we have been invited back each year to celebrate our anniversary. We saved a great deal of money by not using a reception hall, bakery, or band; by not having an expensive dinner with liquor or floral centerpieces; and by not having honeymoon expenses. The bottom line was family, friends, love, and commitment. It was beautiful.

ANNA MARIE AND GLEN McELROY
OCEAN TOWNSHIP, NEW JERSEY

Total budget: $2,900
Guests: 4

We always tell people, if you want a big wedding, have it or you are going to regret it. Glen was married before and I never wanted a big wedding, so I have no regrets. I am a flight attendant and Glen is a helicopter pilot and New Jersey state trooper who used to be a minor-league baseball player. We met when a friend of mine was dating one of the ball players.

We had a beautiful wedding. It was just us and my brother-in-law and his wife who flew down at the last minute on my passes (discounted travel for airline employees). We got married in Jamaica at a resort called Couples, where everything was done for you. The fact that everything was done was great—and it was so inexpensive. They do weddings all day long, every hour on the hour. You just paid for the marriage certificate, which was $40, and for the photographs or the video. I liked it best that you could keep the negatives. You had two package choices for the photography; we got the smaller package, which was around $130 for thirty-eight pictures. You got to pick out your wedding flowers from a book. They had different ones to choose from in different colors and shapes, and the groom got a boutonniere for free.

After the ceremony, we had a little reception with Glen's brother and his wife. The resort provided a cake with three tiers, which was included in the package price, too. The champagne was free, and they kept filling up our glasses. You had a choice of wedding sites: on the beach side in a little gazebo, or on the front of the property in a tropical setting.

It was the most relaxing day! We got up that morning and went horseback riding and then went on a catamaran. After we came back, we had lunch and then got ready in separate rooms. Then we came down for the ceremony.

I chose this type of wedding because I knew I would not have been satisfied just going to a justice of the peace. To do even a small wedding here in the Northeast would have been outrageous. I knew it would have been crazy to try to have a wedding here— my family is in Alabama and his family is in New Jersey. We decided this way sounded romantic and fun and easy.

Wedding gown
I had a dress made by a local seamstress for $350. I had seen a dress in a book that was $2,000 and it was very simple, like the dress Carolyn Bessette Kennedy wore.

Travel expenses
I saved about $800 by using my discount as an airline employee. We flew down on a Tuesday, got married on a Thursday, and came back the following Tuesday.

Hotel accommodations

We booked the cheapest level of room at the resort. When we got there, we weren't satisfied with the location and they gave us a free upgrade. Always ask for an upgrade.

Wedding announcements

After we got back, I sent out a hundred announcements. I sent nice ones; that is probably where I spent the most money. There was a wedding picture of us on the beach that I had made into prints, and I included those with the announcements. Two weeks after the wedding, we had a huge party in our backyard to celebrate.

LISA AND SHAWN MICHAEL
BOZEMAN, MONTANA

Total budget: $2,000
Guests: 80

Shawn and I got married on August 15 in Bozeman, Montana. I'm a wedding and event consultant for Ever After Weddings, so I put into practice some of the advice I give my clients. We both wanted an outdoor wedding, so we set up the ceremony and reception in my parents' backyard. We sent out about a hundred invitations, but only eighty or so people came. The ceremony was scheduled to start at 1:30 P.M., but a light rain shower delayed it until 2 P.M. It was fairly informal. My dress didn't have a train, the groomsmen wore just vests, and Shawn and his father wore jackets.

Ceremony

We really wanted our ceremony to reflect our personalities, so we didn't want to go all out. Plus, we were paying for some of the wedding, so we needed to keep it on a tight budget. Shawn and I are not very religious, so outdoors won out over a church wedding. We did have a minister marry us, though. He was really great in letting us have some latitude in our ceremony. He ended up mailing us a copy of the standard ceremony, and I cut and pasted it with other readings to bring it up-to-date and to fit our styles. Shawn gave me a white rose along with his vows and promised to give me a white rose each year on our anniversary to reaffirm our vows. I accepted it and promised to place it in the same vase each year. That was my favorite part of the ceremony.

Wedding gown
I bought a Ladybug gown for $329, plus alterations and undergarments. I bought it in a town about 200 miles away in a store that has a lot of inventory. I also bought it off the rack, so I saved ordering charges. The biggest way I saved money in this category, though, was with the veil. My mom and I spent an afternoon making my veil. About a yard of tulle, some pipe cleaner, some white silk flowers, ribbon, and glue gun and we were set. Plus, we had a lot of laughs that day! Shawn's parents paid for the tux rentals—$175 for five of them.

Cake
I think this is one of the biggest ways we lucked into saving money. Shawn's aunt makes wedding cakes on a part-time basis, so this was her gift to us. We gave her a general idea of what we wanted, and she produced a beautiful three-tiered cake. Additionally, she made two "extra" cakes, sort of like a groom's cake, one white and one chocolate. We ended up taking one on our honeymoon!

Flowers
Shawn works at a local grocery as the dairy manager, so we went there for flowers. It was definitely the cheapest in town, and we knew the florist there is a great floral designer. We got the pack-

age deal, and it cost us about $200. However, I do have a word of caution: Grocery stores don't specialize in flowers, so they have to order *all* of the materials specific to your wedding. My flowers didn't make it onto the truck going to Bozeman! Because we are friends with the head florist, she called around town and located most of the flowers she needed. Also, be sure the florist you talk to actually arranges the flowers. The other florist working there put together my bouquets, and because I hadn't told her what I wanted, she had to interpret off paper. Thankfully, my aunt did a little rearranging, and they turned out fine. We also paid $10 for a dozen roses for petals for the flower basket. My sister made the flower basket and the ring pillow with white satin and maroon ribbon. It was very customized to my wedding, and it saved us money!

Photography

I hired a college student to photograph my wedding. Jared charged us $100 for the day, plus film and developing ($150). The best thing was that we got to keep the negatives! Some of the pictures turned out a little dark, but all in all he did a great job. My uncle also was taking photos, so we got twice the pictures. Where Jared's pictures weren't that great, my uncle's filled in. We ended up with over 300 prints between the two!

Ceremony site

We had our wedding outdoors in my parents' backyard. I rented folding chairs for 75 cents apiece, flower hangers to line the aisle (eight for $13 each), and a wicker gazebo to get married under (for $85). A family friend helped provide decorations for the gazebo, and Shawn's parents brought about five tables for the reception. We paid the minister $100 and spent close to $250 on all of the ceremony accessories—cake cutter, goblets, nuts, vase for the rose ceremony, guest book and pens, bubbles, and miscellaneous charges.

Invitations

We made our own. I formatted the words on my computer and then printed them out on a laser printer on high-quality paper. We went to a local copy center and copied them onto the 8 × 5 cards we found. It was very, very easy. The cards, envelopes, postage, and copying cost about $70 total.

Music

Since we were trying to save money, we decided to use recorded music. This is another place where a friend pitched in to help. I took various songs to my friend, told him what order I needed them in, and he used his CD recorder to create three wedding CDs. The best part is that they make a great keepsake for me. I'm pretty sentimental, and music is very important. This method worked out great for saving money, too. I only had to buy the blank CDs (about $4 each).

Catering

We had finger foods for the reception. I had a lot of family there to help prepare everything. The total cost was probably $300. My mom and Shawn's mom split the bill.

Transportation

We didn't spend any money here because the ceremony and reception were in the same place. I had a nice surprise, though, when one of my bridesmaids said that we could borrow her father's 1968 Mustang convertible as our wedding gift. We used it to drive around town and formally end the reception. It was the best part of the day!

My dad ended up paying for most of our wedding, but we bought the invitations, all of the accessories, and the flowers. Because we had twelve months to plan, we could spend a little each month on the wedding so there wouldn't be as much to buy at the last minute. This is advisable for couples who are paying for all or part of their weddings.

CHAPTER SEVEN

BUYING THE RINGS

With this ring, I thee wed.

Choosing wedding and engagement rings is a momentous decision. You will wear them every day of your marriage as a reminder of the wedding ceremony and your never-ending commitment to each other.

Because of its circular shape, the wedding ring has always been a universal symbol of betrothal and eternal love. In ancient Egypt, the ring was placed on the third finger of the left hand because it was believed that the vein in that finger led directly to the heart (anatomical but romantic). Anthropologists believe that the first wedding rings were exchanged in Egypt as early as 2800 B.C. The early Egyptians wore rings made of hemp, grass, or woven rushes, which understandably wore out over time and had to be replaced. Prosperous Egyptians could afford sturdier gold rings, which were used as currency and also displayed the bridegroom's wealth and social standing. The ancient Greeks and Romans wore wedding rings made of iron or gold.

In some cultures, it was believed that the wedding ring protected the bride and groom from evil spirits, which were attracted to a couple on their wedding day. According to folklore, if the ring was dropped during the ceremony, it meant the newlyweds were in for bad luck and a rocky marriage.

It wasn't until 1477 that the diamond ring became the traditional standard—after King Maximilian of Germany gave a diamond engagement ring to his betrothed, Mary of Burgundy.

CHOOSING A DIAMOND

It isn't written in stone that an engaged woman must wear a diamond ring, but most do. About four out of five couples choose a diamond engagement ring. More than half choose a round-shaped diamond, which is called a "brilliant" cut. Diamonds also come in other shapes: oval, marquis, pear shaped, heart shaped, and emerald cut.

What determines the value of a diamond? Diamonds range in value according to a global standard that jewelers call the four Cs: carat weight, color, clarity, and cut.

The Four Cs

Carat
Carat is the unit of weight used for diamonds, a word derived from carob seeds, which were used to balance scales in ancient times. There are 100 points in a carat, so a 99-point diamond weighs virtually one carat, and a 45-point diamond weighs a little less than

half a carat. But two diamonds of equal weight may not be of equal value; it all depends on their color, clarity, and cut.

Color

Grading a cut stone for color means deciding the amount by which it deviates from the whitest possible. Completely white (truly colorless) diamonds are rare and therefore the most valuable. To the untrained eye, many diamonds appear colorless, even though the majority contain slight traces of yellow, brown, or gray.

On the flip side, although most diamonds are a shade of white, diamonds come in all colors, including blue (like the Hope Diamond), pale yellow, canary yellow, pink, red, green, and brown. Colored diamonds (called "fancies") are prized for their depth of color, just as white diamonds are valued for their lack of color. Diamonds are rated on a scale beginning with D (perfectly colorless and most valued) to Z (light yellow and least valued).

Clarity

Nature makes each stone one of a kind. Some contain more imperfections, called "inclusions," than others. The fewer the inclusions, the more valuable the diamond. A diamond's clarity is determined by taking into account the size, nature, and placement of these imperfections. (Yet slight flaws cannot be detected by the naked eye and don't affect a stone's beauty.)

A top-clarity grade of FL means the diamond is flawless. At the opposite end of the scale are lesser-grade diamonds with I ratings of 1, 2, or 3, which mean the imperfections are visible to the naked eye.

Cut

Diamonds are cut by skilled craftspersons according to a mathematical formula. A finished diamond has fifty-eight facets, which are the small, flat polished planes cut into a diamond so that the maximum amount of light is reflected. When masterfully cut, a diamond's facets and angles act like light-dispersing mirrors. This reflection, or brilliance, is important in evaluating a diamond's quality, since accuracy in cutting is essential to the diamond's beauty.

Diamond cutting is a painstaking procedure requiring great skill and precision. More than half of all couples choose the round brilliant cut. Also popular are the marquise, emerald, pear, oval, and square-cut diamonds.

Gemstones

Over the centuries, gemstones have been prized for their beauty as well as their romantic folklore. Green emeralds were believed to ensure lasting love, rubies were associated with health and passion, sapphires symbolized sincerity and fidelity, and opals represented hope and purity.

Like diamonds, gemstones are evaluated according to the four Cs. Muted colors or colors between hues are generally less expensive than stones with clear, primary colors.

Couples looking for beauty on a budget should consider a gemstone engagement ring. Like diamonds, no two gemstones are exactly alike. Yet many gems are not necessarily rare and are in less demand, and therefore much less expensive, than diamonds. These beauties often are bargains and are out of the ordinary. Affordable gemstones include amethyst, garnet, citrine, topaz, aquamarine, beryl, opal, turquoise, iolite, peridot, tourmaline, ruby, sapphire, and emerald. Within each variety, quality dramatically affects price. Rubies are the most valuable gemstone, and some fine examples are more costly even than diamonds.

What to Spend

The rule of thumb is to set aside two months' salary on the engagement ring, but this is a personal decision. Think carefully about buying a ring for "investment purposes" or resale value. How many couples do you know who have actually sold their diamonds, even in the face of personal financial crisis?

The Right Fit

Look for a ring that fits properly. It should slip comfortably over the knuckle and hug the base of the finger without sliding around too easily. Because your hands swell slightly in warm weather, keep the "toothpick" rule in mind: There should be enough room to slide a toothpick between the ring and the finger.

Caring for Your Engagement Ring

Even though a diamond is the hardest substance known to human-kind, it can be chipped by a hard blow or damaged by household cleaning chemicals. Don't let your ring come into contact with chorine bleach. Every six months, examine the prongs to make sure none is loose, bent, or broken, or else the stone may slip out. Clean the ring occasionally in a mixture of equal parts cold water and household ammonia. Let it soak for 30 minutes. Gently rinse and air-dry on a clean, soft cloth.

BUYER BEWARE

Buying a diamond is an important investment—and a potentially risky one. We've all heard horror stories of couples who plunked down thousands for what they thought were fine diamonds, only to find out they had purchased worthless stones.

It's a scary thought. Unless you know how to use a loupe (a jeweler's magnifying glass) or know something about stone cut, color, clarity, and quality, it's nearly impossible to tell with the naked eye whether a diamond is flawless or worthless. Generally, a stone that looks dull, lacks brilliance, and is cloudy or yellowish isn't very valuable. (But rare deep yellow diamonds, called fancies, are actually priceless.)

So what's the average consumer to do?

Do a little background reading and then find a reputable jewelry store that has been in business a long time and offers a large selection of diamonds in a range of prices. Ask friends and family for referrals. Check with the Better Business Bureau to see if any complaints have been lodged against the store. Wedding jewelry is sold at local jewelry stores, at chain jewelry stores, at department stores, through wholesale distributors, and even over the Internet.

Before you purchase a stone, have its four Cs (carat weight, color, clarity, and cut) certified. Ask about the retailer's return policy and whether there is an extra charge for sizing the ring. Have the ring appraised by an independent and reputable gemologist (not one recommended by the jeweler). Be aware that appraisals can vary as much as 25 percent. Insist that the final sale of the ring be contingent on your getting the ring appraised and your being satisfied with its quality.

Talk frankly with the jeweler about the diamond shape you want to buy and the amount you want to spend. It isn't necessary to buy an "investment quality" diamond; your goal should be to find the best quality stone for the price.

Remember, the wedding ring is a symbol of love. It needn't be expensive, or big, or studded with sparkly rocks, or even new, to be meaningful.

According to the Diamond Information Center's consumer brochure, *Your Guide to Buying and Caring for Diamonds*, "Gradations within each of the four Cs make for an infinite number of combinations to determine the value of any diamond. But there's a range of beautiful diamonds for any price you want to pay."

It's important to keep all receipts and pay by credit card. If there's a problem, you'll have more legal recourse and can withhold payment until the dispute is settled.

Ask the jeweler to explain each characteristic of the stone and how it adds to the ring's total value. You also should ask him to "plot" the diamond's flaws and inclusions on a drawing of the stone and to give you a written description of its four Cs. That way, you'll have a record of the location of its blemishes. This kind of map is handy both now and years down the road when the ring is repaired. Bring the drawing along when you return to pick up the stone after it has been mounted into a setting. By having a map, you will able to identify your stone and make sure it's the same one you left to be repaired or mounted.

Insurance

If the ring is worth more than $500, insure it as soon as possible, either on a homeowner's or renter's policy. Keep copies of all receipts in a safe place. By doing so, all will not be lost if you go for a swim and accidentally lose it in the Pacific Ocean.

Call the American Gem Society for a free brochure, *Questions to Ask Your Insurance Agent*. The AGS telephone number is 1-800-340-3028.

What Should an Insurance Appraisal Include?

An appraisal for insurance purposes should include the stone's cut, color, clarity, and weight; a thorough description and photograph; the exact dimensions of each stone; the tone, intensity, and hue of colored stones; and a description of the metals used in the mounting.

Is It a Fake?

When purchasing fine jewelry, you get what you pay for. Be wary of "the bargain of a lifetime" or salespeople who pressure you to make an on-the-spot decision. Chances are, if an offer sounds too good to be true, it probably is. If you suspect a jeweler has made a fraudulent claim about the stone you've purchased, contact the local Better Business Bureau and the attorney general in your state, as well as the organization below.

The Jewelers' Vigilance Committee
25 W. 45th St., Suite 400
New York, NY 10036
(212) 997-2002

GREAT SOURCES FOR FREE BUYING GUIDES

Tiffany & Co. has been selling diamond engagement rings for 160 years. Tiffany invented the six-prong "tiffany" setting, designed to hold the stone away from the band and expose more of the diamond. This upscale jewelry store, based in New York City, offers a free booklet, *How to Buy a Diamond,* that covers diamond styles, the four Cs, and frequently asked questions. Call 1-800-526-0649 or visit http://www.tiffany.com.

The Diamond Information Center, an industry association based in New York City, offers a free brochure titled *Your Guide to Buying and Caring for Diamonds.* It includes ten tips for buying diamonds and information on caring for, cleaning, and storing diamond jewelry. For a copy, call 1-800-FOREVER (367-3837) or write to the following:

Diamond Information Center
466 Lexington Ave.
New York, NY 10017
http://www.adiamondisforever.com

Considering a gemstone? Call or write the American Gem Society, an organization of certified gemologists. These jewelers are trained in appraisal methodologies and will provide a professional report of the quality and value of your fine jewelry. This consumer protection organization provides referrals to certified gemologists in your area and offers a free publication, *Information Guide to Satisfaction with Your Fine Jewelry Purchases*. Call the American Gem Society at 1-800-340-3028 or write to:

The American Gem Society
8881 W. Sahara Ave.
Las Vegas, NV 89117
http://www.ags.org

Another good source of information on gemstones is the Gembureau, also known as the International Colored Gemstone Association. Call (212) 688-8452 or write to:

The Gembureau
The International Colored Gemstone Association
3 E. 48th St., 5th Floor
New York, NY 10017

For information on platinum jewelry, call the Platinum Guild International USA at 1-800-990-7528 or write to:

Platinum Guild International USA
620 Newport Center Dr., Suite 800
Newport Beach, CA 92660

WAYS TO SAVE ON RINGS

■ **PICK A SOLITAIRE, OR SINGLE-STONE, ENGAGEMENT RING.** Jewelers note that a solitaire is the best value for a given sum because almost all its value is in the one stone.

■ **FOR WEDDING RINGS, CHOOSE HIS AND HERS PLAIN GOLD BANDS.** Simple gold bands are a timeless classic, and you can have a message of love engraved inside. There are many inexpensive versions of the gold band, with details such as etching, tiny diamond chips, or inexpensive gemstone inserts. Since the stone chips are so small, they needn't be rare or expensive to look sparkly. Cost is $90 to $150.

■ **ASK A CRAFTSPERSON OR ARTIST TO MAKE CUSTOM RINGS FOR YOU.** Visit juried craft shows (meaning the artists are screened by a jury of their peers) to find talented artisans who can help you design your own ring and create something one of a kind.

■ **BUY ESTATE JEWELRY.** This means previously owned jewelry or antique jewelry sold by a family or at auction. You may get a vintage gem in a platinum setting. (Platinum settings were once the standard but now are rare—and coming back into fashion.) Estate jewelry is often sold in antiques shops, jewelry shops, pawnshops, and consignment shops. To ensure you're getting your money's worth, have the ring appraised by a certified gemologist before making the final sale.

■ **CONSIDER VINTAGE REPRODUCTION RINGS.** You can get that estate jewelry look without the high price tag. Many museum shops carry reproduction jewelry with medieval designs and old-fashioned Italianate or Victorian flourishes. Prices range from $50 to $250 for rings in silver or 14-carat gold.

■ **NEGOTIATE.** The average chain jewelry shop charges a full 100 percent markup. Some department store jewelry departments mark up the price even more—up to three times the wholesale cost. That means there is a lot of wiggle room for a discount. Never pay the retail or sticker price until you have shopped around and know you are getting a true bargain.

■ **LOOK IN THE YELLOW PAGES UNDER "WHOLESALE DIAMOND" STORES, OR SHOP IN THE "DIAMOND DISTRICT" OF A MAJOR CITY.** Wholesale outlets may be no-frills shops (no fancy chandeliers or plush carpeting), but the average markup on the stones is generally 10 to 25 percent above cost.

■ **CHECK OUT THE INTERNET.** You don't have to be a jewelry store owner to purchase stones and settings at wholesale prices. The Jewelz Web site (http://www.jewelz.com) is a "gemstone gallery" where anyone can purchase semiprecious gemstones, precious gemstones, rare and collector's gems, gold and sterling silver jewelry, ring settings, and more. The prices are deeply discounted off retail, and the cyber "stock" changes continuously. Gems are available from $1 to $1,000 per carat weight.

■ **WEAR AN HEIRLOOM FAMILY ENGAGEMENT RING OR HAVE THE STONE(S) REMOUNTED IN A NEW SETTING.** This is a meaningful way to honor a relative and create a family keepsake. If your mother or grandmother is widowed or divorced and no longer wears her engagement ring, she may be pleased to have it put to good use.

■ **BUY A FABULOUS FAKE.** If you can't afford a real diamond—or don't care if it's authentic—consider a cubic zirconia (CZ) ring. Some couples postpone buying a genuine diamond until they can afford the kind of quality stone they really want. In the interim, they purchase a fake that looks remarkably real. These fake stones often are called synthetic, faux, or man-made. The shop-at-home television channels often feature them. Purchase a great fake and you'll have enough left over to buy matching earrings! Price is $50 to $150, depending on the quality.

■ **GOLD RINGS DO NOT HAVE TO BE 100 PERCENT GOLD TO BE CONSIDERED REAL.** Most gold contains a mixture of at least two other metals, or alloys. Depending on the mix, the gold may look a little yellow, white, or pink. This is because a pure gold ring is very soft and easily damaged.

■ **KNOW THE DIFFERENCE BE-TWEEN *CARROTS* AND *KARATS*.** A *karat* is a gold measurement term. Karats are measured using a scale of 24. The higher the karat, the higher the proportion of gold. Jewelry that is 100 percent gold is called 24 karat; 18 karat is 18 parts gold and 6 parts other metals; 14 karat is 14 parts gold and 10 parts other metals.

■ **FOR AN EXTREMELY DURABLE WEDDING RING, CHOOSE PLATINUM.** Platinum is a white metal that resembles white gold and silver.

■ **CHOOSE A BIRTHSTONE INSTEAD OF A DIAMOND.** If your birthday is in April, it's a diamond anyway.

■ **CHECK OUT THE STORE'S ENGRAVING AND SIZING POLICIES.** Are these services extra or free?

■ **A DIAMOND'S VALUE DEPENDS ON A COMBINATION OF ALL FOUR Cs.** Many experts, however, believe the most important of all these is the cut. Cut determines the brilliance, fire, and beauty of the stone.

■ **GO FOR THE CLUSTER LOOK.** Purchase six or eight inexpensive small stones and have them mounted in a cluster setting for a lush look.

A Final Note

Don't drop those rings! There are many old superstitions about losing or dropping the wedding ring. Centuries ago, it was considered unlucky if someone dropped the ring and it came to rest on a gravestone in the church floor. If it fell on a man's grave, people believed it meant the bridegroom would be the first to die. If the ring rolled onto the gravestone of a woman, it signified the bride would be the first to die. So be careful. And if you have a ring bearer, be sure to sew the rings onto the pillow!

CHAPTER EIGHT

THE WEDDING GOWN

C ontrary to what you may believe or have heard, not all brides have to or choose to wear white. It's fashionable these days for brides to wear white or shades of champagne, sea-foam green, pink, pale yellow, or other pastels. Many designers are livening up all-white gowns with brilliantly colored sashes or flowers.

A white wedding gown does not signify virginity, fertility, or joy. White dresses became the tradition only after England's Queen Victoria wore one in the 1840s. Until then, brides wore their very best dress on their wedding day, often a homespun brown or black dress. After Queen Victoria created a sensation in a white gown, it became the rage for other women to wed in white and also signified a bride's social standing—only the wealthy could afford to wear a white dress that couldn't easily be cleaned and worn again.

Picture your ideal wedding gown. It should be absolutely beautiful. It should fit like a second skin. Wearing it should make you feel truly lovely. This isn't just a dress; it's the dress that dreams are made of. But a wedding gown doesn't have to be long, or voluminous, or even white, and it certainly doesn't have to be expensive.

Leaf through the pages of wedding magazines and you'll see up to 200 bridal designers and thousands of gowns. Log on to the Internet and view gown styles day and night. There are wedding gowns in every price point and every fabric imaginable—from silk to satin to taffeta to tulle.

The average cost for a gown nationwide is around $800 to $900, or at least $1,300 when the shoes, accessories, undergarments, and headpiece or veil are factored in. OK, that's the national *average*. Now ignore that figure. What a bride *actually* spends has a lot to do with her personal tastes, the quality of the fabric, where and (even when) the gown is purchased, and how savvy a shopper she is.

It's possible to find an elegant wedding gown for $200 or $2,000. You just have to know where to look. Let's take the example of a designer gown that's featured in the bridal magazines and has a suggested retail of $950. Store A might sell it discounted for $750; Store B might sell it above retail at $1,200. Store C might sell it for $450 during a seasonal sale or sample sale. Exact same dress, different price.

The point is: comparison shop!

A wedding gown is an important purchase and an emotional one. It's also a very lopsided investment—the bride is spending a *lot* of money for a garment she will wear just once. You wouldn't buy the first pair of shoes you try on, so don't buy the very first gown (unless you're so bowled over you can't imagine not having it).

Gowns vary widely in price and quality. The quality variance is the bad news. Many bridal gowns on the market are downright cheesy. The fabrics are cheap and the workmanship is poor. For higher-end, designer gowns, the customer pays more for the designer's name but gets far superior fabrics in return—real silk satins and luscious cottons, not shiny polyester that wrinkles and crinkles easily.

I've always been puzzled as to how gown manufacturers get away with this. Spend $700 on a cocktail dress or evening gown and you're assured of the best fabrics and most beautiful construction. Spend the same amount—or even more—on a wedding gown, and the seams may be unraveling, the sleeves poorly set in, and the fabric the same stuff used to make Halloween costumes. What's more, many gown manufacturers glue on the beads, lace, or sequins. That may mean the dress can't be dry cleaned. It's essentially a throw-away purchase.

To get the most value from your wedding gown purchase, ask the salesperson to educate you about dress design, fabrics, and construction. Bring along a friend who is a skilled dressmaker or home sewer. Examine the gown both inside and out.

"Even on a limited budget, you want to look very beautiful and very special—both the bride and groom," says Cele Lalli, former editor in chief of *Modern Bride* magazine. "There is so much available in every price point. Maybe limit how much you spend, but make sure it is extremely attractive."

SAVVY SHOPPING STRATEGIES

Begin the shopping process by looking at gowns in bridal magazines. Tear out the pages and circle the separate elements that appeal most to you. It may be the neckline in one, the sleeves in another. Don't fret if you don't find all the "perfect" features in one dress. Be patient. The more you see, the more you may change your mind. Think of this as the research and development stage.

Next, ignore your limited budget and go to the best salon or fanciest department store in town. Start at the top. Don't panic about the prices. (Who knows, someday you may be able to buy a whole wardrobe there, so don't feel guilty about taking the salesperson's time.) Make an appointment to try on two or three styles. This will give you an idea of which colors, shapes, and styles flatter you most. Do you look better in a shade of ivory, ecru, off-white, blush pink, or bright white? Do long or cap sleeves look prettier? Can you carry off the look of a full ballgown skirt, or does it make you look like a snowball?

Once you have narrowed down the gowns that flatter you most, ask the salesperson to recommend the same basic style but in a gown with a less expensive fabric or made by a less famous designer. Department stores often have women's clothing lines grouped into "good," "better," and "best" categories. The store may carry the "designer original" in one department and a less expensive knockoff of that style in another.

Never shop for a wedding gown when you are tired, hungry, or rushed. Never shop on a Saturday—the stores are crowded with other brides, and you won't get the undivided attention of the sales staff. To avoid too much commotion, bring along just one person whose opinion you trust—not the entire wedding party.

Wear the appropriate undergarments. Bring along a slip (because stiff, crinoline underskirts are scratchy) and wear a strapless bra. Bring shoes with the heel height you plan to wear on the wedding day. Look for the original labels. To prevent price competition, some bridal retailers remove the tags from the gowns so that consumers don't know the name of the manufacturer. Other shops secretly encode the manufacturer's name and style number in their own tags. This is a ploy to keep you from comparison shopping and buying it for less elsewhere.

When ordering the gown, ask to see the designer's measurement and size chart to ensure it is being ordered to the appropriate size. The key measurements are the bust, waist, and hips. Don't be surprised if every gown in your normal size feels tight! It doesn't mean you're getting chunky; most wedding gowns are sized small, another industry mystery. If in doubt, order a size larger than you normally wear. It's much easier to take a gown in than to let it out.

Ask to be measured with a plastic measuring tape, not a cloth or elastic one that's stretched out of size. Record your measurements on the sales receipt, along with the phrase *store-recommended size*. That way, if the gown comes back three sizes too large, you can negotiate for the shop to pay for the additional alterations.

Gabriella Pannunzio, bridal fashion consultant at Hilary S. King Associates in New York, has this advice: "Always have your dress altered by seamstresses who are expert in working with bridal fabrics. That's because chiffon, silk, and organza are very hard to work with, and lots of seamstresses are not experienced in bridal wear and don't know how to work with bustles or with special gown fabrics."

Unless the gown is sold off the rack (with no ordering involved), expect to leave a 50 percent deposit. Deposits are generally nonrefundable, so if you change your mind or find a better deal elsewhere, you've lost the deposit money.

Most shops send the order direct to the manufacturer, where the gown is constructed to your nearest size, not your exact measurements. It often takes months for the gown to come back because manufacturers wait until they have a certain number of orders in the same size and style. Once the gown arrives, the work has just begun. It may take three or four fittings to custom-fit it to your body.

Where to Shop

Wedding gowns are available in bridal salons, department stores, warehouse outlets, mail-order catalogs, and off-price outlets. Vintage and new styles can be found in consignment shops. It's even possible to rent a wedding gown! Use your imagination and be open to "nonbridal" possibilities. You may be able to buy the ultimate dress for next to nothing at a garage sale, craft show, or theatrical costume shop.

WAYS TO SAVE ON THE WEDDING GOWN

Shop the Sales at Bridal Salons

Bridal salons offer the most service, which is important when choosing a wedding gown. A full-service salon typically offers individualized attention, plus salespeople to help the bride try on the gowns and coordinate the accessories and headpieces. Many salons also offer the one-stop-shopping experience, where you can buy shoes, hose, jewelry, gown, accessories, makeup, and bridesmaids' attire in one fell swoop. Think of the time you'll save. (And time is money.)

If a rock-bottom bargain is your ultimate goal, however, avoid bridal salons unless you make a beeline for the clearance rack or find a great deal on a discontinued or overstocked style.

Bridal salons often charge top dollar. In many salons, the sales staff work on commission, which elevates the price and often means more sales pressure to buy. Don't fall prey to a salesperson who gushes that everything looks perfect on you. Use your own judgment or, better yet, bring along one brutally honest friend whose opinion you value.

If you do shop at a bridal salon, consider finding a dependable seamstress to do the alterations at a fraction of the cost of salon alterations. Alterations are a big source of revenue for some bridal salons and can add up to $200 to the tab. Don't be surprised if the salon charges extra for ordering large sizes (over 18) or extra-tall sizes.

Warehouse Outlets

Warehouse and off-price outlets are far cheaper than full-service bridal salons (up to 70 percent off), because the shopper is basically on her own. The gowns are sold off the rack as is, with no special ordering involved. Once a bride selects her dress, she can take it home with her that day.

Warehouse chains are able to slash prices because they keep lean sales staffs, offer few services, and often buy the gowns in bulk or purchase designer samples or past season styles. Some specialize in "designer look" gowns that mimic the current styles but are constructed out of less expensive fabrics and trims.

You may be required to pay in full at the time of sale. Be sure to check out the exchange-and-return policy and alteration fees. If purchasing a discontinued or sample gown, examine it carefully for signs of damage or stains. Chances are it's not returnable.

Have the Gown Made

Buy a pattern and sew the gown yourself, or have it made by a talented friend or professional if you know one. Every fabric store carries patterns for wedding gowns, and these often include instructions for making the veil and other accessories. Patterns cost from $8 to $19. It's the best route to a custom look without the custom price, and if you appreciate fine fabrics, you'll be able to choose a better quality than most bridal gowns are made of.

Before hiring a dressmaker, ask if she regularly alters clothes or makes gowns for brides and bridesmaids. Sewing a wedding gown is a major project that requires specialized skill. The gown must be a perfect fit, and gowns often require linings, beadwork, delicate handwork, or special lace or fabric overlays.

Look at samples of the seamstress's work, inside and out. Are the seams unpuckered and smooth? Do the zippers lie flat? Are the edges finished, meaning the seams won't unravel? Are the sleeves set in smoothly so that they don't bunch or pucker? Does the seamstress have experience working with laces and beading? These details matter.

I remember a bride who was heartbroken when, just three days before her wedding, her seamstress delivered five sloppily sewn bridesmaids' gowns. The dresses were a disaster. The bride had invested hundreds of dollars in expensive lace for overskirts, and the seamstress had botched them badly, leaving pieces ripped and torn. The bride cried for a whole day, then ran out to buy five dresses off the rack at a bridal shop.

Don't know a good seamstress? Call the local high school, fashion design institute, or vocational-technical school for a referral to an aspiring designer or home economics teacher who loves to moonlight. A sewing or fashion design class might be willing to produce your gown as a class project. High school students who have attended proms always know the name of at least one freelance seamstress who is a whiz with formal gowns. Plenty of skilled amateurs are out there.

Keep in mind that having a gown made is not necessarily cheaper than buying one. It all depends on the quality of fabric, the amount of yardage, and the special notions and trims required. Obviously, a gown with 20 yards of fabric will cost more to make than one with 10 yards. Depending on the style, a wedding gown will require as little as 5 yards of fabric for a simple sheath, or as much as 22 yards for style with a multilayered ballgown skirt.

Fabrics range in price from roughly $6 a yard for polyester to $50 to $60 dollars a yard for imported silk or satin.

What do fabric and sewing materials cost? I visited a local chain fabric store and tallied what it would cost to make a classic empire-waist gown with front princess seams, short sleeves, and detachable train.

Sewing Materials and Pattern	Cost
Pattern (size 10)	$12.95
3¾ yards white lamé satin fabric (polyester) (45" wide) @ $8.99 per yard	$33.71
2 spools thread @ $1.10 each	$2.20
3 yards pearl braid trim (1" wide) @ $3.39 per yard	$10.17
1 9" zipper @ $1.50	$1.50
1⅞ yard finishing lace (⅜" wide) @ $1.45 per yard	$2.70
½ yard bridal loops and 6 (⅜") buttons	$3.80
3¾ yards lining fabric (45" wide) @ $3.99 per yard	$14.96
¾ yard interfacing @ $2.97 per yard	$2.23
4¾ yard fabric for train (45" wide) @ $8.99 per yard	$42.70
Sleeve fabric:	
½ yard lace (60" wide) @ $7.99 per yard	$3.99
Sleeve lining:	
½ yard French net lining (60" wide) @ $8.99 per yard	$4.49
Sew-on pearls to embellish sleeves:	
3 packs (5 buttons each) @ $1.30 per pack	$3.90
TOTAL	$139.30

Discount Bridal Service

"The best money-saving tip out there is to buy your gown from Discount Bridal Service. There is nothing better going," says Sue Winner, MBC (master bridal consultant), of Sue Winner and Associates in Atlanta, Georgia.

Discount Bridal Service (DBS) is a national network of local dealers that sells bridal gowns for 25 to 40 percent off retail prices. Based in Scottsdale, Arizona, DBS also offers savings on bridesmaids' gowns, prom dresses, and dresses for the mother of the bride and flower girl. Most nationally advertised gowns are available through DBS, which actually is more a purchasing service than a shopping service.

Once a bride chooses her gown, she works with a DBS representative. The bride provides either the name of the manufacturer, style number, and color, or the issue and page number on which the dress appears in a bridal magazine. DBS verifies the style, quotes a price, orders the gown, and ships it directly to the bride.

"It's virtually any gown the bride wants. She has to do all the research, call the dealer, and tell them what dress she is looking for, the manufacturer and style number, and the dealer will give her a quote. If she likes the quote, she comes in and gets measured," Winner says. "She picks the size ordered based on the manufacturer's measurement chart, and the dress will arrive at her door. DBS will recommend seamstresses in her community. If she is ordering bridesmaids' dresses, they will be able to ship the dresses directly to the bridesmaids so that they can arrive at the wedding ready to walk down the aisle and don't spend the Friday evening before the wedding going to the seamstress."

For more information, call the DBS national sales office at 1-800-874-8794. The DBS Web address is http://www. discountbridalservice.com.

Shop the Department Store Sales

Shop on sale in the "better" dress department or cocktail dress section of a major department store. The fabric quality and workmanship will be invariably better than in a bridal shop, and you'll pay less than for an average gown. Look for a white sheath with matching beaded jacket, a silk or satin suit, or a white evening gown.

Buy a Debutante's Dress

What do brides and debutantes have in common? Long white dresses, of course! Shop for a wedding gown in the debutante department of a boutique or major department store. There's a blizzard of white dresses to choose from, and they are bargains compared to bridal gowns. Shop for a deb gown when the sales begin, which is just after the debutante "season." Although the season varies across the country, many debutantes officially make their "debut" in society in December, early January, or June.

Buy a Bridesmaid's Dress

There are oodles of bridesmaid's styles that can easily double as wedding gowns. The bonus is that bridesmaid's styles are less than half the price of wedding gown styles, and many can be worn again for cocktail parties or special events.

Visit Vintage Clothing Stores

If you love antique clothing, shop for a gown or tea-length dress in a vintage clothing store or antiques shop. For under $100, you may find a treasure that has beautiful laces or intricate beading. (And you won't see the same gown on five other brides.)

Check Out Consignment Shops

Consignment shops sell new and "gently used" clothing at up to 75 percent off the original retail price. They're a smart place to bag a bridal bargain for the simple reason that gowns are worn for a matter of mere hours.

Typically, a bride brings in her gown and veil or headpiece after the wedding, places them on consignment, and then gets a percentage of the selling price (anywhere from 40 to 50 percent). The seller is required to have the gown freshly cleaned and pressed before consigning. Some consignment shops also carry new dresses and discontinued designer styles.

"Often, brand-new dresses that have been dropped from a designer's line are available at consignment shops," notes bridal consultant Lois Pearce of Beautiful Occasions in Hamden, Connecticut. "These dresses have not been pre-owned; they are moved out from the bridal store stock."

Want to save even more? "Buy the gown you want, and after the wedding turn right around and put it in consignment and recoup some money," says Ron Maddox, a certified wedding consultant for A Time for Us Productions in Dallas, Texas. "The consignment market is growing by leaps and bounds. You can find anything from inexpensive dresses to designer dresses and can find a designer gown of your dreams for a fraction of the cost."

Think "Less Is More"

Buy a simple gown with few frills. Lace and beads are labor intensive and boost the price. You can always enhance the gown with pearls, beads, or trims you sew on yourself.

Surf the Internet

It's possible to find a bargain gown on the Web, but be wary. You are expected to pay in full at the time of sale, and you won't be able to try on the gown, feel the fabric, or critique the construction. The gown will arrive in the mail, stuffed in a box, which means you will still need to pay to have it fitted, steamed, and pressed before wearing.

Shop the Sample Sales

To make way for the new, designers and manufacturers clear out their old styles by holding sample sales. Samples are the dresses worn by models when the styles are shown to buyers. Most major wedding gown manufacturers are based in New York City, but if you live in that part of the country or are willing to travel, you can buy a gown for as much as 60 to 80 percent off retail. Sample sales tend to be held in April and May, and again in October and November. Call the manufacturer and ask, "When is your next sample sale?" It may be worth a trip. Be sure to ask what size samples they sell—most sample gowns are in small sizes (6 to 8) because they are worn by models.

Bridal shops nationwide also hold sample sales. But in this case, "sample" means the dresses tried on by women in the shop. Because stocking every gown in every size is too costly, shops often stock just one sample size per style (usually a 10, 12, or 14) and then temporarily pin it to fit on the bride. That's why if you're a size 6, it's hard to get an idea of how a gown *really* will look if you're forced to try it in a size 12. When shopping a sample sale, realize that the gown probably has been tried on many times before. Examine it carefully for makeup stains, open seams, or loose beading. But don't be scared off. Most shops take excellent

care of their samples, and you could wind up with an unbelievable bargain. Again, call the shop for more information.

Scan the Classified Ads

Ever wonder what brides do with their wedding gowns when they
don't go through with their weddings? They donate them to charity or sell them. Look in the classified ads for "never been worn"
wedding dresses at a bargain. Don't feel guilty—sometimes the
gowns are for sale because the bride decided to wear her mother's
gown or found another gown she liked even better.

Rent a Gown

Formalwear shops have been renting tuxes to the groom for years;
at long last the bride can rent her gown, too. There are a growing
number of gown rental shops across the country. To find one, look
in the Yellow Pages under "Wedding" or "Bridal," or call a formalwear shop and ask for a referral.

"We do have a place or two here in Dallas that offers gown
rentals," says Dallas wedding consultant Ron Maddox. "When you
are looking at how much you have to spend, it can be better to rent
a fabulous gown for $199 than buy a cheap one for $199."

Wear an Heirloom Gown

The most sentimental way to save on a wedding gown is to wear
your mother's or grandmother's. Chances are the gown will need
some cleaning and/or repair. It may have yellowed with time or
have rust stains or blotchy spots from being exposed to heat, light,
or air. Unless you're a trained cleaning specialist or textile conservator, don't attempt to clean or refurbish it yourself. Call the local

historical society, gown preservation company, or textile specialist for professional advice.

If the gown is in good shape fabricwise but just needs alterations or a makeover, you have several options:

- ✤ A too-large gown can be taken in and made smaller.
- ✤ A too-small gown can sometimes (but not always) be made larger. This may involve opening the seams or adding gussets or lace to the shoulders and sides. Remember, it's easier to take a gown in than to let it out.
- ✤ Sleeves can be added, lengthened, shortened, or removed.
- ✤ A high neckline can be converted to a low scoop, V-neck, or sweetheart neckline.
- ✤ The bodice of one gown may be removed and attached to a different style "skirt."
- ✤ A long gown can be transformed into a knee-length or tea-length dress.
- ✤ Lace can be "cut away" in sculpted designs and replaced with illusion netting.

Christine Morrissey is president of National Gown Cleaners, a gown-cleaning and preservation company based in San Jose, California. She offers the following advice for remaking or repairing an old wedding gown.

**What can be done to refresh or
remake a previously worn or vintage gown?**
"First, consult with a textile conservator or gown cleaner before attempting any handling yourself. To refresh a gown can be as simple as hanging it out in a cool location for a few days. To change the smell of aging or remove any dust requires some form of cleaning. If the gown is in need of alterations, consult with a dressmaker, then follow up with a dry cleaner or [specialized] gown cleaner.

In many cases, cleaning first is appropriate. On the other hand, there are some cases where you are better off doing the alterations first. It really depends on the condition of the garment."

Should you ever try to attempt cleaning
or remaking the gown yourself?
"Speak with a textile conservator first, so that you can walk away knowing all the options. One option may be doing the work yourself. I have given instructions to many brides on how to handle a cleaning or alteration on their own. I would not ask this question of a normal dry cleaner. Textile conservators are trained to keep the integrity of the garment yet make recommendations based on knowledge of fabrics."

How can you find a reputable person or company
to repair or restore a gown? What questions should you ask?
"I would always look for a company that specializes in doing this type of work and has at least twelve references within the last year. More important, does it have the proper type of insurance to cover the damage from improper handling?

"Ask the company how long it has been around. This doesn't always make it better, but it gives you an idea of the business it is. I would also ask what methods of cleaning are available. What kind of damage should you expect, if any? Does the company have experience in matching or dying fabrics, which may be necessary in a restoration requiring an alteration, and what value of insurance is it willing to commit to? Does it have an appraiser it can consult? The bottom line is, check references before hiring. These should include the AIC (The American Institute for Conservation of Historical and Artistic Works), the Better Business Bureau, museums (call them directly!), bridal shops, a good dressmaker, the Internet, wedding planning books, and in some cases a few dry cleaners."

What are the most common questions brides ask about restoring or repairing an old gown?
"How much does it cost? What color can I expect to get? My company takes a sample piece of fabric off the gown and tests the cleaning first. We basically do a restoration on the swatch. That way, the customer can see the color somewhat like it should be after services. The next question is, what is the time frame? It normally takes six to eight weeks to complete a job including a follow-up cleaning and pressing. This time frame doesn't include any repairs or alterations. In most restoration jobs, we wait for the cleaning result to determine what kind of alterations will be needed."

What are some of the most common things you can do?
"We probably do more free consultations than anything else. It is the only way to give the customer information they can walk away with and think about before making the huge commitment to time and money. We use a wet-cleaning method using a slow-acting bleach to restore most of the gowns we work on. We also use ovis paste on many old and historical textiles. This is a paste-type product that is used by most textile conservators. This is a good question to ask so-called gown-cleaning specialists. If they don't use it, then they really don't know what they should know about old fabrics and cleaning them. We also do a huge job with matching textiles or fabrics to be used in the alterations following the cleaning. Basting down areas that are fragile is also a must before handling many older gowns. A good dressmaker would also recommend this prior to cleaning."

WAYS TO SAVE ON ACCESSORIES

Shoes and Hosiery

■ **DON'T BUY "BRIDAL" SHOES IN A BRIDAL SALON.** You'll pay top dollar for what is essentially a white pump with fabric rosettes or sequins glued on. Instead, buy a pair of plain white pumps in a theatrical- or dance-supply store. They'll be inexpensive *and* incredibly comfortable. (Comfortable shoes are critical on the wedding day! The bride stands, walks, or dances for most of the day. Be sure to break in your shoes before the big day.)

■ **WEAR BALLERINA SLIPPERS.** They're graceful and feel like cozy bedroom slippers.

■ **SHOP THE MIDSUMMER SALES.** You'll find white shoes in all styles and heel heights.

■ **DON'T WASTE MONEY ON WHITE "BRIDAL" STOCKINGS.** These cost $15 to $20 a pair. They may have fancy designs, but no one sees them under a long gown, except for a few seconds during the garter toss.

The Wedding Veil

■ **FORGO THE VEIL AND HEADPIECE.** Wear a cluster of flowers in your hair or a pretty barrette decorated with fresh floral sprigs.

■ **IF WEARING AN UPSWEPT HAIRDO, SHOW IT OFF AND SKIP THE VEIL.** Ask the hairstylist to insert tiny rosebuds, pearls, or baby's breath into your hair. Shop for bobby pins with tiny pearls on the end or make them yourself by attaching seed pearls with Krazy Glue.

■ **BUY A GOOD-QUALITY COMMUNION VEIL.** It may sound a little ridiculous to wear a child's veil, but you'll get the same look as a bridal veil on a limited budget. No one will know the difference. Or buy a white headpiece or satin wreath in the children's communion accessories department. Many of these are lovely and already decorated with satin flowers and ribbon streamers.

■ **BORROW A VEIL FROM A RECENTLY MARRIED SISTER OR FRIEND.** The look can always be changed a little by adding or removing laces or decorations.

■ **MAKE YOUR OWN VEIL.** Visit the wedding section of a large craft store and look for how-to guides. Most craft stores stock all the pieces for making a veil: the headband or headpiece, tulle, pearls, trims, ribbons, and barrettes. Ask the manager if the store offers any veil-making classes or seminars. For under $20, any bride can create a custom veil, even if she's all thumbs.

■ **BUY A PLAIN SATIN HEADBAND OR OVERSIZED PLASTIC BARRETTE IN THE WEDDING DEPARTMENT OF A CRAFT STORE CHAIN AND SEW OR GLUE SHIRRED TULLE TO THE UNDERSIDE.** Tulle for bridal veils is conveniently available in precut and preshirred lengths. It comes with the edges raw (unfinished), trimmed with narrow satin ribbon, or neatly turned under. Ready-to-use floral and pearl sprays are available with bendable wrapped wires.

■ **BUY A PLAIN PLASTIC HEADBAND AND WRAP IT WITH WHITE GROSGRAIN OR SATIN RIBBON.** Tuck or glue in the ends. Take a hot-glue gun and decorate with seed pearls or small fabric flowers.

■ **USE AN ALTERNATIVE TO A VEIL AND HEADPIECE.** Try a simple mantilla (a light scarf) of beautiful lace you've borrowed from a grandmother or purchased in a fine fabrics shop. Wear a wreath of fresh flowers that match the bridal bouquet. Shop the after-Easter sales for a glorious hat.

CHAPTER NINE

THE WEDDING PARTY

Think of the wedding party as your personal dream team. They are the people you treasure most in the world and the ones with whom you most wish to share the joy of your wedding day. On a practical level, they are the people you can count on to help with the planning and to support you throughout the process of preparing for marriage. They're a circle of love.

Despite the warm, fuzzy feelings you'll get from being surrounded by lots of friends as you walk down the aisle, resist the temptation to ask *all* your sorority sisters or *every* childhood friend you ever played dolls with to be your bridesmaids. Do yourself a big favor and keep the wedding party small. You'll save time and money and avoid stress.

Gone are the formal days when a bride was expected to have at least five bridesmaids and five groomsmen and a troop of little children as ring bearers and flower girls. (Your grandmother's wedding portrait probably had a group shot of at least a dozen people, didn't it?) Weddings just aren't that formal anymore—and few people observe the old rule of thumb that you need at least one usher for every fifty guests.

The more people included as attendants, the higher the costs for the ceremony and reception. Imagine the wedding party has four bridesmaids, four groomsmen, a best man, a matron of honor, two flower girls, and a ring bearer. That's only an extra thirteen people to invite, right? Wrong. You can't include the bridesmaids, groomsmen, and honor attendants without their spouses or dates. And, understandably, young children must be escorted by their parents. That's twenty-nine people.

But that's not all. Sure, they pay for their own attire, but each person represents hidden additional costs, like boutonnieres, bouquets, gifts, an extra two people at dinner, an extra two people at the reception, a larger limousine, hotel accommodations, an extra person at the bridesmaids' luncheon, and extra table centerpieces, linens, and favors. Don't forget more time for the photographer to set up and shoot portraits of each one of these people and their respective spouses, dates, or parents. Plus, you've got the stress of long-distance telephone calls, travel arrangements, dress fittings, airport pickups and drop-offs, a baby-sitter for the flower girl's baby brother, and trying to get the members of a large bridal party to agree on dresses, flowers, accessories, shoes, and tuxes. Whew!

Consider choosing two bridesmaids instead of three, and you can easily trim the following amounts.

Bouquet	$75
Floral headpiece	$30
Gift	$35
Rehearsal dinner (with spouse or escort)	$70

Reception meal (with spouse or escort)	$100
Bridesmaids' luncheon	$30
Accommodations (two nights)	$200
Transportation to/from airport	$70
TOTAL	$610

Granted, many of the people the couple considers close enough to be in the wedding party are people they would otherwise include as guests. But it's easy to see how it all adds up and how much can be saved by cutting back just a little. (And the bride and bridegroom could take that extra $610 and put it toward a longer honeymoon or a new dining-room set.)

When it comes to the wedding party, keep in mind the following practical ways to save.

WAYS TO SAVE ON ATTIRE FOR THE MAID OF HONOR AND BRIDESMAIDS

■ **ASK ABOUT GROUP DISCOUNTS.** Some shops offer a free dress when a minimum number of dresses is ordered (say three or four), or a 20 percent discount when several dresses are ordered together. Even if a discount is not advertised, ask for one. It can't hurt.

Don't take all the bridesmaids shopping at the same time. It will be chaos. It's difficult enough finding one "perfect" dress for one body type; try finding five for people of all different sizes, shapes, and personal tastes.

Be considerate. Pick a style in keeping with the bridesmaids' budgets. You get the final say on what your attendants wear, but understand that being a bridesmaid can be a real financial hardship for some people. (How would you like to have a $300 fuchsia dress hanging in your closet that somebody else chose and that you may never wear again?)

If your attendants are embarrassed about disclosing their weight, dress size, bust size, or height, give them each an index card and envelope and tell them to write down their measurements and seal it in the envelope. Label all the envelopes and hand them to the sales clerk while ordering hosiery or dresses.

■ **WISE IS THE BRIDE WHO HAS JUST ONE OR TWO BRIDESMAIDS.** That means she doesn't have to worry about finding multiples of a dress style, which makes it easier to snag bargains in outlets, vintage clothing stores, and consignment shops.

■ **AVOID BRIDAL SALONS UNLESS YOU MAKE A BEELINE FOR THE CLEARANCE RACK OR FIND A BARGAIN ON A DISCONTINUED OR OVERSTOCKED STYLE.** Bridal salons often charge a premium for anything "bridal," which includes bridesmaids' dresses.

■ **VISIT THE "BETTER" DRESS DEPARTMENT OF A LOCAL DEPARTMENT STORE.** Surprisingly, a designer cocktail dress or evening gown may cost $75 to $100 less than a bridesmaid's dress at a bridal salon. The fabric and quality will be better, and the bridesmaid will have something she can truly wear again.

■ **WHEN SHOPPING, CONSIDER THE "WEAR AGAIN" FACTOR.** A dress that costs $100 is no bargain if the bridesmaid wouldn't be caught dead wearing it again. However, investing $200 on a dress that can be worn many times to a cocktail party, holiday party, business affair, or other special event is a great value.

■ **SHOP THE CLEARANCE SALES AT STORES THAT HAVE CHAINS NATIONWIDE.** When I was a bridesmaid for my sister-in-law, I found a great tea-length dress on sale at a Laura Ashley shop for $40. The salesclerk held the dress a few days until I could call the other two bridesmaids (in two other states) and tell each to look at the dress in the store's mail-order catalog. When they both approved the style and the price, the shop called stores around the country to find two more in the sizes we needed. The bride was so impressed, she ordered one in another color for herself for her honeymoon. The total for the four dresses was $160, less than what each of us expected to pay for one dress.

■ **LOOK FOR A PROM DRESS** There are plenty of sophisticated, elegant styles to choose from, and it's easy to find something pretty and flattering for around $100. Better yet, wait until the after-prom season for clearance sales.

■ **SKIP PRICEY ACCESSORIES SUCH AS OPERA GLOVES, DECORATIVE SHOE CLIPS, COORDINATING JEWELRY ENSEMBLES, HAIR CLIPS, OR FANCY DESIGNER HOSE (WHICH NO ONE REALLY SEES ANYWAY).** If you want the bridesmaids to wear special pearls or drop earrings, consider making these your gift to them.

■ **IF THERE ARE LITTLE GIRLS AND GROWN-UPS IN THE WEDDING PARTY, LOOK FOR COORDINATING "MOTHER-DAUGHTER" DRESSES IN STORES OR MAIL-ORDER CATALOGS.** These styles were popular in the late 1960s and early 1970s and are making a comeback. Mail-order companies such as Land's End (1-800-356-4444) and Talbot's (1-800-992-9010) now carry seasonal mother daughter styles featuring matching or coordinating dresses for women, teens, and young girls. *Voilà!* An instant ensemble look for everybody.

Check out the party and cocktail dresses in the Chadwick's of Boston mail-order catalog (1-800-525-6650). The company sells well-known designer brands at a discount in women's, children's, and petite sizes. Many of the dressier styles are perfect for bridesmaids and come with matching shoes.

■ **PICK A SEWING PATTERN AND HAVE THE DRESS MADE BY A PRO-FESSIONAL SEAMSTRESS OR A TALENTED FRIEND.** Most major fabric stores have a bridal fabric section, as well as trims, pearl sprays, and materials for making a matching headpiece.

Keep in mind that sewing a dress is *not* necessarily cheaper than buying one! It all depends on the quality of the fabric, the amount of yardage needed, trims, lining, interfacing, notions, and so forth, and the labor involved. A basic bridal or bridesmaid's gown pattern costs $10 to $20. Seamstresses charge anywhere from $15 to $50 an hour, depending on their skill and experience and whether the dress requires laborious hand beading or lining. A dress style with simple lines and little decoration is quickest—and therefore the least costly—to make.

■ **IF YOU'RE LUCKY ENOUGH TO HAVE BRIDESMAIDS WHO ARE ALL THE SAME SIZE, LOOK FOR SAMPLE SALES.** Most stores carry wedding and bridesmaids' gowns in sample size 10. These can often be taken in or taken out. Be wary: buying the sample means buying a dress many people have tried on. You may get a bargain, but check it carefully for makeup stains around the neck, perspiration stains at the armholes, open seams, or other signs of damage. If it's in terrible shape, it's not worth any price.

■ **BUY UNDERGARMENTS ON SALE AT A LINGERIE SHOP OR WARE-HOUSE OUTLET.** "Bridesmaid" and "bridal" slips, bras, and bustiers are no different from those sold in lingerie shops and often are priced exorbitantly because a tiny rosebud or bit of white "bridal" lace has been added.

■ **BORROW A POUFY CRINOLINE SKIRT, OR SPLIT THE COST WITH ANOTHER BRIDESMAID WHO MAY USE IT LATER IN THE YEAR AT ANOTHER WEDDING.** Why spend $40 to $80 for a stiff, Scarlett O'Hara–style crinoline skirt when you truly will never wear it again (unless it's under a Halloween costume).

■ **PURCHASE SHOES AT A DISCOUNT STORE.** The plainer the style, the less expensive. You can always dress up plain satin pumps with clip-on pearl earrings, or take a hot-glue gun and attach a decoration or fabric rosette, advises bridal consultant Lois Pearce of Beautiful Occasions in Hamden, Connecticut. "Purchase satin pumps from a local shoe store, use a glue gun, and apply an appliqué from a craft store to dress the shoe up," she says.

■ **IF THE SHOES ARE TO BE DYED, BRING ALL OF THE PAIRS OF SHOES IN TO BE DYED AT THE SAME TIME.** This avoids variations of color from different dye lots. If the bridesmaids live in different parts of the country, suggest they each buy the same shoe style at a major national shoe chain and have them mail the shoes to one designated person, who will arrange for the dyeing of all the pairs at the same time. When everyone arrives a day or two before the wedding, dole out the shoes at the rehearsal dinner.

■ **FOR A UNIFORM LOOK, PURCHASE HOSE FOR ALL THE BRIDES-MAIDS AT THE SAME TIME.** You may get a discount for the bulk purchase and will be assured of having the same color and style for all. Pick up a few extra pairs in case there are any last-minute snags or runs.

WAYS TO SAVE ON ATTIRE
FOR THE FLOWER GIRL

■ **"FOR KIDS, SHOP AT EASTER TIME OR AT AFTER-EASTER SALES,"** advises Charisse Min Alliegro of Princeton Event Consultants in Princeton, New Jersey. From late January through early May, stores are full of pretty Easter dresses, often with matching hats and accessories and little coordinating baskets or purses. During the after-Easter sales, there are bargains galore on tights, dresses, gloves, hats, and underslips. Having a midwinter wedding? Shop the after-Christmas sales for beautiful holiday dresses in satins, brocades, and velvets.

■ **SHOP FOR A COMMUNION DRESS.** Once traditionally all white, communion dresses are now also available in pale pastels or in white or ivory with colorful trims. Look for a plain white dress with simple lines and give it a custom look by tying a wide satin ribbon ($3 a yard) around the waist. For a coordinated look on a shoestring, you can add the same-color-ribbon bows to the child's shoes, hair, or flower basket. Most children making their First Holy Communion attend the religious ceremony in early spring, so the best time to find an outfit at an after-communion sale is in April through June. Some mail-order catalogs specialize in communion dresses, veils, headpieces, and accessories (like little purses, gloves, baskets, and Bibles). Call the office at your local Catholic church and ask if it has any catalogs or can recommend a supplier.

Communion clothes departments are also a gold mine for hair decorations and veils. Many communion veils are absolutely perfect for flower girl wear, and there are loads of pretty headpiece styles with fabric flowers, pearl sprays, and trailing ribbons. Whereas you might spend $75 for a child's headpiece or wreath in a bridal salon, you can find similar styles for $10 to $15 in a communion department.

■ **DON'T EVEN *THINK* OF BUYING KIDS' PARTY SHOES IN A BRIDAL SALON OR RETAIL SHOE STORE.** Mothers will tell you: for the best buys on patent leather party shoes, ballet slipper flats, or Mary Jane styles, visit a shoe outlet store or the shoe department of a large national discount chain such as Target, Bradlees, or Kmart. You will find dozens of styles at under $10 a pair, versus $40 to $70 a pair at retail and bridal salons. White party shoes are a mess after a couple of wearings anyway, and kids' feet grow so quickly that it's a crime to spend too much on a pair of children's shoes for a wedding.

Remind the child's mother to have her break in the shoes before the wedding. There's nothing worse than a cranky flower girl who won't walk down the aisle because her feet hurt. If the mother needs advice, tell her to put each shoe into a clear plastic bag, or wrap each shoe in plastic wrap and urge the child to walk around the house in the shoes for a few days. Kids think this is a fun game and will be happy to oblige.

■ **DON'T WASTE MONEY ON FANCY TIGHTS WITH DELICATE PATTERNS OR DECORATIONS.** Nobody sees them under long dresses, and you'll really need to buy two pairs of tights anyway, because young children don't stay clean in dress-up clothes for long. Flower girls invariably run around and get their tights dirty or snagged. That's why seasoned photographers always take the portrait of the flower girl first!

■ **SHOP FOR PLAIN WHITE GLOVES IN A CRAFT STORE.** No kidding. For less than $2 a pair, you can find basic styles that are pretty the way they are or can be jazzed up with a glue gun and rosettes or ribbons.

WAYS TO SAVE ON ATTIRE FOR THE BEST MAN AND GROOMSMEN

■ **BRING ALONG FABRIC SWATCHES OR COLOR PICTURES OF THE DRESSES TO CHOOSE COMPLEMENTARY TUXEDO AND TIE COLORS.** It may seem obvious, but be sure the styles coordinate well with the bridesmaids' and maid/matron of honor's attire. It's important that the men's and women's outfits and accessories look good together for the group portraits.

■ **ASK FRIENDS FOR REFERRALS TO REPUTABLE FORMALWEAR SHOPS KNOWN FOR SERVICE, QUALITY, AND VALUE.** If the wedding date is near prom or graduation season, be sure to reserve the tuxes several months ahead.

■ **ADVISE THE MEN TO HAVE THEIR MEASUREMENTS TAKEN BY AN EXPERIENCED TAILOR.** Don't hand them a tape measure and trust them to ask their mothers or roommates to do it. Getting the measurements exact is critical for a proper fit, and most people don't know how to do this correctly.

■ **RENT OR BUY? FORMALWEAR EXPERTS NOTE THAT ANY MAN WHO WEARS A TUXEDO MORE THAN TWO TIMES A YEAR IS PROBABLY WISER TO BUY THAN TO RENT.** Compare the cost of renting versus buying. You may be surprised.

■ **COMPARISON SHOP.** Formalwear shops vary widely in the quality of the lines they carry and the prices they charge. Visit several to get an idea of their range of selection. Does the stock look fresh and up-to-date? Are the accessories current? Does the shop offer a wide range of prices and package deals? Does the shop cater mostly to the high school prom trade? Does it carry an extensive selection of wedding attire? Does it have tuxedos for little boys, too?

■ **ASK ABOUT QUANTITY DISCOUNTS.** Most formalwear shops offer the fifth suit free with the rental or purchase of four others. That usually means the groom's rental is free. But if the groom already has a tuxedo or will wear a military uniform, ask if the groom's father can get the freebie.

■ **ASK WHAT THE RENTAL PACKAGE INCLUDES.** The average package includes tux, shirt, cummerbund, bow tie or tie, and shoes. You'll need to arrange for all the guys to wear the same-color socks. Purchase the socks in bulk at a discount store and dole them out at the rehearsal dinner while the bridesmaids are picking up their dyed shoes.

■ **SAVE YOURSELF A LOT OF AGGRAVATION BY REMINDING ALL THE MEN TO CHECK ALL THE PIECES IN THE RENTAL PACKAGE BEFORE TAKING IT OUT OF THE SHOP.** Are they the right color and size? Did you get *two* left shoes? Horror stories abound of groomsmen who walk down the aisle in borrowed tennis shoes or oversized, droopy shirts because they didn't open the rentalwear box until they arrived at the ceremony.

■ **IF THE WEDDING IS NOT FORMAL, SUGGEST THAT THE MEN WEAR DRESSY ATTIRE THEY CAN USE AGAIN.** A smart look is a classic navy blazer, crisp white shirt, khakis or gray wool pants, and a silk tie. To give the outfits a snazzy, coordinated look, make your gift to each groomsman a colorful vest or matching silk tie.

WAYS TO SAVE ON GIFTS
FOR THE ATTENDANTS

It's customary to give a thank-you gift to each attendant. They deserve it—wedding party members really are expected to come through for the bride and groom. A gift need not be expensive, but it should be thoughtful and selected with the person's tastes and personality in mind.

The old standbys are faux pearls for the women and cuff links or money clips for the men. Frankly, these choices have been done to death. The gifts need not all be the same. Some couples choose to give the best man and maid/matron of honor a more substantial gift than the other attendants to reflect the honored role they play in the wedding. It's up to you. Consider the following ideas that run under $25.

For the Female Attendants

❖ Aromatherapy candles or essential oils

❖ A gift certificate for a manicure or pedicure

❖ Monogrammed stationery

❖ Designer makeup brushes

❖ Long-distance calling card

❖ A gift certificate for a cooking class

❖ Travel-size shampoos, conditioners, and soaps in a pretty zippered travel bag

❖ Pretty hair ornaments: barrettes, floral hair clips, or headbands

❖ A fine silk scarf

❖ Candlesticks

❖ A charm with a wedding motif or something else sentimental (if she has a charm bracelet)

❖ A long-running tape of her favorite music

❖ Pretty jewelry-organizing compartment boxes for her drawers

❖ Gift certificates for several nights at the movies
❖ A tree seedling

For the Male Attendants

❖ A monogrammed baseball cap
❖ A desk clock
❖ A gift certificate to a bookstore or music store
❖ A personalized coffee mug filled with specialty coffee beans
❖ A pocketknife
❖ A vest or tie
❖ A CD case
❖ A brandy snifter
❖ A long-distance calling card
❖ A gift certificate for movie tickets

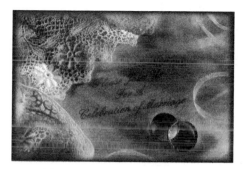

CHAPTER TEN

WEDDING INVITATIONS

First impressions count. When a wedding invitation arrives in the mailbox, it has an important job to do. It announces a couple's impending special day and their wish to be surrounded by loved ones.

But an invitation gives more than just the date, time, and venue of the ceremony and reception. It reflects the style and formality of the wedding and even gives guests an idea of what's appropriate to wear. A handwritten invitation suggests guests should expect an informal, small wedding. An engraved invitation indicates a more formal affair. If the invitation notes a 7 P.M. ceremony, guests know that evening gowns and tailcoats may be in order.

Invitations should be ordered as soon as the date is set and the guest list is complete, which should be at least three to six months in advance. This allows time for ordering, proofreading the text, and addressing the invitations yourself or hiring a calligrapher. Set aside at least a week for addressing the invitations because it always takes longer than expected. It's more fun when a friend helps out. Ask a friend with beautiful penmanship to spend some quiet evenings with you addressing the invitations without distractions. They should be mailed four to six weeks before the ceremony, and up to eight weeks ahead for a summer or holiday wedding, especially a June date when guests often have competing social obligations for both graduations and weddings.

Expect to spend anywhere from $80 to $1,000 for a hundred invitations. Custom, handcrafted, and engraved invitations are the priciest. Why such an enormous difference when it's only paper? It all depends on the quality of paper stock, the little extras (liners, inserts, colored inks, gold seals and decorations), whether the invitation has labor-intensive laser cuts or lace cutouts, and the printing method used.

Wedding stationery may be ordered through a commercial printing company; at a stationery store; through a bridal consultant; in a bridal shop, jewelry shop, department store, or office supply store; or through mail-order catalogs.

PRINTING METHODS

About fifteen years ago, wedding invitation choices were pretty much limited to ivory or cream paper with a single fold and plain black ink. That look is still elegant and timeless, but brides also can choose from a rainbow of colored inks, theme designs (including cowboys, flowers, entwined hearts, or cartoon characters), and unusual papers such as translucent vellum and textured rice paper.

Some couples shudder at the idea of using anything but the classic cream invitation with engraving or thermography. If that style doesn't reflect your personality, don't feel compelled to use it. There are seemingly endless choices at every price point.

Engraving

This is the most elegant, most formal, and most expensive option. Engraving is a centuries-old printing process in which the text is cut (engraved) into the surface of a copper or brass plate. Ink is applied to the metal surface, which is then wiped clean, leaving ink inside the impressions. Paper is laid on the die, and a press forces the paper into the cavities of the die, creating a raised-letter effect. The letters can be felt from the back. Engraving is beautiful but costly and time consuming, since a plate must be custom-made for each client. Unless you have money to burn, skip engraving.

Embossing

Embossing isn't technically a printing process, but it does press dimensional designs, text, borders, or artwork into the paper, creating a raised surface. It's pretty but pricey. If money is tight, consider using embossing for just a single design or a raised initial.

Thermography

A less expensive alternative to engraving, thermography is the most popular printing method for wedding invitations. In this heat process, wet ink and a resin powder are fused together on the paper to create a raised-lettering effect. The print is raised and slightly shiny, and the letters cannot be felt from the back. The average person can't tell the difference between engraving and thermography. A great choice for the couple on a limited budget.

Laser printing

This is an inexpensive form of printing in which the ink lies flat on the paper. The look is attractive, but it's not the highest quality and isn't appropriate for formal invitations. Laser printing is best used for casual or informal invitations.

Personal computer printing

Many personal computers now have software programs for print-ing invitations for weddings and special events. These are super for informal invitations, and the price is certainly right. Be sure to set the printer "properties" for the sharpest quality printing and buy extra print cartridges before printing the invitations. You don't want to run out in the middle of the project.

Handwritten invitations

For a small, informal wedding or a wedding at home, buy beautiful plain invitations or note cards at a stationer and write them your-self using a fine-quality pen.

Computerized or handwritten calligraphy

Calligraphy is an elegant form of script featuring flourishes and curls. The look can be achieved by computer (done at most sta-tionery stores) or by hand. A calligrapher usually creates a master, which is then replicated by engraving, thermography, or offset printing. Unless the guest list is very small, it is far too costly for a calligrapher to write every single invitation by hand, so most peo-ple have only the envelopes addressed by hand. Expect to pay any-where from $3 to $15 to address each envelope.

It All Adds Up

If you think basic invitations and envelopes are the only expense, think again. The following are two invitation packages and prices (from two well-known stationery companies) for simple ecru invi-tations with a single fold. The first is for thermographed invita-tions, the second is for engraved invitations. *Note:* These packages contain different pieces and are intended as a general comparison.

"Although traditional genuine engraved stationery has been synonymous with the best in fine wedding stationery, brides can save money by ordering thermographed 'raised printing' wedding stationery," advises Linda Hiniker, a marketing executive with Carlson Craft® stationery in North Mankato, Minnesota. "This process simulates the appearance of engraving and the cost is much less."

100 thermographed invitations

Invitations with filigree border	$80.95
Informal/thank-you cards	$31.95
Enclosure cards	$31.95
Response cards and envelopes	$36.95
Printed outer envelopes	$13.00
Lined inner envelopes (gold)	$12.00
Burgundy ink	$5.50
TOTAL (before postage)	$212.30

100 engraved invitations

Invitations (no border)	$273.90
Response cards and envelopes	$173.90
Reception cards	$115.90
At-home cards	$115.90
Burgundy ink	$18.00
TOTAL (before postage)	$697.60

"There are so many invitation companies out there that provide discounts, you don't have to pay full price and can still get lovely invitations," says Beverly Ann Bonner, MBC, owner of The Beautiful Wedding Inc. in Norwood, Massachusetts. She notes that invitation prices vary widely and there is "lots of price flexibility out there."

Bonner advises couples to shop around for quality invitations and ask the vendor for the best possible price. "It doesn't hurt to ask. You may be pleasantly surprised. Tell them, 'Listen, I saw this in another place, but I really like your service and your quality. Could you give us a small discount?' Even if it's only 10 percent, you are still ahead of the game."

Don't stop there. Bonner says another great way to save is to print your own save-the-date cards using a personal computer. "You don't need to pay an expensive printer for this. You can do it yourself with desktop publishing," she notes. "Do something ahead of time with a save-the-date letter with information about hotels, airline, and directions."

To get an idea of what's available, borrow an invitation sample book from a stationery store or send away for free mail-order catalogs. Many will send free samples of invitations as well as samples of liners, envelopes, ribbons, and place cards. (See phone numbers on pages 146–148, or look at the back pages of bridal magazines for free resources.) Compare styles and prices. It's amazing how much they vary. Catalogs are gold mines of information and usually have pages devoted to sample invitation wordings, hotline numbers to call for help, and explanations of what all the papers, cards, and envelopes are used for.

But be wary: many of the paper stocks offered in these catalogs are thin, even cheesy. Always ask for a paper sample to determine if the quality is up to your standard. Even if you don't particularly like what the catalogs offer, it's a good way to research what's out there and get a feel for fonts, inks, paper stocks, and invitation styles.

Generally, a couple will want to order invitations, matching envelopes, response cards, thank-you notes, informal cards (folded notes printed with their married name or monogram on front), and at-home cards to inform friends of their new address. If the entire ensemble is ordered at the same time, the printer sometimes will provide a discount.

Making the Guest List: His, Hers, and Theirs

The guest list usually is compiled from several sources: the bride's friends and co-workers, the groom's friends and co-workers, the bride's relatives, the groom's relatives, and any friends or colleagues they have in common. It's customary to send invitations to each member of the wedding party as well as to the officiant and all guests over the age of sixteen. If the officiant is married, include his or her spouse.

To calculate the number of invitations to order, figure one for each couple, plus one for each single guest. Some etiquette experts say it isn't obligatory to invite dates, but I've been to too many affairs where single guests were invited without escorts and felt resentful. Likewise, don't invite a married person without his or her spouse, even if you are struggling to stretch your budget and have never met the spouse. The usual offenders are couples who invite their co-workers but tell them to leave their spouses behind. Or worse, they invite the spouses of some colleagues but not others. No one will care that you are trying to save money; they'll just feel hurt and may even consider staying home.

Do You Really Need All Those Cards and Envelopes?

The most confusing aspect of choosing invitations is keeping all the pieces straight. What fits into which envelope, and why is so much stationery needed? The truth is, the groom and bride really don't need all the pieces the sample books list as necessary. Save money by ordering only what you really want and need.

Response cards

These are small rectangular cards enclosed with the invitations. They are filled out and returned by guests to give you an accurate reception guest count. As a courtesy, enclose stamped, self-addressed envelopes with the response cards for easy mailing. The response card sometimes includes a choice of entrée for guests to indicate, as well as a deadline for guests to respond: *The favour of a reply by December 10, 2001, is requested.*

Reception cards

These cards state the time, date, and place of the reception. They are used to invite guests to the reception following the ceremony and need not be mailed back by the recipient.

Ceremony cards

These are used when everyone is invited to the reception, but only a select few also are invited to the ceremony.

Within-the-ribbon cards

Sometimes called pew cards, these printed cards are sent with the invitations to special guests for whom you wish to provide reserved, assigned pew seats. A white ribbon usually is draped across the seat. The guest presents this card to the usher. He or she is escorted to the seat, and the ribbon is removed. Within-the-ribbon cards were once used exclusively for royal and ultraformal weddings, but many contemporary couples are using them as a way to honor guests and give them exclusive, preferred seats at the ceremony.

At-home cards

These cards inform recipients of your new address and the date you'll be moving there. At-home cards may be inserted with the wedding invitation or wedding announcement. This is an old tradition that goes back to the days when ladies in society were available during certain times of the week to "receive" callers at home.

The cards traditionally read:

Mr. and Mrs. Joseph Gorini
Will be home after May 24th
161 West Hill Drive
Greenwich, Connecticut 06820
(203) 772-1234

Tissue paper

Sheets of delicate white or ecru paper may be placed between the invitation and the envelope. The tradition of inserting tissue originated when a printer in a hurry used tissue paper as a blotter instead of waiting for the ink to dry naturally.

Informals

These folded note cards are printed with your married name or monogram on the front.

Wedding programs

These one-page or fold-over (resembling a brochure) cards list the wedding party, parts of the ceremony service, the musical selections, and any special sentiments from the bride and groom.

Wedding announcement

Often, there are people you'll want to notify of your wedding but don't feel inclined to invite for any number of reasons—they might live too far away or be casual acquaintances. In this case, a wedding announcement will do. Wedding announcements are never sent before the ceremony has taken place and the license has been signed. (So don't be tempted to mail them on the way to the church—you never know what might happen.)

The announcement should be in the same paper, style, and color as the invitation. It includes the wedding date but not the location, and therefore is not an invitation to attend. People who receive wedding announcements are not obligated to send a wedding gift.

Save-the-date mailings

These printed cards are mailed at least three months before the wedding and urge friends and relatives to "save the date" for your wedding. A save-the-date mailing is helpful for alerting guests who will travel a distance and need to plan well ahead, or when your wedding is in June or at another busy time of year. Guests may be invited to other weddings or graduations, and you want to get to them first. If a block of hotel rooms is being reserved for guests with a special rate, it's thoughtful to include this information on the save-the-date card, along with the hotel's phone number and deadline for reservations. You also might include information on sightseeing and nearby attractions.

Envelopes

The outer envelope is the larger one with glue on the inside flap. The guest's name and address are written on the front of the outer envelope; your return address is written on the back envelope flap. The inner envelope is the one without glue. On it is written the guests' surnames with their appropriate title, such as *Mr. and Mrs. Kenneth Gibson* or *The Reverend James McArthur*.

How do all those cards and envelopes go together? Have the stationer demonstrate and also give you an assembled set to take home as an example. The wedding invitation is placed fold-side down in the unsealed inner envelope, along with all enclosures (response card and envelope, reception card, etc.) and a piece of tissue paper. Then the inside envelope is placed into the larger outer envelope, face-side up toward the flap, for addressing and mailing. See? It's not so hard.

WAYS TO SAVE ON INVITATIONS

■ **CHOOSE A CLASSIC STYLE.** You can't go wrong with the traditional single-fold white or ivory invitation with black ink. It looks elegant and upscale, and many companies make them with inexpensive but substantial-looking paper stock. Best of all, the traditional style requires no fussy inserts, illustrations, or liners, so there's no need to spring for costly extras.

■ **UNLESS YOU HAVE YOUR HEART SET ON ENGRAVING AND HAVE VOWED TO CUT BACK ELSEWHERE, CHOOSE THERMOGRAPHED INVITATIONS INSTEAD.** Most people don't notice the difference between thermography and engraving anyway, and thermography is often one-third to one-half the price.

■ **AVOID OVERSIZED INVITATIONS AND ENVELOPES.** Nonstandard sizes always cost more, and the added weight translates into extra postage. This doesn't sound like much, but realize that invitations require one or two stamps for the outer envelope, plus another stamp for the response card envelope. Multiply that (3 stamps at 33 cents each) by about 150 invitations, and the tab for postage alone is almost $150!

■ **WHEN CONSIDERING ORDERING INVITATIONS OR ACCESSORIES BY MAIL, FACTOR IN THE ADDED COST OF SHIPPING, HANDLING, AND INSURANCE.** It may be cheaper to buy the item locally.

■ **AVOID HEAVY PAPER STOCK, ENVELOPE LINERS, AND EXTRA INSERTS AND FRILLS.** Bows, pearls, heavy cardboard decorations, fabric, and so forth are all priced separately, and the added weight means more postage.

■ **LOOK FOR DISCOUNTED INVITATIONS.** These may be ordered by mail, through a bridal consultant, at a bridal salon, in a stationery store, and even at formalwear shops and office supply stores. There's absolutely no reason to pay retail. Also, purchase paper and envelopes by the pound, or in packets or reams, from discount office supply and stationery stores.

■ **LOOK FOR SALES AND POSTHOLIDAY CLEARANCES.** After the holidays, it's easy to pick up plain note cards and envelopes for a song.

■ **COMPARE PRICES.** Most wedding invitations are printed by a handful of manufacturers nationwide. (Look carefully at the return addresses in the mail-order catalogs. You may get three different catalogs whose invitations are all printed by the same company.) The prices will vary for the same thing depending on the markup in that catalog. This also applies to the big sample books found at local stationers. Couples choose an invitation, then place an order through the stationer that is passed on to the manufacturer. Manufacturers set suggested retail prices and give the dealers a choice of markups. Your goal is to find a dealer who discounts at least 25 to 30 percent. (Wholesale prices for dealers are generally up to 50 percent off retail.)

■ **MAKE YOUR INVITATIONS BY HAND.** "One of my favorite tips on saving money, as well as a way to add a personal touch to your wedding, is to make your invitations by hand. There are many ways to do this depending on your style," says Sherry Richert of Mad Moon Creations in San Francisco (http://www.MadMoonCreations.com).

She adds, "Your local art store probably carries a lot of beautiful handmade papers that you could use. Laser-print the invite on some lovely vellum paper and tie it to a square of the handmade paper with a pretty little bow. You could also make great color copies of your favorite photo of you and your partner and use that on your invitation. Invite some of your closest friends to help you make copies of the invitation—not only will the time fly by, but it will help everyone feel more involved in your special day."

If making your own invitations, buy the paper and envelopes at the same time. They must be a perfect fit—you'll go crazy trying to find the right match if the pieces weren't purchased together.

■ **MAKE YOUR OWN LAYERED INVITATIONS.** Purchase good-quality, paneled 6 × 8 inch ivory note cards (the kind with an embossed panel around the perimeter) and matching loose envelopes. Write out the invitation in a calligraphic style in the center of the panel. Then place a piece of translucent ivory vellum paper (cut to the same size) over the note card. Using a hole punch, place two holes at the top. Thread a ¼-inch translucent or satin ribbon through the hole and tie a small bow. You can align the invitations vertically or horizontally.

■ **ALWAYS ORDER MORE INVITATIONS AND ENVELOPES THAN YOU THINK YOU'LL NEED.** There may be last-minute invitees, and people often make mistakes while addressing the envelopes. It's more economical to order a larger print lot up front, because if more are needed later, many companies charge an extra setup fee or have a 25- or 50-invitation minimum for reorders. Besides, it's nice to have a few extra invitations to keep in a scrapbook or frame as a memento.

■ **SKIP THE EXTRAS**

- *Do without colored inks.* Companies charge more for them than standard black ink (an extra $5 to $15). Bright colors can look garish on a wedding invitation anyway.

- *Skip reception cards.* "If everyone is invited to both the reception and ceremony, include the reception as the last line or a 'footnote' on the wedding invitation," suggests bridal consultant Betty Jackson of Friend of the Bride in Indianapolis. "Not only is this a savings in the cost of an additional reception card and printing, but it may save postage as well. This is appropriate for formal invitations, too."

- *Eliminate printed place cards.* Make your own or purchase them in packages of twenty-five to fifty in party stores or stationery stores. Neatly handwrite the names using a fine-point pen.

- *Skip printed map cards and save around $25 per 100 invitations.* Ask the church or reception site for their standard map and directions and make photocopies at work or the local library. Or log on to the Internet and find one of the many sites that make maps.

- *Omit double-lined envelopes.* You'll save $25 to $30 per 100 invitations.

- *Eliminate the matching printed accessories.* Napkins, matchbooks, bookmarks, plastic cups, streamers, embossed envelope seals, paper scrolls, programs, and ashtrays aren't necessary.

- *Do without printed at-home cards.* Instead, type up your new address and phone number on a home computer and make photocopies. Mail them after the wedding or tuck them in with thank-you notes.

- *Omit response cards entirely.* Some couples prefer their guests to send a formal handwritten note along the lines of: "Mr. and Mrs. Gregory Flagg accept with pleasure (or regret that they are unable to accept) your kind invitation for Sunday, the fourth of March."

■ **CONTACT THE GRAPHIC DESIGN DEPARTMENT OF A LOCAL COLLEGE OR HIGH SCHOOL AND SEE IF A TALENTED STUDENT ARTIST OR DESIGNER IS WILLING TO CREATE CUSTOM WEDDING INVITATIONS FOR A MODEST FEE.** Graphic designers tend to be highly skilled at desktop publishing and can usually print them or give you a master disk to take to a printer. Many designers also work closely with commercial printers, so you may get a referral to a high-quality, inexpensive print shop.

■ **INSTEAD OF HAVING YOUR RETURN ADDRESS PRINTED ON THE OUTER ENVELOPE FLAPS, WRITE IT OUT YOURSELF AND SAVE $30 PER 100 INVITATIONS.** Or, order an embosser and press your address into each envelope. An embosser costs roughly $30 (the same as having addresses printed), and it comes in handy after the wedding for all future correspondence.

■ **SAVE TIME BY PENCILING A NUMBER ON THE UPPER RIGHT-HAND CORNER OF THE BACK OF THE RESPONSE CARD THAT CORRESPONDS TO THE NUMBER ON YOUR GUEST LIST.** This is a clever trick from bride Elizabeth Pisaretz. If the respondent fails to write her or his name on the card, you'll have a way of comparing it to the master list to figure out who the mystery guest is. You'll also be able to keep track of people who forget to mail their cards back and can follow up to see if they are coming.

■ **ORDER BLANK THANK-YOU NOTES WITH THE REST OF THE STATIONERY.** Notes that don't have "Thank You" on them can be used anytime.

■ **DISCOVER THE ARTIST WITHIN.** "There are many artistic calligraphers out there, but you don't need to hire a calligrapher. Every single library has a section on the fine arts and calligraphy. Go to the library, check out a book, buy a [calligraphy] pen, and practice," says consultant Beverly Ann Bonner. "You don't even need to buy a kit! With some practice, you can do it yourself. And there are also machines right now that do calligraphy. They have really upgraded the technology and it doesn't look computerized. It looks nice."

■ **USE STAMPS AND BORDERS TO CREATE CUSTOMIZED INVITATIONS.** Order plain ivory or cream invitations and fancy them up with gold or silver stamping or any ink color you wish. Stamp a border of tiny flowers or stars around the invitation, and stamp a matching design in the corner of the outer envelope. Why stop there? You can stamp coordinating designs on the napkins, place cards, and wedding programs. Rubber stamps cost less than $6; inkpads are around $2.

■ **KEEP THE INVITATION TO THE LENGTH STIPULATED BY THE PRINTER.** Some charge an extra fee per line for printing more than fourteen lines of text.

■ **INSTEAD OF HAVING THE WEDDING PROGRAMS PRINTED COM-MERCIALLY, MAKE THEM YOURSELF USING A DESKTOP PUBLISHING PROGRAM.** Many paper suppliers sell folded blank wedding programs that are compatible with laser printers. The results are fabulous, and the price can't be beat. Call Paper Direct, Inc. at 1-800-272-7377; or It's Your Wedding by Rexcraft at 1-888-796-1184.

Keep in Mind

❖ Don't try to save a few dollars by not putting stamps on the response card envelopes. That's tacky. Guests expect to be able to fill in their response and just mail it off.

❖ It used to be that the only correct response to a wedding invitation was a handwritten reply. Unfortunately, this bit of wedding etiquette has passed many guests by, and they may not know they are expected to take the time to write a formal reply. The note should be written on white stationery in blue or black ink, paralleling the wording on the invitation.

✤ It's appropriate to include on the shower invitation where the bride is registered, but not on the wedding invitation.

✤ A wedding invitation should never be issued by a deceased person. This may sound ridiculous to mention, but it's not unusual for a bride or groom to wish to honor a dead parent by including the parent as a host on the invitation: "Mr. and Mrs. Peter O'Malley request the honour of your presence . . ." If Mr. O'Malley has passed away, he technically is in no position to invite people to a wedding. Think of another way to memorialize the loved one; otherwise guests will be very uncomfortable.

✤ It's not appropriate to write phrases such as "no gifts, please" or "instead of gifts, please donate to charity" on an invitation. If gifts are not expected, quietly spread the word by phone or ask the maid of honor to tell people.

✤ Traditional, formal wedding invitation papers are made from cotton or wood fibers. The traditional ink color is black, but dark gray is sometimes used for font styles that are too difficult to read in black. (The standard size for most invitations is $5\frac{5}{8}" \times 7\frac{1}{2}"$.)

✤ A stationer will provide guidance on appropriate wording, especially in confusing cases such as military titles or when the parents are divorced and remarried. Many mail-order catalogs have hotline numbers to call for a free consultation.

♦ Do your homework. Make sure guests' names are spelled correctly. Double-check whether a friend spells his name "Steven" or "Stephen." Those little details show you care.

ENGAGEMENT AND WEDDING ANNOUNCEMENTS

Placing an engagement and/or wedding announcement in the local newspaper spreads the news to a wider circle of friends in the community. You may place announcements in both your and your future spouse's hometown newspapers as well as in the towns where you live and/or work.

For most newspapers, the announcement service is free. Others charge a modest fee of $15 to $30. Generally, newspapers will accept only black-and-white photographs. Call the paper's features or community editor and ask if it has standard forms to fill out. If not, just clip the newspaper's bridal page and mimic its format.

INVITATION RESOURCES

Below are resources and toll-free numbers to contact for free invitation catalogs. After you receive the catalogs, many of these companies invite you to mail in an enclosed postcard to request free samples. Customers usually are allowed up to three free invitation samples, along with swatches of ribbons, layers, or wraps.

American Stationery Co., Inc.
100 Park Ave.
Peru, IN 46970-1701
1-800-822-2577
Fax: 1-800-253-9054

Carloon Craft®
1750 Tower Blvd.
P.O. Box 8700
North Mankato, MN 56002-8700
(507) 625-0879
Fax: (507) 386-2330

Creations by Elaine
6253 W. 74th St., Box 2001
Bedford Park, IL 60499-2001
1-800-452-4593
Fax: 1-800-388-0086
E-mail: Elaine@myprinter.com

Idea Art
P.O. Box 291505
Nashville, TN 37229-1505
1-800-433-2278
Fax: 1-800-435-2278

Promotional papers for desktop printers.

It's Your Wedding by Rexcraft
Rexcraft
Rexburg, ID 83441 0100
1-888-796-1184
Fax: 1-800-826-2712

Catalog includes invitations and papers for ordering, as well as
laser-compatible blank papers, cards, and envelopes for creating
your invitations and wedding programs yourself on a home
computer.

Jamie Lee Fine Wedding Stationery
P.O. Box 42038
Phoenix, AZ 85080-2038
1-800-288-5800
Fax: 1-800-288-5822

Now and Forever: Wedding Invitations and Accessories
P.O. Box 820
Goshen, CA 93227-0820
1-800-521-0584
Fax: 1-800-421-3965

Includes invitations inspired by Disney characters and Spanish-language invitations.

Paper Direct, Inc.
P.O. Box 2970
Colorado Springs, CO 80901-2970
1-800-272-7377
Fax: 1-800-443-2973
http://www.paperdirect.com

A wide variety of do-it-yourself plain papers for personal computers and printers, including embossed and die-cut designs for wedding programs, invitations, postcards, note cards, envelopes, and more.

Weddingware
P.O. Box 1466
Coshocton, OH 43812
1-800-622-4489
Fax: 1-740-622-5352

Wedding stationery featuring watercolor designs.

For a comprehensive Web site that offers more than a dozen free catalogs featuring invitations and accessories, including catalogs from Canada, Sweden, Europe, and the United Kingdom, log on to the following address:

Wedding Orders Catalog Index Headquarters
http://www.catalog.com

CHAPTER ELEVEN

FAVORS AND ACCESSORIES

Does your family favor favors? In some cultures, wedding favors are always expected and considered a gracious thank-you gift to the guest. Those little porcelain Cadillacs with the couple's name written across the hood are deemed downright necessary. In other cultures, favors are regarded as frills—or even tacky

Consider the preferences of your family and guests. Will they feel deprived going home without a wedding goodie?

Bridal favors and accessories are one budget category in which a couple can save a bundle. Many accessories are fun but not exactly critical to the success of the wedding. You may wish to put that money elsewhere. Sure, heart-shaped puffed rice for throwing is adorable, but at $21 a bag the bride could easily forgo it in favor of more hors d'oeuvres. Do you really *need* personalized bridal bookmarks at a cost of $90 for 200? (If people are reading at your wedding, you've got a problem!)

Think in terms of time. It's certainly cost-effective to make your own favors, but if the bride works long hours or doesn't find crafting relaxing, it may not be wise to spend nine hours dipping homemade petit fours, stuffing them into little boxes, tying tulle bows, and handwriting a calligraphy label. Whew.

Realize that while you, your parents, and your spouse will get all choked up looking at bud vases engraved with your wedding date for the next thirty years, no one else will. Skip the personalized guest favors unless they're solely for your own pleasure.

WAYS TO SAVE ON WEDDING FAVORS

■ **CONSIDER GIVING JUST ONE FAVOR TO EACH COUPLE OR FAMILY.** Do the math: it all adds up. Even $4 a favor times 200 guests means an $800 expenditure.

■ **BE CREATIVE. MAKE THE FAVORS PERSONALIZED BUT NOT PRICEY.** Are you fanatic bridge players? Give your guests packs of cards tied up with tulle. Coffee lovers can give specialty coffee beans inside mugs. Seed packets are a thoughtful gift from gardeners. Is the bride or groom a professional chef? Share a favorite recipe with guests. Write the recipe on a card or parchment paper and tie it to a wooden spoon. Wine lovers might want to give unusual wine stoppers.

■ **REGIONAL FOOD FAVORITES ARE ALWAYS WELCOME FAVORS!** You may think the goodies are commonplace in your part of the country, but guests will regard them as exotic treats. Give maple syrup, homemade jam, apple butter, cider, and honey from New England; coconut patties from Florida; barbecue sauce or hot sauce from the South; dried cherries from Michigan; blueberries from Maine; cheddar cheese from Wisconsin; spice rubs or chilies from the Southwest.

■ **BUY BULK CANDY FROM YOUR LOCAL WHOLESALER OR OUTLET SHOP.** "Miniature candy bars are ideal favors," says Master Bridal Consultant Karen DeKay of KD Productions in Daphne, Alabama. "Use your computer and good-quality paper to print a cover for the candy bar. You can personalize the covers and make something really special. You can even scan and insert a photo of the couple on the wrapper, along with the date of the wedding and a 'Thank you for sharing our day' message."

■ **WHEREVER POSSIBLE, MAKE IT YOURSELF.** A little packet of almonds tied with tulle will cost $1.50 apiece if purchased from a salon, or about 55 cents each if the almonds are bought in bulk and tied up in tulle circles bought at a craft store. (See directions on page 155.)

Craft and floral supply stores are invaluable resources for favor-making ideas and supplies. Ask the owner or manager to show you how to make a few basic styles, and cost out the price per favor. Many have free craft-making classes or offer pamphlets with step-by-step instructions.

When Michigan bride Jeanna Okley married Arthur Rosen, she made attractive guest favors that doubled as place cards. The bride bought clear Lucite picture frames (3" × 5") and used a personal computer to print out each guest's name and table assignment in an elegant calligraphic font. She inserted a name into each frame and decorated the upper left-hand corner with dried green leaves and tiny porcelain flowers. "When you went to the [seating assignment] table, you picked up a frame with your name on it, you put it at your guest table, and when you went home, you could use it with any picture you want!" says Cele Lalli, former editor in chief of *Modern Bride* magazine, who was a guest at the wedding.

Chocolate stirring spoons are easy to make by dipping plastic spoons in melted chocolate. Let the chocolate set, wrap the dipped end of the spoon with heavy-duty cellophane wrap, and tie with a bow. When guests stir the coffee, the chocolate melts into the cup.

IDEAS FOR INEXPENSIVE FAVORS

❖ Phone card for free long-distance calls

❖ Fragrant sachets

❖ Flower bulbs for planting

❖ Personal message rolled into a scroll

❖ Decorative soaps tied up in tulle

❖ Heirloom family recipe tied to wooden spoon

❖ Regional food delicacy (maple syrup, jam, salsa, etc.)

❖ Coasters

❖ Place-card holders in unusual shapes (Adirondack chairs, houses, etc.)

❖ Miniature glass vase with silk flowers

❖ Cookie cutters or kitchen gadgets

❖ Create a mix of your favorite songs on a tape (or have professionally duplicated)

❖ Crossword puzzle with pen (make your own using clues about a hobby, like shell collecting, or references to your family history)

❖ Bag of "designer" coffee or tea

DO-IT-YOURSELF IDEAS

Jordan Almonds in Tulle Netting

In some European countries, these candy-coated almonds are given at weddings as a symbol of fertility and happiness in marriage. Almonds in tulle are probably the most classic wedding favor of all.

For each favor, place five almonds in the center of the tulle netting. Gather the edges of the netting to form a pouch. Take a 6- to 8-inch piece of ribbon, thread a plastic wedding ring on it, and tie the bundle together.

1 5-pound box Jordan almonds (500 almonds per box)	$29.95
4 packages precut tulle netting circles (25 to a pack) @ $2.97 each	$11.88
100 gold-tone wedding rings (@ 5 cents each)	$5.00
4 rolls white ⅜" satin ribbon with frothy edge (6 yards each) @ $1.99 per roll	$7.96

Makes 100 favors at approximately 55 cents each   TOTAL $54.79

Fragrant Potpourri Bundles

Scoop approximately one-half cup potpourri into center of a tulle circle. Tie up the bundle into a little pouch using an 8- to 10-inch curling ribbon. Curl the ribbon ends.

15 10-ounce bags potpourri (@ $3.96 per bag)	$59.40
4 packages precut tulle netting circles (25 to a pack @ $2.97 each)	$11.88
3 rolls gold metallic curling ribbon (66 feet each @ 66 cents per roll)	$1.98

Makes 100 favors at approximately 74 cents each   Total $73.26

WAYS TO SAVE
ON POPULAR ACCESSORIES

Walk into a bridal salon or flip through the pages of a wedding invitations catalog and you'll be amazed by the sheer number of bridal accessories on the market. Some are lovely, others are ridiculous. Some are bargains, others are outrageously priced. Do a lot of comparison shopping. Many of these items can be easily skipped or made yourself.

Accessories truly gild the lily. They can pull together a wedding "theme" by coordinating the colors and personalized designs. It's possible to order perfectly matched wedding invitations, napkins, matchbooks, heart-shaped wedding pillows, thank-you notes, cake knives, and cake toppers.

Compare prices. Many mail-order catalogs offer the identical accessories at different prices. For example, while researching this book I found one catalog advertising "Heart-Shaped Designer Wedding Rice" (white heart-shaped grains of puffed rice) for $21 a bag, while another was selling the exact same product for $16!

Keepsake Planner "Bride's Box" File

Why pay designer prices for what is basically a white recipe card box with index cards, when you can purchase the same thing at an office supply store for a few dollars? File the index cards alphabetically by guest's last name and use them to record names, addresses, phone numbers, how many guests have accepted/declined, gifts received, and when thank-you notes were mailed. (Approximate savings: $30)

Bride's Accordion File

Step into any upscale bridal salon and you'll find brocaded and beribboned white accordion files for the bride. Pretty? Yes.

Necessary? No. A good office supply store will carry virtually the same thing (no fancy fabrics or ribbons, though) for under $10. An accordion file is a great way to organize receipts, contracts, fabric swatches, and other important items. And you can always spiff it up with a glue gun, some ribbons, and silk flowers. (Approximate savings: $30 to $40)

Cake Knife

It's puzzling why newlyweds are supposed to supply their own cake knife for the cake-cutting ceremony at the reception. Go figure. Especially since these basic cake servers run upward of $150 for keepsake crystal and china varieties. Save by bringing your own cake server from home or asking the caterer to supply a long-handled knife, and dress it up with a poufy French-wired ribbon or cluster of fabric flowers. *Voilà.* (Approximate savings: $25 to $150)

Wedding Organizer Calendar

Purchase a calendar with bridal motifs for $25, or buy a plain calendar and fill in the important dates and deadlines yourself. To make a pretty and personalized keepsake, visit a quick-print shop and ask for a plain, undecorated calendar. Thread satin ribbons through the pages to bind them. Then add collages or color photographs to each month's page. Every month, take a photograph of you and your fiancé and paste it in as a remembrance. (Approximate savings: $15 to $20)

Guest Book and Pen

Would you normally spend $20 on a plastic pen decorated with lace and satin rosettes? That's what you'll pay when you search for "bridal" guest book pens in bridal salons, stationery stores, and mail-order catalogs.

And wedding guest books at an average of $15 to $30 are no bargains, either. A wedding guest book is nothing more than a white book with lined pages for guests to record their names. For a more personalized and much less expensive version, look for blank books at a local bookstore for $2 to $6 each. These often are used for journals and diaries; the pages are lined or blank. Feeling like Martha Stewart? Take a glue gun and cover the book with a beautiful damask fabric. You can seal the edges on the front and back covers with grosgrain or satin ribbon. (Approximate savings: $10 to $18)

Personalized Matchbooks and Napkins

Skip them! Most brides say these are a waste of money—the napkins get thrown away and few people smoke anymore. (The reception site usually provides napkins and ashtrays anyway.) Trim these items and save an average $30 per 200 personalized napkins and about $60 per 200 matchbooks.

If your heart is set on decorated napkins, buy colored paper napkins at a warehouse-style paper store, buy an interesting rubber stamp design ($5), and stamp the designs yourself.

Bridal Bookmarks

Bookmarks are one of those favors that nobody really uses except the bride and groom. Skip them and save about $90, or make them yourself with supplies purchased at a paper or office supply store.

Etched Crystal or Silver Toasting Goblets

Unless you long for expensive toasting goblets to keep as mementos, borrow a set from friends or use your parents'. Or, buy one pair to be used by all the siblings in your family and passed down. Shop for a mismatched pair at a consignment, antiques, or thrift shop. It's easy to find high-quality "orphan" crystal pieces at these shops or at garage sales, because people usually want sets of six or more glasses. If the "his" and "hers" goblets you find are antique crystal and cost only a few dollars apiece, who cares if they don't match? (Approximate savings: $40 to $150)

Cake Topper

Borrow the one your parents or grandparents used. The vintage topper will have great sentimental value both for you and for the person lending it. Or invest in a topper that can be handed down from one sister or brother to the next family member. (For more money-saving ideas on cake toppers, refer to the chapter on wedding cakes.) (Approximate savings: $10 to $60)

Wedding Programs

Make them yourself using a home computer! Many office supply stores carry paper suitable for wedding programs. Any single-fold or double-fold stock used for printing business brochures will do nicely. Refer to the chapter on invitations for more ideas and resources. (Approximate savings: $30 to $50)

Embroidered Ring Bearer Pillow

Save on a ring pillow by making one yourself. At a craft or fabric store, purchase a small foam pillow or foam square (about 8 to 10 inches square) and cover it with lace or fabric. (Consider wrapping it with leftover alteration fabric from the wedding gown or bridesmaids' dresses.) You can decorate the center with flowers, embroider the couple's initials, sew a covered button into the center for a tufted look, or glue on faux pearls with a hot-glue gun. Remember, it's prudent to let a child carry fake rings down the aisle. If the couple insists on the real rings, be sure to sew ribbons to the pillow so you can securely tie the rings.

Chiffon Bow Candle

Order a "bridal" bow candle from an accessories shop or catalog and it will cost $34. Make one yourself by tying French-wired white chiffon ribbon around a 6-inch-tall pillar candle and you'll spend only $11 ($3 for the ribbon and $8 for the candle). (Approximate savings: $23)

Here's a tip from bridal consultant Lois Pearce of Beautiful Occasions, Hamden, Connecticut: "Have the groom's cake cut, boxed in tiny boxes, and ready to go for guests to take home with them as favors. Create a keepsake favor including your wedding program, a listing of bridal party members, the reception menu, and a special note from the bride and groom. Roll and tie it as a scroll, or attach a tassel to create a booklet."

RESOURCES FOR UNIQUE FAVORS AND ACCESSORIES

For a brochure on place-card holders/favors in whimsical shapes (including chairs, teapots, picture frames, handbags, and music stands):

Placeframes
825 Olive St.
Scranton, PA 18510
1-800-756-6184

For pewter place-card holders/favors shaped like twig chairs, Adirondack chairs, benches, and lawn chairs:

Coldwater Creek
One Coldwater Creek Dr.
Sandpoint, ID 83864
1-800-262-0040

For cake-pull charms to insert within the wedding cake layers:

Rexcraft
Rexburg, Idaho 83441
1-800-635-3898

For a brochure on custom-wrapped chocolate wedding-bar favors:

Carson Enterprises, Inc.
630 Towne Square
Fairfield, OH 45014

For a brochure on live-tree seedling favors and seed packets:

Tree and Floral Beginnings
273 Route 34
Locke, NY 10392
1-800-246-0252

For a catalog of party and wedding favors and novelty items (Mardi Gras masks, hula skirts, tiaras, feather boas, and much more) for theme parties:

Oriental Trading Company, Inc.
P.O. Box 2308
Omaha, NE 68103-2308
1-800-228-0475
http://www.oriental.com

CHAPTER TWELVE

THE WEDDING CEREMONY

O nce you've set the wedding date, everything else seems to fall into place. Finding a ceremony venue—whether it's a church, synagogue, or the same spot as the reception—is the piece of the planning puzzle that everything else depends on. Couples often pencil in the date and then forget about the ceremony itself until a few weeks before the wedding, when the minister wants to know which readings they've chosen or whether they plan to write their own vows.

Don't lose sight of the fact that the ceremony is the *real* reason for all this fuss. It's the ceremony that makes it a wedding. Even if you aren't particularly spiritual, you should realize that the wedding ceremony is more than just a prelude to the reception party. Take time to make it meaningful and memorable. There are many ways to personalize a ceremony that don't cost a dime and will leave guests talking about your wedding for years. You can sing to your spouse, wear your grandmother's veil, or carry a replica of your mother's bouquet.

SETTING THE DATE

Why is June so popular for weddings? According to the Association of Bridal Consultants (ABC), June was the traditional month because in an agrarian society, it was after planting and before the harvest. If people wanted to marry right out of school, June was the month when school ended. And since roads in those days were unpaved and travel was difficult, by June the dirt roads had dried out, making it easier for guests to get there. Today, none of these reasons applies, and weddings are becoming a year-round business. In some parts of the country, August, September, and October are just as favored by brides as June.

Planning the wedding ceremony involves two basic decisions: What's your ideal date? Will it be a civil or religious ceremony? Whatever type of ceremony you prefer, the planning should begin as early as possible.

Many churches, synagogues, and secular sites are booked a year or more in advance. Many houses of worship impose restrictions on days when ceremonies can be performed, such as no marriage ceremonies on holy days, on the Sabbath, or during certain religious feast days or festivals. In some religions, a waiting period of six months to a year is expected because marriage is considered a sacrament requiring spiritual preparation. It's a commitment not to be rushed into lightly. (Now you know why so many couples book a date so far into the future!)

If you're marrying in a short time frame either by choice or by chance, it's certainly possible to find a ceremony venue on short notice (there's always city hall), but it may not be the one you want most. If your dream site is booked, asked to be put on a waiting list. Cancellations happen all the time.

Give yourself plenty of time to complete all the necessary pre-ceremony paperwork. You may need to track down divorce papers, citizenship papers, and birth and baptismal certificates.

Divorce and interfaith marriage also can cause additional delays, and a couple may not be able to marry until they meet specific requirements. In the case of an interfaith marriage, it's important for the bride and groom to meet with officiants from both faiths to discuss important issues, such as how you will continue to observe your religions after marriage and in which faith(s) you will rear your children.

Couples are sometimes taken aback to learn that if they are not practicing members of a particular church or temple, the officiant may turn down their request to marry there. Or you may be bumped to the end of the waiting list, behind church members. Also, some congregations don't allow "visiting" clergy to perform weddings there—only the resident or "home" clergy can officiate.

Another big surprise is the fee factor. Couples are expected to pay a fee to the officiant for performing the ceremony. The fee may be a donation of your choosing or a standard rate of anywhere from $100 to $600. You may even have to pay an additional fee for use of the church or the secular venue, which can be hundreds or thousands of dollars, depending on how historic or popular the site is and how much it is in demand. On top of that, there may be an additional fee for the house organist or vocalist—payable even if you don't use them and bring in your own musicians. Even if the ceremony is being performed in the same room as the wedding reception, you may be charged a fee for setting up chairs or moving tables around to make a cozy ceremony spot.

When choosing an outdoor ceremony venue, keep the comfort of guests in mind. A sunset ceremony on a mountaintop may be romantic, but what if it rains or snows? How are elderly guests expected to climb up the rocky slopes? The same goes for a ceremony on a beach, near a waterfall, or anywhere guests will be asked to walk a distance. It's essential to provide chairs and some sort of overhead protection such as a tent or canopy.

What will the climate be like at that time of year? Is it near hurricane or tornado season? Is an ice storm or blizzard possible? How will you arrange to keep guests from being baked in the sun or chilled to the bone? These things matter during a ceremony. No one wants her outdoor wedding to be remembered as the one where guests were treated for sunstroke. Consider moving the date.

WAYS TO SAVE

Choosing the Site

To keep costs down, choose a free or nearly free ceremony site. Begin by creating a list of possible venues that are beautiful and in keeping with the style, level of formality, and size of your wedding. Is that historic church large enough to hold all the guests? If the site seats only seventy-five comfortably, it may be out of the question.

Don't worry, many fabulous sites can be had for the asking. It just takes time and a little research to find them. When calling to check availability, give your preferred date, but have alternate dates in mind. Sometimes it's necessary to be flexible, even if it means booking a Friday or Sunday instead of a Saturday.

Call the local chamber of commerce or visitors bureau for information on local sites. Many regional books list ceremony venues and give detailed information on their prices and special features ("Come to Briarwood and exchange vows in a lush rose garden!"). Unusual sites include yachts, museums, college campuses, and aquariums. Several times a year, major bridal magazines run regional advertising pages devoted to ceremony and reception venues just in your area.

Utilize the free services of the on-site ceremony coordinator. This person may be the officiant, the rectory secretary, or the "resident" ceremony planner. She's done it all many times before and knows the insider secrets for making the ceremony proceed smoothly. She will know the site's regulations and restrictions ("no secular music!") and all the important details, such as how the ceremony will be conducted, what each part signifies, what kinds of readings you may choose, where you can place flowers or decorations (and where you can't), and ways to include children in the ceremony. She will have suggested lists of musical selections to choose from and referrals to florists and musicians who have worked at the site before.

The officiant or ceremony coordinator will fill you in on where you should stand and what you should do every step of the way. Pencil in a date for a ceremony rehearsal a day or two before the wedding so that the bridal party members and parents know exactly what their roles are. Designate someone who is not in the wedding party to take notes at the rehearsal and make copies for everyone. Officiants tend to zip quickly through the rehearsal, forgetting that while they can do this with their eyes closed, the bride and groom will be nervous and terrified about forgetting the instructions.

Sharing the Flowers

Find out if any other wedding ceremonies are being performed before or after yours that day. It's good to know whether you must keep to a rigid schedule and how much time there will be between weddings. If other couples are also being married that day, you may want to share the cost of wedding flowers or music with them.

Let the flowers do double duty at the ceremony and reception (see chapter 14 on flowers and decorations) and hire musicians who are versatile enough to play both ceremonial music and music for dancing (see chapter 18 on music and entertainment). The officiant will advise you on any music restrictions for the ceremony. For example, some churches prohibit any selections that are secular, which means your favorite song from *The Phantom of the Opera* may have to wait until the reception.

Rice Is Nice, Bubbles Are Better

Find out if the church or synagogue allows guests to throw rice. This wedding tradition is a safety hazard (guests may slip and fall), and some churches prohibit rice because it is believed that when rice is swallowed by birds, it expands and injures them. (Animal experts now say this is an urban legend, yet it still persists.) Alternatives include birdseed or flower petals. For a pretty effect in pictures, have guests blow bubbles or throw rose petals at the couple. Petals may be purchased in bulk from a wholesale florist. Scatter them along the wedding aisle or give them to guests to shower on the bride and groom. "Bridal" bubbles are available in bridal salons for about a dollar apiece for a tiny white bottle, but you'll pay a lot less by purchasing them in craft or toy stores (four bottles for a dollar).

Before throwing or blowing anything, check with the officiant to see if it's allowed inside or outside the church. If you get the green light to throw birdseed, make little bundles of it and place them in baskets at the end of each pew or at the back of the church. Guests can pick up a bundle on the way in. To make birdseed bundles, take a half-cup of birdseed, pour into a cellophane bag, and tie up with curling ribbon. Makes about ninety-six packages.

Birdseed Bundles for Throwing	
2 10-pound bags birdseed @ $3.99 each	$7.98
8 packages decorative cellophane bags (12 bags each) @ $1.99 each	$15.92
4 rolls of curling ribbon @ 66 cents each	$ 2.64
TOTAL	$26.54

The Aisle Runner

Save money by skipping the aisle runner. It will cost $30 to $100 to rent and is unnecessary, especially if it's rolled out over carpeting or a perfectly polished floor. This tradition dates back to the time when the bride had to walk on mud or straw, and a runner was laid down to protect her shoes and gown. Unless you're getting married on a barn floor—or in a royal ceremony in a palace—forget about it. If your heart is set on a runner, make one yourself and decorate it with hand-painted or stenciled designs. Then pass it along to the next bride in the family to marry.

The Receiving Line

Here's a special touch that doesn't cost a penny. The receiving line is a gracious way for the bride and groom to greet every guest and thank each one for coming. It is traditionally done at the reception. However, if there is to be no reception, or if there are many more guests at the ceremony than at the reception, it's fine to "receive" at the ceremony, usually at the back of the church or on the outside steps or landing. If the ceremony is a civil one or a small at-home wedding, the newlyweds usually turn and greets guests after the ceremony, and the line forms right there.

Who goes where? The bride's mother stands at the beginning of the line and introduces each guest to the groom's mother, who stands next to her. Next comes the bride, then the groom. The maid of honor stands next, then the bridesmaids. (To speed things up a bit, it's perfectly appropriate to leave the bridesmaids out of the line. Chances are they won't know most of the people anyway.) The two fathers are traditionally left out of the line, but if one chooses to join, the other should as well. It's a nice touch for both of them to join the line if one of them is from out of town or has never met most of the guests.

SPECIAL TOUCHES
THAT DON'T COST A FORTUNE

Add meaning to your wedding ceremony with simple things that are unforgettable.

■ **CHIME THE BELLS OF THE CHURCH.** Says consultant Beverly Ann Bonner, "There's nothing so exhilarating and exciting as a couple who has just been married standing outside of the church, with family and friends hugging and wishing them well, and hearing the steeple bells ringing away."

■ **SING TO YOUR SPOUSE DURING THE CEREMONY OR RECEPTION.** Or create a long-running tape of your favorite songs to play at the reception.

■ **WRITE A CARD TO YOUR FIANCÉ THE NIGHT BEFORE THE WEDDING AND HAVE IT HAND-DELIVERED JUST BEFORE THE CEREMONY BEGINS.** It could include a love poem or a special message from you.

■ **WRITE YOUR OWN VOWS.** There is no better way to personalize the ceremony—and collaborating with your fiancé on your vows gives you special time together to talk about what marriage means to you.

■ **WEAVE TOGETHER TRADITIONAL AND CONTEMPORARY READINGS.** Before trying to write a new ceremony from start to finish, keep in mind that many houses of worship impose restrictions on where and if you can tinker with the script. This is a very important consideration. There are sometimes complex rules about special prayers or procedures that are inviolate if the ceremony is to be legally and/or religiously binding. You don't have to start from scratch or struggle to make everything sound wildly romantic or poetic. A good way to start is to think about what the concepts of love, marriage, fidelity, friendship, companionship, trust, and respect mean to you. If in doubt, just write a "message" to each other. After all, wedding vows are essentially a promise.

■ **WHEN ORDERING A BOUQUET, CHOOSE FLOWERS FOR THEIR TRADITIONAL MEANING.** Red roses stand for passion, bluebells for constancy, ivy for fidelity, yellow tulips for hopeless love.

■ **IF EITHER OF YOU HAS CHILDREN FROM A PREVIOUS MARRIAGE, CONSIDER WRITING SPECIAL VOWS TO THEM.** This is a wonderful way to reassure children that, despite your new marriage, your love for them will remain committed and constant—and that no one can take their place in your heart.

■ **WEAR THE WEDDING GOWN WORN BY YOUR MOTHER OR GRANDMOTHER.** If it has been stained or discolored by age, take it to a textile conservator or bridal gown restorer for expert cleaning and restoration. Don't try to fix things yourself. (See chapter 8 for more information.) Carry a re-creation of the bouquet she carried, too. A talented florist will be able to reconstruct the bouquet if you can provide a wedding portrait.

■ **A HANDKERCHIEF ONCE CARRIED BY YOUR MOTHER OR GRAND-MOTHER CAN BE TUCKED INTO A BOUQUET OR SEWN INTO THE HEM OF THE WEDDING GOWN.** If your mother saved the bonnet or cap from your christening gown, it can be easily made into a handkerchief.

■ **HAVE A CANDLELIGHT CEREMONY.** If the ceremony is at dusk or later, create an elegant look and romantic mood by illuminating the entire house of worship with twinkling candles. Place them in windows, on the altar, or at the end of pews. Be sure to check with your officiant before planning a candlelight ceremony. There may be special fire ordinances or restrictions on where candles may be used. Make a point to check drafty windows or air conditioning that could cause accidents. Because of fire codes, you may need to enclose candles in hurricane lamps or use candlelike tapers that are actually battery-powered lights enclosed in metal containers. Do a trial run before the wedding. Light all the candles at around the same time as your ceremony time. Does it look too dark? Will guests be able to see one another and the altar? You may need to leave a few well-placed lights on.

■ **IF FIRE ORDINANCES PERMIT, HAVE A UNITY CANDLE CEREMONY.** Each guest is given a candle at the beginning of the ceremony. The couple walk down the aisle, stopping at each row to light the candle of the nearest person, who in turn lights the candle of the next person, until the entire congregation has lighted candles—and the community is joined.

■ **HANG PHOTOCOPIES OF OLD WEDDING PICTURES OF YOUR GUESTS AND RELATIVES ON THE ENDS OF PEWS.** They'll be delighted and will have something to talk about during the long, sometimes boring wait for the bride to arrive. Before the wedding, computer scan or make photocopies of their wedding portraits (ask their children or parents to help provide them and to keep it a secret). Place a paper-matted frame around the photos, or just glue them to a sturdy cardboard backing. Hang them on the end of each pew using a pretty ribbon. Guests will be surprised and have fun guessing who is who. After the ceremony, give the portraits to the people pictured in them.

■ **PERSONALIZE THE WEDDING PROGRAM.** Include a poem, spiritual reading, or message to guests from the two of you, and bind the pages together with vellum paper or a pretty ribbon.

■ **ARRANGE WITH YOUR VIDEOGRAPHER TO BEAM THE WEDDING CEREMONY—LIVE, AS IT'S HAPPENING—INTO CYBERSPACE OVER THE INTERNET.** With the right software, you can also download still photos yourself and send them over the Net. Or ask the videographer or photographer to send proofs or an unedited video within a day or two, and mail them to family and friends.

■ **MAKE GOODIE BAGS WITH CRAYONS, COLORING BOOKS, AND STICKERS FOR YOUNG CHILDREN ATTENDING THE CEREMONY OR RECEPTION.** At the ceremony, you may wish to usher children to the church "crying room" or have special seats set aside for children.

■ **MAKE A WEDDING QUILT.** Have the ushers hand a fabric square to each guest as she or he enters the church. Ask guests to sign their names and write a little message to the couple on the fabric. After the wedding, sew all the squares together for a keepsake memory quilt.

■ **CREATE A SPECIAL GIFT TO BE USED LATER.** Have all the guests sign a magnum of champagne to be opened at a future special event, such as your first anniversary, the birth of a child, or the completion of a graduate degree.

■ **PUT ON A PARADE.** "I worked on a wedding at a cathedral in New Orleans where they had a line parade from the church to the hotel," says consultant Fran Casler of Party Consulting by Fran in St. Petersburg, Florida. "If the church is in close proximity to the reception, you can have a little band and do a parade down the streets. It's very, very European and so festive! Everyone just hails the couple and showers them with good wishes. It's wonderful."

■ **GIVE A SPECIAL GREETING TO THE PARENTS.** After the bride and groom exchange vows, they may turn and face the guests and ask their parents to join them on the altar. This is a nice time to say a few words to their parents in front of the congregation, thanking them for their love and support over the years and for welcoming their new "son" or "daughter" into the family.

■ **PRESENT A TOKEN OF APPRECIATION TO THE MOTHERS-IN-LAW.** "We recommend that the bride and groom give their mothers-in-law a nonred, dethorned rose as a surprise at the end of the ceremony," says the Reverend Robert Dittler of the White Robed Monks of Saint Benedict in San Francisco, California. "We also recommend a family blessing where children are involved."

■ **HAVE ALL THE GUESTS STAND ON THE STEPS OF THE CHURCH FOR A GROUP SHOT.** You can later duplicate the photo and send copies as mementos or tucked in with the thank-you notes.

■ **INCORPORATE THE "VESSEL AND THE ROSE" CEREMONY INTO THE WEDDING CEREMONY.** Written by the Reverend Roger Coleman, a Protestant minister and president of Clergy Services, Inc. in Kansas City, Missouri, this ceremony highlights marriage as a life-long relationship. In it, a clay vessel symbolizes love's strength and endurance and the power of God as the Creator. The rose symbolizes the potential and beauty contained in love's promise. The officiant hands the vessel to the groom, and the bride places the rose in the vessel, which the couple hold together as they proclaim their desire to grow together. For information, call Clergy Services, Inc. at 1-800-237-1922.

■ **GIVE GUESTS REAL BUTTERFLIES TO RELEASE JUST AS THE BRIDE AND GROOM EXCHANGE THEIR VOWS.** This is an unforgettable sight. The Butterfly Celebration is a company in Shafter, California, that "raises" butterflies and encases them in little paper pyramids, secured with elastic bows. Rather than shipping live adult butterflies, the company ships chrysalides that hatch into adult butterflies a few days prior to their release at the wedding. Here's the contact information.

The Butterfly Celebration
P.O. Box 1535
Shafter, CA 93263
1-800-548-3284
http://www.butterflycelebration.com

■ **REMEMBER LOVED ONES.** Getting married can be a stressful or emotional time if the bride or groom has recently lost a loved one, especially if a parent has passed away. The loss may seem all the more painful just at a time when you're supposed to feel joyful.

Think of ways to honor the person at the ceremony. Consider dedicating a special reading or poem or writing a few memorial words in the wedding program. At the rehearsal dinner, it's fine to raise a toast and say something like, "Here's to Mother, who is surely missed today at this special occasion. Mom, we know you are with us in spirit."

But whatever you do, don't mistake a wedding for a funeral. This sounds crass, but avoid getting overly maudlin or sentimental—this is not the appropriate occasion, and it will make guests feel uncomfortable. I've heard stories of couples who drag their entire wedding party to a gravesite to "visit" a dead relative before the ceremony or leave an empty chair at the ceremony or reception for the dead person. Think of something less depressing, or guests will squirm in their seats.

QUESTIONS TO ASK THE OFFICIANT
OR CEREMONY SITE MANAGER

❖ Is there a place for the bride and bridesmaids to prepare for the ceremony?

❖ When and where do we sign the marriage certificate? How many witnesses are needed?

❖ Are there any restrictions on wedding attire (no bare shoulders or backs, veil mandatory, and so on)?

❖ What is the fee or honorarium for performing the ceremony?

❖ Is there an additional fee for using the ceremony site?

❖ How early should ushers arrive to seat guests?

❖ Can we bring in our own soloist or organist, or must we use the house performer?

❖ May we write or choose sections of the ceremony, such as our vows or favorite religious passages?

❖ Must all readings be religious?

❖ Are there any other wedding ceremonies being performed before or after ours?

❖ If we write our own vows, where can we keep copies during the ceremony? (At a podium? Will the officiant hand them to us? Must we memorize them?)

❖ What kind of microphone does the officiant use? (Its frequency may interfere with the mikes worn by the bride and groom for the videography.)

❖ Can we include family or ethnic traditions?

❖ Are guests allowed to throw rice? Birdseed? Flower petals? Inside the sanctuary or out on the steps?

❖ Are there prohibitions on photography during the ceremony? If not, where may the photographer/videographer stand?

❖ Is the use of lighting or flashbulbs prohibited?

❖ Can you suggest ways to include children or special guests in the ceremony?

❖ Where can we hold the receiving line?

❖ Where should we stand in the receiving line?

❖ Will the entire wedding ceremony be printed on a bulletin or program (to make it easy for guests to follow)?

❖ Are there restrictions on music for the ceremony?

❖ If we use taped music or a CD, does the site have a tape player or CD player we could use? How is the sound amplified?

❖ May we hold a candlelight ceremony? What are the restrictions on using candles?

❖ Are any accessories provided (aisle runner, pew decorations, chuppah, candelabra)?

❖ Can you explain the order of the processional and recessional to us?

❖ When can we schedule a dress rehearsal for the ceremony?

CHAPTER THIRTEEN

THE RECEPTION AND CATERING

Let the celebrating begin!

A wedding reception is the party of a lifetime. After all, when else will you celebrate one of the happiest moments of your life, with the companion you've chosen for life, in the company of the people you love most?

As you plan the reception, give special consideration to making it personal and meaningful. Caterers and reception site managers may pressure you to make choices that seem like cookie-cutter replicas of every other wedding you've been to—same cake, same rubber chicken, same cheese tray. Don't stand for it! The party should be uniquely the bride and groom's.

The wedding reception represents more than half of the entire wedding budget. That's a lot of cash! But don't panic just yet. Some of the most memorable celebrations are those that don't cost a fortune. Over the years, I've interviewed couples who hired ballroom dancing instructors and treated everyone to waltz lessons at the reception. Another couple held a square dance in their barn. A Connecticut bride and groom invited a gospel choir to sing. One couple entertained guests with a tarot card reader who told fortunes. Another couple held a clambake on the beach.

The point is, these were parties where the guests had good food, good drink, and good company. That's all you really need. If the setting is comfortable, the food delicious, and the company made to feel welcome and appreciated, the wedding reception will be an absolute hit whether you have $2,000 or $20,000 to spend.

Most wedding planners agree that the reception is for the comfort of your guests. They should have good seats (away from the band or swinging kitchen doors), not be squeezed in with too many bodies to a table, and have something good to eat and drink. Treat them as you would friends in your own home (if you had a dining room large enough for 200 people).

If you don't have a king's ransom to spend, then scale back the party, trim the guest list, shift the date to off-season, or change the time of the reception so that there's no need to serve a large meal, but *don't* scrimp on refreshments.

There is nothing worse than going to a wedding where the food was positively awful or the caterer didn't prepare enough. When Carol and Tom of New Jersey were married, the caterer failed to heat up the Swedish meatball hors d'oeuvres thoroughly. Guest bit into hot balls with frozen centers.

"As a catering manager, I don't recommend saving money on the food. You need to meet your required food minimum because you want to provide enough food for your guests," says Susanne Smith of the Garden Court Hotel in Palo Alto, California. "Look for other cost-saving avenues: flowers, cake, favors, and so forth. Utilize the reception site's resources and analyze your budget. Most hotels offer centerpieces, linens, tables, and chairs, as opposed to renting the equipment through a caterer. If someone has the creative genes in the family and they offer to help, have them do the flowers or cake instead of a wedding gift."

WAYS TO SAVE ON THE RECEPTION

Trim the Guest List

The most obvious (and most overlooked) way to cut costs is to trim the guest list. Unfortunately, couples fight it tooth and nail. The reality is that you can't have a formal wedding for 250 guests with extravagant extras—antique linens, truffles, a thirty-piece orchestra—on a tiny budget. It just isn't going to happen, no matter how hard you try to cut corners.

You can have the wedding of your dreams and indulge in all the luxury items if the guest list is whittled down to thirty guests. A small wedding has its advantages. Most couples know right off the bat the core group of twenty-five or thirty who are their "must invite" choices. They can spend less and enjoy more because they're able to indulge in every splurge they fancy. And a small wedding won't plunge them into debt.

It's a disturbing trend that couples would rather go into debt than cut the guest list. They'd rather settle for mediocre food and surroundings just to squeeze in Dad's golf buddies, Mom's college roommate, and all the third cousins they see once in a lifetime. Even though there are ways to wring maximum value from a limited budget, creativity and planning go only so far. Don't let the guest list spiral out of control, or you'll be forced to make compromises that really will be sacrifices. Or worse, you'll be making payments on your wedding for years to come. Even trimming the list by five people can mean a savings of $250 to $1,000.

Shift the Date

The month, day of the week, and season all affect sticker price. Most brides want to be June brides, and most want to marry on a Saturday. There are only four Saturday evenings in June each year, which means these dates are at a premium. All vendors charge their highest, or "premium," rates for Saturday nights, especially in June. If cost is a factor, consider having your wedding during the week instead of on the weekend, or plan an off-season wedding (January through March) instead of a peak-season one (May through October). Even a Friday night booking may cost less than a Saturday or Sunday.

Occasionally, you may get a price break for the most popular booking dates if the vendor has a last-minute cancellation or is willing to book two weddings in a single day to get another "turn" on the room. The downside, however, is that you may be forced to stick to a rigid schedule. If the party is just gearing up but you've got to vacate the reception room by 5 P.M. sharp to make way for another wedding, it will be depressing to watch the cleaning crew "tear down" the room to prepare for the next bride. Or, conversely, your wedding might be delayed while stragglers from the previous wedding clear out.

Shift the Time of Day

Schedule the reception for a time when guests won't expect a full meal, such as midmorning, midafternoon, or late evening. There is no law that says a couple must serve a large wedding luncheon or dinner.

Consider a "simple" reception that lasts two hours. It may be a wedding breakfast with baskets of fresh muffins and croissants, eggs Benedict, fresh-squeezed orange juice, and champagne punch. Or it could be an afternoon tea party with sweet and savory finger sandwiches, pastries, and fresh fruit. Consider a cocktail or champagne reception in which hors d'oeuvres are passed butler style on trays and guests sip drinks. Some couples prefer a wedding-cake-and-punch reception with classical music playing in the background. Or think about having a dessert reception with a show stopping wedding cake, champagne, and a buffet of sweets.

When holding a simple reception, keep in mind the style and formality of the wedding, the tastes of your guests, and whether they have traveled a great distance to attend the ceremony. (Travelers arrive tired and thirsty and expect to be fed!) It's important to let guests know ahead of time what kind of reception you are having. This may be done on the response or reception card with wording such as "Cake and Champagne Immediately Following Ceremony."

Consider a Free or Nearly Free Reception Site

Did you know that some reception sites charge both for the use of the site and for the catering? For mansions and private clubs, the site fee alone can be upward of $25,000! That's in addition to the $50 to $250 per person fee. On top of that, many facilities expect clients to use vendors from a "required" list or a "preferred" list. A "required" vendor is one you must use if you use that facility, which means you may be forced to hire the most expensive caterer in town—who may or may not be the best. A "preferred" list of vendors means those the facility staff regularly works with and usually highly recommends. Find out how much leeway you have in assembling your own team.

"Reception sites owned by the public or run by the government are a lot less expensive than privately run facilities," says certified meeting planner Joyce Scardina Becker of Events of Distinction in San Francisco, California. "Here in San Francisco, we have government-type office spaces, we have city hall, and one of the performing arts spaces is available. Check with your local venue books. One of the best resources for the newest venues are the convention and visitors bureaus and the chambers of commerce. They are the first to know where these venues are and what's opening up, and they will give resources for free. *Every* town has a chamber of commerce, and every major city has a convention or tourist bureau."

Free and inexpensive sites are everywhere! Consider having the wedding in a private home, at a public park with lush grounds or gardens, at a church or club hall, in an art gallery, at a racetrack, at the beach, or in a space at a college or university (alumni sometimes get reduced rates, too). You may need a city permit for park or beach parties, but these are generally under $10. Many aquariums, zoos, and museums are opening up their facilities to weddings as a way to boost revenues during off-hours. The local historical society may have a landmark house available at a nominal charge for private parties. Just ask.

The bonus of choosing landmark sites or historic properties is that they tend to be great backdrops for the wedding portraits. The mansion may have carved wall panels, stained-glass windows, romantic balconies, a winding staircase with a polished banister, or fabulous tapestries.

When choosing any gallery or landmark site, be aware of potential extra costs and hidden restrictions. You may be limited to using only certain rooms or floors of the facility. There also may be an extra charge to ensure the facility against damage to its artwork or collections.

Limit the Hours for the Reception

Have a three- or four-hour reception instead of the standard five. You'll save on liquor and wait-staff charges, the photographer will bill for fewer hours of coverage, and the band won't need to play as long. Most people won't notice—and guests who need to hire a baby-sitter will thank you for it.

Avoid a Holiday Wedding

On a major holiday, reception sites charge more because they must pay their own cooking, serving, and cleanup staff more in overtime wages. They will pass those increases on to you.

On the flip side, the downtime dates *between* major holidays can present a golden opportunity for saving! For example, the period between Christmas Day and New Year's Eve is a sluggish one for restaurants and reception sites. They've finished catering holiday parties for business groups, and their regular customers are home attending parties with friends. That means you may get a reduced rate for booking the wedding during this narrow window of opportunity. And chances are, friends and family are in town for the holiday season anyway, so you'll all be together. As an added incentive, many sites are already decorated for the holiday season with evergreens, trees, swags, ribbons, lights, and candles, so you'll save on the floral bill, too!

Look for an All-Inclusive Site

Want to know one of the great insider secrets for an elegant, low-cost wedding? Have the ceremony and reception at a hotel or resort with all-inclusive rates.

Besides being a stress-free way to have a wedding (it's all in one place!) the per person fee at these places usually includes an impressive range of extras: the linens, music, flowers, cake, candles, photography, decorations, and bridal bouquet. Many also offer discounts on the rehearsal dinner and guest accommodations, or give a free wedding night stay for the newlyweds or a free anniversary dinner for the couple a year later. By having the ceremony and reception at the same place, there's no need to rent limousines, and you'll save on music and flowers.

Have a Destination Wedding

Get away from it all and tie the knot in an exotic or romantic locale without eloping or leaving loved ones behind. Also called a honeymoon wedding or getaway wedding, the destination wedding is one where the couple marries at their honeymoon location and invites guests to come along.

Some resort managers and wedding consultants specialize in destination weddings and take care of every detail, from travel arrangements, hotel accommodations, flowers, and photography to finding a justice of the peace and taking care of the legal documents and red tape associated with having a wedding away from home. Popular destination wedding sites include Disneyland in Anaheim, California, and Walt Disney World in Orlando, Florida, as well as the Greek Isles, Africa, Hawaii, Italy, and the Bahamas.

Be forewarned: Not all destination weddings are cost-effective. But if you are willing to limit the guest list and plan to take a honeymoon anyway, having all the services in one place can end up a true bargain.

"I do destination weddings in Italy—the scenery is so romantic and it's storybook," says wedding consultant Fran Casler of Party Consulting by Fran in St. Petersburg, Florida. "The backdrop is not a Disney World castle, it's a *real* castle in a medieval town in the lake country or in Rome or Florence. It can be a money-saving alternative, too. If the bride and groom are not interested in having 150 guests and would like to have ten or fifteen closest relatives join them, they can do it for the same amount of money—or even less."

At some destination weddings, the couple pays for all travel and hotel expenses for their guests. At others, the guests pay their own way, or the couple picks up the hotel bill or airfare for the entire group. Often, the travel agent or wedding coordinator arranging the wedding can find discounted group travel and accommodations for everyone.

Another cost-effective form of destination wedding is to marry onboard a cruise ship. Many cruise lines offer special wedding, honeymoon, and anniversary packages for couples. Pay one price, climb aboard, and leave all the planning to the ship's cruise director or banquet manager. Once the ceremony is over, you're already at the honeymoon site.

For example, Caribbean Cruise Lines (1-800-421-1700) offers Grand Princess wedding and reception packages. The wedding package (starting at $1,400 per couple) includes a ceremony performed by the ship's captain, champagne, engraved champagne glasses, bouquet and boutonniere, video, framed formal portrait, and more. The reception package (starting at $70 per person) includes champagne, hors d'oeuvres, three tier-wedding cake, petit fours and sweets, live or taped music, and more. These rates, of course, are in addition to the cruise fee, but when you factor in the cost of a honeymoon and reception, the price is still a bargain.

Avoid a Tent Wedding

One of the biggest myths of wedding planning is that a reception in a tent in someone's backyard will be low-cost. No way! If the budget is limited, don't even think about it. First, there's the rental cost for the tent itself, which can be $3,000 to $20,000 depending on the size. In case of inclement weather, you'll need to rent flooring and window flaps. The caterer will need work space, refrigeration, and cooking and electrical facilities (that means renting worktables, a generator, cooking stove, and fridges). Depending on the time of year, you may need to bring in air-conditioning or heating equipment. Don't forget about renting tables, chairs, portable toilets, linens, china, crystal, and lighting. See how it all adds up?

 **How big is a dance floor?** If the reception site will include dancing, you'll need about 3 square feet of dance floor per guest. Some sites use roll-up portable dance floors that can be laid out in interlocking squares. A typical dance floor measures approximately 24 × 24 feet, or 600 square feet.

Inspect the Site

Before signing the contract, always tour the entire reception site and inspect the kitchen and every place guests will enter, including the bathrooms and parking lot. Look for telling details. Are the rest rooms clean and pleasant? Is the dining room attractively decorated with up-to-date furnishings? Is the wallpaper fresh? Do the carpets or curtains show signs of dirt or wear? If the site looks shabby, it may be a sign of financial problems. Don't risk booking a venue that is in disrepair; it may unexpectedly close, leaving you in the lurch.

WAYS TO SAVE ON LIQUOR AND BEVERAGES

■ **CUT BACK ON LIQUOR, WINE, AND CHAMPAGNE.** An open bar that runs for several hours can cost thousands of dollars. Think about ways to curb the liquor consumption, such as skipping the cocktail hour or limiting it to thirty minutes. Or consider serving just boutique beers, or serving wine only at the guest tables, or having a "mineral bar" with bottled waters from around the world. Some couples offer a cappuccino bar or exotic tea bar instead of wines and spirits. Or go entirely alcohol-free. It's perfectly acceptable. Don't worry about what the guests will think.

■ **DON'T EVEN CONSIDER HAVING GUESTS PAY FOR THEIR DRINKS.** You would never ask guests to pay for drinks when entertaining them in your home, so don't even think about doing it at your wedding.

■ **IF THE BARTENDERS PLACE TIP JARS ON THE BAR, INSIST THAT THEY REMOVE THEM.** The reception site will already be charging you a gratuity (and a tax on top of that), and guests should not be expected to tip at a wedding reception.

■ **ASK THE CATERER OR RECEPTION SITE MANAGER IF YOU CAN BRING IN YOUR OWN LIQUOR.** This may or may not be a savings; it depends on whether the site charges a corkage fee for opening bottles brought from off the premises. This fee ranges from $7 to $15 per bottle. Reception site managers will insist the fee covers opening the bottle, keeping it properly chilled, and pouring the beverage, but couples regard it as an incentive to pressure them into buying the house liquor.

■ **IF NO CORKAGE FEE IS IN EFFECT, PURCHASE THE WINE, BEER, LIQUOR, SODA, AND MIXERS AT A WHOLESALE BEVERAGE DISCOUNTER.** You'll spend less than a third of what it would cost to buy them from the reception site. The markup is staggering— sometimes double or triple the wholesale cost! Many liquor stores will accept returns of unopened bottles for credit or a refund. Remind the catering staff that you want the bottles opened only as needed—not all at once. Some states have laws prohibiting opened bottles to be taken off the premises. At my brother's rehearsal dinner, the waiters realized that the guests were light drinkers and purposely uncorked all the rare wines brought in by the bride and groom. The waiters had a grand party after the wedding and finished off the wine, since the opened bottles could not be removed from the restaurant. My brother and his wife were furious but couldn't do a thing.

■ **A GOOD ALTERNATIVE TO AN OPEN BAR IS TO SERVE THREE WINES: RED, WHITE, AND SPARKLING; A GOOD BEER; AND ICE WATER, COFFEE, AND NONALCOHOLIC PUNCH.** "This gives something for everybody to drink. If there is extra money left in the wedding budget, put it into extra food," says Master Bridal Consultant Karen DeKay of KD Productions Company in Daphne, Alabama.

■ **CONSIDER SERVING THE HOUSE BRAND OF WINES, SOFT DRINKS, AND LIQUORS.** The house brand is the one served when you don't specify a particular brand. It usually is offered at a more reasonable price than a premium brand, but it may not be up to your standards. Ask to sample the house brands before approving them.

■ **SKIP THE CHAMPAGNE TOAST, OR HAVE GUESTS TOAST WITH WHATEVER THEY ARE DRINKING.** "The tradition of making sure everyone has a glass of champagne in their hands for the toast turns out to be very costly. Not everyone drinks champagne," notes Dallas wedding consultant Ron Maddox of A Time for Us Productions, Inc. "They will take a sip and then put it down, and you see all these full glasses of champagne sitting around. There is a huge amount of waste involved. Allow them to toast with whatever is on hand."

■ **COME UP WITH AN ALTERNATIVE TO HARD LIQUOR AND WINE.** Serve a light champagne punch and also offer a nonalcoholic punch made from fresh fruit juices, or club soda with fruit puree or sorbet.

■ **SKIP THE CHAMPAGNE "FOUNTAINS" THAT GUSH CHILLED BUBBLY LIKE A WATERFALL.** These are expensive and unnecessary, and guests often mistake them for fruit juice or seltzer bars. (Boy, do they have hangovers later!) If you like the look of the fountain, ask the caterer to fill it with a nonalcoholic beverage such as lemonade or grape-fruit juice.

How much liquor/beverages do we need?

- 1 case of champagne pours 72 drinks
- 1 26-ounce bottle of punch or soft drinks yields 8 glasses
- 1 half keg of beer yields 260 8-ounce glasses
- 1 bottle of champagne yields 6 or 7 glasses
- 1 bottle of wine (750 ml) pours 6 4-ounce glasses
- 1 liter of liquor yields about 22 drinks (1½ ounces each)

Be sure to check with the site's beverage manager about quantities. He will want to know how many guests, the general age range of guests, and whether the crowd prefers wine, beer, or soft drinks.

WAYS TO SAVE ON CATERING

Compare Package Pricing

While researching caterers and banquet sites, call for a price list, sample menu, and color photographs or brochures. Compare prices! Although some sites include just the food in their per person charge—and everything else is billed separately—others include pricey extras such as fine crystal and china and specialty linens and napkins. Ask the caterer to break down every single charge for you.

Package pricing usually is negotiable. If you don't want the monogrammed napkins and matchbooks, ask to swap them for more hors d'oeuvres or nicer flowers. If the catering package includes a buffet with cheese and fruit platters, consider using them for the cocktail hour. (Just be sure this won't deplete the buffet too much.)

Insist on a taste test. It doesn't matter if the site has incredible ambiance. If the food tastes lousy or there isn't enough of it, the food will be the *only* thing guests remember about your wedding.

Never assume that anything is free. Extra, hidden charges may include silk flowers for the restrooms, parking attendants, microphones for the toast, extension cords for the sound system, music stands for the musicians, the dance floor, food station servers, cake-cutting fee, and skirting/garlands for the banquet tables.

Ask about the guaranteed minimum. This refers to the minimum number of servings to be paid for by the client. For example, if you guarantee 175 guests and only 135 show up, you are still expected to pay for the 175-person guarantee.

Menu Considerations

"People assume that you have to order off a menu and pay the price that's listed. However, those are adjusted retail prices, and there are a number of ways to custom tailor a menu so that the cost will be considerably less," says Joyce Scardina Becker. "You can order steak and serve it as an entrée, but instead of a 7-ounce steak, you can serve a 4-ounce steak. The portion can be controlled. It's really a matter of meeting with the executive chef, who can sit down and custom tailor your menu and then cost it out to you."

"Pasta is a great filler-upper," says Karen DeKay. "Realize that 85 percent of your invited guests will probably attend your wedding—with or without an RSVP—and they will be hungry! Pasta dishes are reasonable to make, hold well on the table, and fill up your hungry guests."

Foods that are in season cost less. Find out what fruits and vegetables are grown locally and what the regional specialties are— they will lower your cost.

Don't feel compelled to offer a choice of entrées. One is enough if it's delicious and attractively presented. (When you entertain dinner guests at home, do you make three or four entrées?) Guests really don't need a thousand choices, and they seldom remember what they "ordered" on the response card any- way. The important thing is to serve food that is attractively pre- sented, delicious, and made from the finest ingredients. If there are guests with special dietary needs, ask the caterer to provide a special meal for them.

If children will be at the wedding, consider ordering meals for them with a different size or type of entrée. "There are children's meals that might be $15 instead of $150, so if you are having chil- dren three to twelve years old, they will appreciate chicken fingers and hamburgers and spaghetti more than the adult entrées," Joyce Scardina Becker recommends.

Be aware that hors d'oeuvres vary tremendously in cost. Depending on the hors d'oeuvres you choose, the price could be pennies apiece or several dollars each! Since guests gobble an average of five hors d'oeuvres per person, per hour, the price can quickly soar. Skip the cheese tray with the little cubes of rubbery cheese and the bland crackers. Cheese trays are never cheap, and guests always eat them last (after the more interesting hot hors d'oeuvres have been devoured).

Don't even think of having a fresh "raw" bar. Fresh oysters, clams, and shrimp add precipitously to the cost, and you'll need huge amounts to satisfy guests (they tend to zoom in and devour these treats first). If you must serve expensive seafood, limit the amount and have it passed butler style by waiters.

Reception Style

Avoid a buffet reception. It's a common misconception that a buffet is always cheaper than a sit-down meal. This isn't necessarily so. Less portion control means a caterer must prepare more food per person to keep the buffet looking full and presentable.

Skip food stations. They're festive and provide an element of entertainment (it's fun to watch the chef toss crepes in a pan), but depending on the station, the price will rise $10 to $18 per guest—and that's on top of the per person fee. You're paying for both the specialty food (crepes, carved roast beef, Chinese food, omelets, shucked oysters, gourmet pizzas) and the extra chef or food server to operate the station. Instead, save that money or put it into a better-quality entrée or more unusual side dishes.

 **How many hors d'oeuvres should we serve?** For a reception that also will include a meal, you'll need about five hors d'oeuvres per person, per hour. For a simple reception with just cocktails or champagne and hors d'oeuvres, figure on at least twice that amount and be sure to have a mix of hot and cold hors d'oeuvres.

Hire Your Own Caterer

Some reception sites allow clients to bring in their own (off-site) caterer. Others insist you use the house chef. If using an off-site caterer, contract for just the food only. Arrange to pick it up yourself, then delegate a team of family and friends to help set it up and clean up afterward. Or divvy up the food-preparation responsibilities with the caterer. Perhaps have her make the entrées, side dishes, and canapés, while you make the salad and provide the rolls, wedding cake, and beverages.

Never choose a caterer on cost alone. A good caterer will work within your budget, even if it means paring down the whole event or choosing less-expensive ingredients and food-preparation techniques that require less labor.

Remember, a large part of catering costs are directly related to labor costs. Avoid foods that require carving at the table or time-consuming kitchen prep. Skip the cherries jubilee or shrimps grilled tableside. Obviously, in-season foods cost less than out-of-season items. Nationwide, chicken is generally less expensive than beef, beef is less expensive than shellfish, and items like imported caviar and fresh salmon, shrimp, and lobster will send any catering bill sky high.

Staff Meals

Joyce Scardina Becker offers this insider tip for stretching a reception budget. It's a kind gesture to feed vendors such as the photographer and musicians, but it isn't mandatory, and you can negotiate this in the contract. Find out if there is a staff meal you can order or an employee cafeteria they can use. "You may be able to send the photographer down to the employee cafeteria for six dollars," she says.

Rent or Buy?

Rent tablecloths and napkins from a restaurant supplier rather than a rental shop. One Connecticut bride estimates she saved $2 per napkin and $4 per tablecloth this way and got a larger selection of colors and styles to choose from. If you've got 200 guests and twenty tables, that's a savings of $480.

If you insist on purchasing rather than renting, buy cloth tablecloths and napkins in large quantities from a wholesale supplier. Use them later for parties and family reunions. Depending on the style and fabric, it may be cheaper in the long run to buy them.

What size linens do we need? The reception site manager can help you determine the tablecloth lengths that will look best. Decide whether you want the cloths to reach about 10 to 15 inches past the tabletop, or reach the floor, or extend past the floor in a "puddle" of fabric.

What size guest tables do we need?

- Generally, a 54-inch square table seats 4 people.
- A 60-inch round table seats 6 to 8 people.
- A 72-inch round table seats 8 to 10.
- A 72-inch long rectangular table seats 6 to 8.
- A 96-inch long rectangular table seats up to 10.

SPECIAL TOUCHES AT THE RECEPTION

■ **HAVE THE CATERER PREPARE SOME OF THE WEDDING MEAL FOOD TO BE SENT OR TAKEN TO YOUR HOTEL ROOM AFTER THE RECEPTION.** Says consultant Amy Connor of An Affair to Remember in New York City, "You'll probably have little time to eat during the reception, and you'll be starving by the time you get to the hotel."

■ **INSTEAD OF TOSSING THE BOUQUET, GIVE IT TO SOMEONE SPECIAL.**
Amy Connor gave her bridal bouquet to her grandmother, who
was recently widowed and was the single woman she "most wanted
to have it."

■ **DRINK CHAMPAGNE FROM THE FLUTES YOUR PARENTS USED AT
THEIR WEDDING.**

■ **DEDICATE A SPECIAL DANCE AT THE RECEPTION TO A SELECT
GROUP.** The group might be all married couples, or couples celebrating their anniversary that month, or couples who have celebrated
milestone anniversaries.

■ **IF THERE IS A HANDFUL OF CHILDREN AT THE WEDDING, INVITE
THEM TO SIT AT THE HEAD TABLE FOR DESSERT.** It's an incentive to
keep them well behaved until then and makes for adorable pictures, too.

■ **IF THERE ARE CHILDREN AT THE WEDDING, SET UP A SPECIAL KIDS-
AND GRANDPARENTS-ONLY TABLE.** Children tend to behave and
have a much better time when they have a "special" table with
other children or with Grandma and Grandpa.

■ **INVITE GUESTS TO HOLD HANDS DURING THE BLESSING.** When
Stacy Darragh and Frank Garnett were married, the minister
noted that the wedding ring symbolizes the never-ending love
between a husband and wife. In celebration of that eternal love, he
invited all the guests onto the dance floor for the blessing and
asked them to hold hands in a circle.

■ **PEN A TAKE-HOME REMEMBRANCE.** Instead of favors, write a personal note to each guest and roll it into a scroll. Tie it with a ribbon
and leave it on their dinner plates. Yes, this takes time, but guests
will never forget it.

QUESTIONS TO ASK THE RECEPTION
OR CATERING MANAGER

- Is a wedding package offered?
- If so, what exactly is included? What is the cost?
- May we make substitutions?
- What ways can you suggest to make the most of a limited budget?
- What do clients value about this site (view, scenic setting, food quality, historical appeal)?
- Is there a guaranteed requirement for the number of guests?
- Are all taxes and gratuities included in the per person cost?
- Do you provide catering, site rental, or both?
- Can the site be used for both the ceremony and reception?
- Is there an appropriate place for the receiving line?
- If the site is in a historic mansion or museum, how much space will be available to guests (entire building, one section or wing)? What is off-limits?
- Do we need to purchase insurance in case of damage to the site's collections or furnishings?
- Is there a dance floor? How large is it?
- What is the ratio of waiters to guests?
- What does a place setting look like and consist of?
- What are the arrangements for a head table?
- When are the deposit and balance due?
- Do you provide a written contract?
- What kind of health permit and liability insurance do you carry?
- What are the liquor laws in this state regarding guests who are served too much alcohol and later injure others or cause an accident while under the influence?

- Do you work from a set menu, or can we request a menu tailored to our preferences?
- Is the cost of the service staff included in the price?
- Will the caterer/banquet manager I've hired be present at the reception on the wedding day to oversee the event and make sure all goes smoothly?
- When is the final guest count due?
- What if unexpected guests show up? Can you accommodate them? What is the additional charge?
- Have you ever catered a wedding at this site before?
- Will there be another wedding here on the same day?
- How will the servers be attired?
- Are all charges clearly stated in a contract? Does this include types and amounts of food, number of guests, complete menu listing, per person charge, liquor and beverage charges, setup charges, cleanup charges, and equipment charges?
- Will you provide special dietary meals on request?
- Can we supply our own liquor?
- How are drink costs calculated?
- What brands of beer, wine, liquor, champagne, and soft drinks are served? Is there a corkage fee?
- Do you supply the wedding cake?
- Do you provide the flowers?
- Until what date are these prices in effect (price escalation clause)?
- What is your cancellation or postponement policy?
- Is any part of the deposit refundable?
- Do you supply plates, glasses, silverware, and linens?
- Do you handle the cleanup and rental returns?
- Are there adequate rest room and cloakroom facilities?
- What are the arrangements in case of rain?

CATERING YOUR OWN WEDDING

Doing it yourself has many advantages—the price can't be beat, and the menu is *exactly* what the bride and groom long for. But think long and hard about attempting anything as labor intensive as catering your own wedding or having an at-home wedding.

It takes time and the organizational skills of a military general. There's the consideration of cooking space, counter space, refrigeration, and storage space. Is there enough space to seat people comfortably in your home? Do you have a backup plan in case it rains and everyone runs into the dining room? Who is going to heat up all those canapés while the bride is slipping into her gown?

I remember a humorous article in *Gourmet* magazine years ago titled "The Bride Wore Oven Mitts," about a gutsy bride who catered her own wedding—from fussy appetizers to towering cake—and was so exhausted in the process that she forgot to change her shoes and wore sneakers under her wedding gown. It was hilarious, but it convinced me I needed to find a caterer when I got married.

Obviously, if you choose to cater your own wedding, or even just provide some of the main dishes or appetizers and let the caterer do the rest, it takes a lot of advance planning and testing of recipes that are quick, are easy to triple or quadruple, and can be conveniently made ahead and frozen. You'll need to find a legion of helpers—maybe local church members or teenagers to help cook or serve or clean up. It will take more rolls of aluminum foil and more boxes of garbage bags than you ever dreamed possible. But the results may be well worth it.

As a former food writer, I've been impressed by couples who take the time to feed and nurture their guests. The ones who take pride in shopping for the finest ingredients and lovingly preparing them for a wedding feast seem to discover a side of the wedding celebration that the rest of us miss. They get satisfaction from serving special recipes and watching friends savor the special meal. They literally share their love on their wedding day.

Perhaps you'll want to have the wedding at home, but leave the food preparation to someone else. Janice Anthony of Connecticut is a veritable professional at producing at-home weddings. She's done them for all five of her children. For each, she hired a caterer through word-of-mouth recommendations from other wedding professionals, and for each, she booked a disc jockey. She also rented tables, chairs, linens, and china. "We didn't feel we had enough space for a band, and a band is a bigger expense," she says. The five weddings ranged in size from 35 to 165 guests. "There are so many benefits. People can be there as long as you want them to be, and it doesn't have to end after four hours. It's more comfortable and personal, too. People seem to feel that personal warmth that I don't think you can find at a hotel or inn somewhere."

Each of the five weddings was held outdoors in the family's backyard. Luckily, it never rained on any of them. "The big disaster at the first one was not preparing adequately for the caterer to have a place to prepare the food. It was a real hot day, and we had rented a small tent thinking they could set up there, but they ended up using the basement," Anthony recalls. "The caterer kept saying, 'Clear this and clear that!' and we kept clearing off the tops of the washer and dryer."

Anthony offers the following mother-tested tips for planning an at-home wedding:

- ❖ Rent enough portable toilets. Have separate ones for the men and women, and make decorative "Ladies" and "Gentlemen" signs to hang on the doors.
- ❖ Warn the neighbors ahead of time about the noise from music and guests. (Or invite the neighbors.)
- ❖ Borrow, rent, or buy an additional refrigerator—or, at the very least, ask a neighbor to clear out shelf space in theirs.

It's essential. Anthony checked into renting one and found it was cheaper to buy a secondhand refrigerator for $75. She found the fridge in a newspaper classified ad.

❖ Consider borrowing utensils and serving platters instead of renting them. Rentals and tents are pricey. It may be cheaper in the long run to buy a small tent rather than rent one. Look in discount hardware and home supply stores.

Planning the Menu

When planning the menu, choose items that are inexpensive, are easy to prepare ahead of time, and freeze well. To get ideas, collect menus and price lists from caterers, hotels, and reception sites. Keep in mind that although you don't need to offer several entrées, it's thoughtful to provide at least one vegetarian main course or several vegetarian side dishes for people who can't eat meat or prefer not to. The foods should be in keeping with the season of the year, the number of guests, and the guests' preferences.

Ronnie Fein, a food journalist, author of *The Complete Idiot's Guide to Cooking*, and director of the Ronnie Fein Cooking School in Stamford, Connecticut, makes the following menu and recipe suggestions:

For a wedding buffet dinner
Sliced filet mignon, Caesar salad (with or without grilled shrimp), marinated vegetables, and several colorful salads made from starches or grains, such as barley, corn, and tomato salad; rice with peas and olives; or couscous with macadamia nuts and lemon.

For a sit-down dinner
A first course of salad or crab cakes, followed by stuffed chicken breasts or filet mignon, crispy potatoes, fresh asparagus, and/or pureed carrots with dill. Or make the main course an upscale shrimp-and-eggplant lasagna served with a green salad.

For dessert

Chocolate truffles; fresh strawberries with custard sauce, cream, or aged balsamic vinegar; fruit sherbet; or chocolate or lemon mousse.

Chicken Breasts Stuffed with Wild Mushrooms and Fontina Cheese

20 boneless and skinless chicken breast halves	40 ounces (10 cups) finely chopped mushrooms
Salt and pepper	14 ounces grated fontina cheese
10 tablespoons butter	
5 tablespoons olive oil	10 tablespoons olive oil (about ½ cup)
5 large shallots, chopped	2½ cups fresh plain bread crumbs
5 cloves garlic, chopped	

Preheat the oven to 425 degrees Fahrenheit. Place the chicken breasts on a cutting board and cover them with waxed paper. Pound the chicken breasts with a meat mallet or the flat side of a cleaver or chef's knife until they are about ⅛-inch thick. Place the breasts shiny side down. Sprinkle the chicken with salt and pepper. Keep in refrigerator until ready for stuffing.

Heat the butter and olive oil over moderate heat in a sauté pan. When the butter has melted and looks foamy, add the shallots, garlic, and mushrooms and cook over moderate heat, stirring constantly for 5 to 8 minutes until the vegetables have softened and the pan juices have evaporated. Remove the vegetables to a mixing bowl and stir in the cheese. Let the mixture cool. Place equal amounts of the mixture in the center of each chicken breast. Fold the chicken to completely enclose the filling. Brush or rub the chicken with enough olive oil to coat the surface. Coat the stuffed breasts with the bread crumbs and place them on baking sheets, seam side down. Bake for 30 minutes or until completely cooked through. Serves 20.

Roasted Filet Mignon

2 beef filets, preferably thick ones, each about 4½ pounds (or 4 center-cut filets, each about 2 to 2½ pounds)

4 tablespoons olive oil

Salt

Freshly ground pepper

Garlic salt to taste

Preheat the oven to 425 degrees Fahrenheit. Brush or rub the oil onto the meat. Sprinkle the meat with the salt, pepper, and garlic salt. Place in shallow roasting pans and roast for 10 minutes. Reduce the temperature of the oven to 350 degrees. Continue to roast until a meat thermometer inserted into the thickest part of the meat reaches just below 120 degrees (rare) or just below 130 degrees (medium). The time will depend on the thickness of the roasts and whether two large or four smaller roasts are used; from about 25 to 40 minutes. Serves 16 to 20.

Pureed Dill-Scented Carrots

5 pounds carrots	1½ teaspoons salt (or salt to taste)
Lightly salted water	
15 tablespoons butter (one stick, plus 7 tablespoons)	5 tablespoons minced fresh dill weed or 5 teaspoons dried
2½ teaspoons sugar	1¼ to 1½ cups cream

Preheat the oven to 350 degrees Fahrenheit. Peel the carrots and cut them into bite-size chunks. Place the carrots in a saucepan and cover them with lightly salted water. Bring the water to a boil, lower the heat, and simmer the carrots 15 to 20 minutes until they are fork tender. Drain the carrots. Place the carrots in the work bowl of a food processor with the butter, sugar, salt, and dill weed. Process until the carrots are pureed and have a uniform texture. Stir in the cream. Put the mixture in a serving or baking dish. Reheat in the oven until hot (6 to 7 minutes; if the mixture has been refrigerated, then heat for about 15 to 20 minutes). Serves 20.

Sautéed Potatoes with Rosemary

54 "new" or small red Bliss potatoes

Lightly salted water

6 tablespoons butter

6 tablespoons vegetable oil

1½ teaspoons salt (or salt to taste)

¾ teaspoon freshly ground black pepper

4½ tablespoons minced fresh rosemary, or 4½ teaspoons dried, crushed rosemary

Place the potatoes in a large saucepan and cover them with lightly salted water. Bring the water to a boil, lower the heat, and simmer the potatoes 15 to 20 minutes until they are fork tender. Drain the potatoes and peel them when they are cool enough to handle. Heat the butter and vegetable oil over moderate heat in a large skillet. When the butter has melted and looks foamy, add the potatoes to the pan. Sprinkle the potatoes with salt, pepper, and rosemary. Sauté the potatoes 15 to 20 minutes, shaking the pan occasionally, or until the potatoes are browned on all sides and are lightly crispy. These may be reheated in a preheated, 425-degree oven for about 6 to 8 minutes. Makes 18 servings.

Gougeres (crisp pastry balls with herbs and cheese)

2 cups water

½ pound unsalted butter, cut into chunks

2 cups all-purpose flour, sifted

1½ teaspoons salt

8 large eggs

1 cup grated Parmesan cheese, optional

4 tablespoons finely chopped fresh herbs, optional

Dash cayenne pepper, optional

Egg wash: 2 eggs beaten with 4 teaspoons water

Heat the water and butter in a medium-size saucepan. Bring the mixture to a boil over moderate heat. Add the flour and salt all at once. Stir vigorously with a wooden spoon until the mixture is blended and begins to come away from the sides of the pan. Remove pan from the heat and let it cool for 4 to 6 minutes. Add the eggs, one at a time, blending well after each addition. Add the cheese, herbs, and cayenne pepper and blend them in thoroughly.

Preheat the oven to 400 degrees Fahrenheit. Butter and flour several baking sheets. Pipe small balls (about ¾" to 1") of dough out of a pastry tube or drop from a teaspoon onto the sheet. Brush the balls with some of the egg wash. Bake in a preheated, 400-degree oven for about 18 to 20 minutes, until golden brown. Turn off the heat. Pierce the puffs with the tip of a sharp knife. Return puffs to the turned-off oven for 2 to 3 minutes. Remove the puffs from the oven. Serve hot or at room temperature. Serve whole or slit the gougeres in half crosswise and fill with dips, spreads, salads (such as curried egg salad), or chopped vegetables (such as bruschetta tomatoes) just before serving. Makes about 72.

CHAPTER FOURTEEN

FLOWERS AND
DECORATIONS

Ever notice that romance and roses go hand in hand? Flowers make every wedding more festive and breathe life into the celebration. They add color, beauty, and fragrance.

The good news about wedding flowers is that easy substitutions make for pretty, not pricey, designs. Plus, no one will know the difference. Flowers range dramatically in cost depending on rarity, demand, and time of the year. You might look at two bridal bouquets—both stunningly beautiful—and one might cost $50 and the other $500.

Flowers represent a significant portion of the wedding budget—10 to 20 percent—and like the gown, they make a striking visual statement and set the tone for the style and formality of the wedding.

Begin by looking at the glossy color photographs of bouquets and table arrangements in bridal magazines. Tear out the pages that appeal to you and put them in your wedding file or binder. You may like the shape of one bouquet or the rare flowers of another. Take notes about which color mixes appeal to you: Are they soft pastels? Bold jewel colors? The soft green garden look?

The next step is to put yourself in the hands of a talented florist. Like photographers and cake bakers, some florists are more artistic and creative than others. Floral designs are much like fashion designs; styles come and go. You can expect a florist who has earned the AIFD (American Institute of Floral Design) designation to be professional and on top of the latest floral trends. There are only 1,068 AIFD–certified florists in the world. This nonprofit organization is dedicated to education about flowers and horticulture.

Choose a florist who has extensive experience with weddings. How do you find one? Call the catering managers at the three best hotels and three best country clubs in town. Ask for three recommendations from each. The same one or two names will be at the top of everyone's list. As you interview florists, you'll get a feel for who leans toward standard cookie-cutter designs and who has a flair for the more unusual styles.

Ask if the florist charges a consultation fee. Most are happy to talk with you for free. Of course, if the florist makes up a sample bouquet or arrangement at your request, expect to be charged for their time and raw materials. This is reasonable and worth it to gauge what the finished product will look like. If you're considering having samples made up, schedule it for a time when you're having the engagement party or a dinner with both sets of parents. You can use the flowers as centerpieces.

When it comes to florists, don't be scared off by a designer who usually does upscale, expensive events. A good florist will work within any budget or floral scheme. High-priced floral designers often have told me they will work within tight wedding budgets if the bride honestly admires their work. Many top designers have experience working on fund-raising galas for nonprofit organizations (whose budgets are limited, like yours), so they know glamorous ways to make more from less.

Consider using an independent florist rather a retail shop, says floral designer W. Donnie Brown of Five Star Floral Design and Events in Dallas, Texas. "The retailer has to mark up its product at least 350 percent to pay for the expensive inventory that it must keep on hand at all times," he explains. "The independent has less overhead and therefore can cut at least 100 percent from that pricing structure."

No matter who you hire, ask to see a portfolio of the florist's work first. Must you choose from standard arrangements in an FTD book, or can you experiment with different stems and unusual ribbons for a special look? Ask if you can come back while the store is preparing for another wedding, to get an idea of how well the staff manages under pressure of a full-scale wedding production.

Be sure to inspect the flowers going out the door. Are they at the peak of freshness, or slightly tired and discolored? Ask how far ahead the arrangements will be assembled and where they'll be stored. Also, find out if the florist will be working on another wedding that day. If so, does she have the refrigeration and storage capacities to handle both events?

When consulting with the florist about centerpiece designs, know the size of the guest tables being used for the reception and the sizes of any banquet tables for food buffets. Size matters. There's a big difference in cost and style of centerpieces for a round table that seats six versus a rectangular table that seats twelve. You also should know the color scheme of the reception room, including the carpeting, table linens, walls, and curtains, so that the florist can design centerpieces in a complementary style and color. It doesn't make sense to choose centerpiece flowers that match the bride's bouquet if those colors will clash with the reception table-cloths or carpeting.

Come prepared with a budget in mind. Be frank about how much you want to spend and what you need to order: how many bouquets, arrangements, headpieces, boutonnieres, altar sprays, and so on. Remember that a good florist can show you ways to get the most value from your money and may suggest any one of the following ideas.

THE SIX RULES
FOR SAVING ON FLOWERS

Rule #1: In-season and locally grown flowers cost less than exotic and imported ones.

"The price really depends on what the flower is, the quantity of them, and the time of year," says Christine Hockin, an AIFD–certified florist and co-owner of Oakhurst Flower Shoppe in Oakhurst, New Jersey. Before Hockin designed a lily-of-the-valley bouquet for a fall wedding, she warned the bride about the steep cost. "I told her that in November I would have to bring them in from Holland, and the flowers alone would be $500. She was in shock! But lily of the valley is only in season in the end of May, and it's only in for about a week or two."

"Go with flowers that are in season," she advises. "Ask your florist what's in season at the time of year of your wedding. If you want sunflowers in December, they will be pricier than in summer. We can get tulips in July, but they will be more expensive than in the months when it's cold."

Wedding consultant Robbi Ernst III, founder of June Wedding International, a Las Vegas–based national certifying organization for wedding and event planners, and author of *Great Wedding Tips from the Experts,* notes that flower prices range so widely that simply substituting one flower variety for another can reap huge savings. "Lily of the valley costs about $150 for a bunch of ten or twelve flowers. It's not that many. So for what you'd spend on *one* bunch of lily of the valley, you could get two or three table arrangements of less costly flowers."

"If you must have lily of the valley or another expensive flower, use it for accent only, like in the boutonnieres, and use just one," Ernst suggests. "It gets you away from the ordinary, mundane stephanotis, and using just two or three strands in the bouquet is especially rich and meaningful."

Rule #2: Anything that requires a lot of labor will cost more.

Most of the cost of a wedding bouquet or formal arrangement comes from the labor. It takes time to trim, hand-wire, and hand-tie flowers into a bouquet. Arrangements don't just jump into the oasis foam and arrange themselves. A bouquet that requires hours of hand-tying will cost more than a bouquet composed of a few long stems tied with a single ribbon. It makes sense, doesn't it? For a chic effect that costs next to nothing, carry a single, perfect long-stemmed rose tied with the most beautiful ribbon you can find.

Rule #3: Avoid major flower-giving holidays.

The floral bill for a wedding date near a major flower-giving holiday such as Mother's Day, Thanksgiving, Easter, or Valentine's Day will be invariably higher than at other times of the year when flowers aren't in peak demand. Florists are charged more for their flowers by wholesalers and then pass along the seasonal increases to you.

But there's an even better reason to schedule a date away from these holidays: florists are pressed to fill orders at these frantic times of year and won't be able to give your wedding the time and attention it deserves. Do you want an exhausted, overworked florist who has eighty Valentine's Day orders to fill before she starts on your wedding, or do you want someone who has the time to lavish on only *you*?

Rule #4: Avoid traditional "bridal" flowers.

All of the traditional wedding flowers also happen to be expensive, no matter what time of year. These include white roses, gardenias, dendrobium orchids, orange blossoms, tulips, and camellias.

Rule #5: Spend your money where people will see it.

Ceremony flowers tend to be a big expense (altar arrangements must be formidable to fill the big, open space), but guests see them for the shortest amount of time. Put your money toward the reception flowers instead.

Rule #6: Let the flowers do double duty.

Have the ceremony flowers designed with the idea of using them again at the reception. The bridesmaids' bouquets can be arranged on the head table, the altar sprays can be used to decorate the banquet tables, and the pew bows can be used again to decorate the bride and groom's chairs or to make the doors at the reception look more festive.

Utilize the centerpieces elsewhere, says designer W. Donnie Brown. "I do topiaries or iron stantions or rented brass aisle stantions to make for a dramatic entrance for the processions. The aisle designs are later moved to the dining tables to create topiaries," he says. "Sometimes the stantions are height adjustable for varying the dimensions to fit the aisle and the tables. You get an elaborate aisle decoration and pay only a transfer, labor, and waiting-time fee for the centerpieces. This is a fraction of what it would cost to have both done independently on such a large scale."

CHOOSING THE BRIDAL BOUQUET

For the initial consultation with the florist, be sure to bring a pho tograph of your gown and swatches of the gown's fabric and lace. The same is true for the bridesmaids' attire. When designing the bouquet, the florist will want to examine the silhouette of the gown and its style, level of formality, and fabric before designing the flo- ral accompaniment. Your height, body shape, and complexion all play a part, too. That's because the bouquet should complement the total look and be in proportion to you. It may seem obvious, but too large a bouquet will overshadow you and too small a bou- quet will seem skimpy. The lopsided effect will look even more ridiculous in the photos.

Floral experts pay special attention to scaling the flowers to fit the bride. They often create the attendants' bouquets in a size scaled to the average size of the bridesmaids.

Bouquet Styles

Cascade
A large, tear-shaped arrangement in which flowers gracefully spill downward. The traditional cascade is the most popular bridal style. Avoid a cascade that's too large, or it will look like the floral arrangements that drape caskets (what's known in the trade as a funeral spray bouquet).

Nosegay

A tightly bound cluster of small flowers, round in shape. A small nosegay is sometimes called a posy. A nosegay typically requires two dozen or more flowers, so it's not an inexpensive choice.

Arm bouquet

A graceful crescent shape designed to be cradled in one arm. The arm bouquet usually includes just one to six long-stemmed blooms tied together by a ribbon or greenery.

Biedermeier bouquet

A bouquet featuring concentric circles of tightly packed flowers in different colors. This highly stylized bouquet has a very formal look and tends to be pricey since it requires so much labor and many flowers (dozens of them).

Hand-tied bouquet

A simple cluster of long stems tied with a luxurious ribbon. This is different from a hand-wired bouquet, which means any bouquet style in which the flowers are all individually tied by hand with florist tape before being assembled in a cluster.

Spray bouquet

Usually a triangular-shaped cluster of flowers.

Pomander

A tightly packed ball of flowers suspended from the wrist by a decorative ribbon.

Instead of Carrying a Bouquet:

- Carry a prayer book or family Bible.
- Hold a warm, furry muff.
- Carry a beautiful fan. You can find them at museum gift shops or craft stores.
- Hold an ostrich feather or plume tied with a satin ribbon.
- Carry a basket filled with silk flowers or baby's breath.
- Drape a floral boa (made of wired flowers and greenery) around your shoulders.

Breakaway

A bouquet containing a detachable minibouquet for tossing.

Tussie mussie

A bouquet style popular in Victorian times. The tussie mussie is a small, hand-tied bouquet consisting of stems tied together and trimmed to a uniform length. Sometimes, but not always, a tussie mussie is inserted into a cone-shaped holder made of metal or stiff paper, or even crocheted yarn.

WAYS TO SAVE ON FLOWERS

■ **PICK UP THE FLOWERS AT THE FLORIST SHOP YOURSELF.** You'll save up to $100 on delivery and setup fees. If you won't have time on the morning of the wedding, ask a trusted friend or relative to do it. Just be sure you have a large enough car or van to transport the flowers and a cool place to store them. Don't forget to ask the florist for last-minute instructions on care and arrangement.

■ **FIND OUT ABOUT TRANSFER FEES.** "For a fairly nominal fee, the floral designer I work with will transfer the altar arrangements to the reception and use them on the buffet tables. That is quite a savings of money," says consultant Ron Maddox of A Time for Us Productions in Dallas, Texas. "He charged one bride $100 to transfer her arrangements, and that $100 would certainly not have gone far for flowers for a reception."

The floral designer created two large, three-sided floral arrangements to place on either side of the altar. After the ceremony, he transported them to the reception and placed them back to back to create the look of one imposing arrangement. "You couldn't tell it was two arrangements," Maddox recalls. "It was quite lovely and very worthwhile."

■ **ASK THE FLORIST TO DO A MARKET BUY.** The florist visits a wholesale flower distribution mart the day before the wedding or early in the morning on the day of the wedding, buys what's on special for that day, and creates the floral designs using those blooms. If you really trust your florist's judgment and talents, this can be a great way to save money.

■ **SHARE THE COSTS WITH ANOTHER COUPLE BEING MARRIED THAT DAY OR WEEKEND.** This is easier than you think, and reception site managers and florists usually are eager to cooperate, since it makes planning easier for them, too. Ask the caterer or site manager if she thinks you and the other couple have similar tastes and budgets. You may want to swap phone numbers or explore the option of shared items over a cup of coffee. If you're going to rent a trellis or chuppah, or have expensive fabric swags or balloon arches installed, it makes sense to leave them up one more day for the other bride—and cut the bill in half.

"I think sharing costs is the best money-saving tip of all," says bridal consultant Michelle Hodges. "I remember a bride who just amazed me. This bride [who was being married on a Sunday] got together with the bride from Saturday, and they used the same caterer. They upgraded linens, chairs, and other rental items that could be used for both days and then split the cost."

The caterer was thrilled because he was at the same venue for two days in a row and could produce two high-end events with ease in setup. In return, the caterer gave both brides excellent service and a choice of additional menu options.

"Of course, it helps if you at least have similar tastes with the other bride," Hodges says. "These two tried to share large floral arrangements but found they had different tastes in flowers, so they decided to skip that idea. But the shared aspects worked out great."

■ **USE THE BOUQUETS AS CENTERPIECES.** "If you have a limited floral budget and a large bridal party, have the attendants' bouquets designed to be used as table centerpieces once the pictures are finished and before the guests are asked to enter the ballroom," advises wedding consultant Toni DeLisi of Memorable Events in Waldwick, New Jersey. "If you have 120 guests seated at twelve tables, and you have six bridesmaids, your florist will have to make only an additional six centerpieces for the reception."

■ **COME UP WITH AN ALTERNATIVE FOR THE FLOWER GIRL TO THROW OR CARRY.** Instead of ordering fresh rose petals for the flower girl to throw, purchase confetti at a party supply store or make your own using colored paper or glittery wrapping paper. Kids love doing this! Or set the children loose in the family garden and have them gently pluck petals off fresh flowers.

■ **FOR AN INEXPENSIVE AND UNDULATING LOOK, ALTERNATE TALL AND SHORT CENTERPIECES ON THE GUEST TABLES.** Shorter-stemmed flowers are often less expensive. Be wary of too-tall centerpieces, unless the base is narrow enough for guests to look around it (like a topiary or narrow vase with the widest part of the display higher than head level). Otherwise, a maximum height of 12 to 14 inches is a good rule of thumb.

■ **AVOID WHITE-ON-WHITE ARRANGEMENTS.** "One thing that brides seldom think about in the floral department is to use color," advises Master Bridal Consultant Sue Winner of Atlanta, Georgia. "When you do all-white flowers for a wedding, it takes a whole lot more flowers to look like you've got anything. Adding splashes of color goes a long way."

■ **DON'T SKIMP ON CENTERPIECES.** An arrangement should look lush and big enough for the table. This doesn't mean you need dozens of roses, as long as the design is a suitable focal point and doesn't look as if the florist got lazy and left something out. Use "filler" flowers and greens generously. For example, combine a few exotic blooms such as bird-of-paradise with many eucalyptus leaves and other less expensive but colorful flowers such as gerbera daisies and big chrysanthemums.

■ **FRESH FRUIT—AND EVEN PARSLEY—ARE GREAT FILLERS TO SUP-PLEMENT FLOWERS.** Pineapples, red and green grape clusters, apples, and pomegranates provide interesting color and texture. Look for the most perfect, unblemished fruit you can find.

■ **AVOID TALL OR VERY LARGE VASES.** Tall vases require long-stemmed flowers, which are often pricey. Large vases require huge amounts of flowers to fill them up properly. Instead, group together many little vases.

■ **SCHEDULE THE WEDDING NEAR THE CHRISTMAS/NEW YEAR'S HOL-IDAYS.** Most sites will already be decorated with evergreens, red ribbons, trees, and poinsettias. You won't have to spend a penny on flowers and decorations!

■ **USE SEVERAL SHADES OF ONE COLOR FOR VALUE AND DRAMA.** A variety of different flowers in the same shade will create dimension and texture. Avoid predominately white arrangements. White wedding flowers tend to be expensive (think orchids and roses), and you'll need many more of them to make a statement.

■ **ARRANGE SOME OF THE FLOWERS YOURSELF.** Or have a friend or local garden club member do it.

■ **USE SMALL FLOWERING PLANTS AS PARTY FAVORS.** When arranged in a tight cluster, eight little plants in pots look like one large arrangement.

IDEAS FOR
INEXPENSIVE CENTERPIECES

There are many options for inexpensive, nontraditional floral centerpieces. Amy Connor of An Affair to Remember in New York City suggests: "For a Christmas wedding, fill a bowl in the center of the table with inexpensive glass tree decorations. They are available in many colors, prices, and sizes. They can be used on the couple's Christmas tree for years to come. For a great favor, write each guest's name on one in a swirling font with a gold pen."

■ **PLACE GROUPINGS OF FRAMED PICTURES OF FAMILY AND FRIENDS ON THE GUEST TABLES.** Include vintage photos of family members, as well as childhood or baby pictures of the older relatives in the family. These sentimental groupings are a great conversation piece, as everybody will try to figure out who's who.

■ **SCOUT FLEA MARKETS FOR VINTAGE WEDDING PHOTOS.** "You can often find boxes and boxes of such items for a pittance. Cheap frames can be painted to match, and the pictures can be gathered in groups on tables," says Amy Connor.

■ **COME UP WITH A CENTERPIECE THEME.** Sarah and James, a Connecticut couple who met and fell in love at an Ivy League college, placed framed drawings of their favorite campus buildings at their guest tables. Each landmark had a special meaning for them. ("This is where we studied together; this is where we first kissed," etc.)

■ **PURCHASE TALL, INEXPENSIVE GLASS VASES AT A CRAFT OR WHOLESALE FLORIST SUPPLY STORE AND FILL WITH FRESH LEMONS (OR LIMES) AND WATER.** The effect is simple but colorful and very dramatic.

■ **FOR AN AUTUMN WEDDING, PURCHASE PLUMP GOURDS OR PUMP-KINS AND SCOOP OUT THE SEEDS.** Fill the natural container with sheaves of wheat, fresh flowers, branches, Halloween masks, or leaves.

■ **ARRANGE CANDLES OF DIFFERENT HEIGHTS AND THICKNESSES IN AN ARTISTIC GROUPING.** For more reflected light, place them on a round or square mirror. You can find these inexpensive mirrors at craft and party stores or in the bathroom wall tile departments of local home improvement stores.

■ **INCORPORATE CANDELABRAS.** "Alternate florals on tables with candelabras decorated with freeze-dried rose petals at the base. Rented candelabras are less expensive than floral centerpieces," suggests wedding consultant Patricia Bruneau of L'Affaire du Temps in Milpitas, California.

■ **USE CANDLES, CANDLES, AND MORE CANDLES.** "All shapes and sizes of candles on a table can be very romantic and cost-effective. Be sure to check with the facility on open- or closed-flame restrictions," Bruneau adds. "And floating gardenia bowls with votives at the base are an inexpensive and beautiful look."

■ **RENT OR BORROW SILVER BOWLS AND FILL WITH PERFECT FRESH FRUIT.** For a more unusual look, dip the fruit in an egg-white-and-sugar mixture and allow to dry for a crackly, sparkly finish.

■ **USE BLOSSOMING BULBS AS CENTERPIECES.** Hyacinths and daffodils are colorful and fragrant, too.

■ **FLOAT MINIATURE CANDLES OR BIG BLOSSOMS IN SHALLOW, CLEAR CONTAINERS.** The blossoms can be spider mums; snip the flower part off the stem.

■ **FILL A GLASS BOWL WITH REAL GOLDFISH.** Wedding guests will love watching them swim, and you can float one or two large flower heads on top for added color. Be sure to bring along a scoop net and resealable plastic bags so that when the reception is over, the fish can go home with any children at the wedding. (Plan ahead and purchase a little container of fish food for each child who gets a goldfish goodie bag.)

■ **SPRAY TREE BRANCHES, TWIGS, AND LEAVES WITH GOLD METALLIC OR WHITE PAINT.** Place in tall vases or make a natural "nest" in the center of the table. Put a wide candle in the middle.

■ **TAKE A PLASTIC TOY BEACH BUCKET AND FILL IT WITH SAND AND CANDLES.** Scatter seashells around the table for a dramatic seascape look. Use children's crayons to rub pretty colors on the shells. It really works!

IDEAS FOR DECORATING
AN OUTDOOR SITE

■ **FOR AN OUTDOOR WEDDING, DRESS UP THE RECEPTION SITE WITH TALL POLES AVAILABLE AT HARDWARE AND GARDEN SUPPLY SHOPS.** These poles have hooks on one end for attaching hanging baskets of flowers (under $15 each) and are made to be pushed into the grass or inserted into wooden buckets filled with sand. Place the poles around the tent or yard to serve as focal points or arrange them in a line to serve as a backdrop for the ceremony. After the wedding, use them in your backyard.

■ **PURCHASE A TRELLIS OR PERGOLA AT A HOME AND GARDEN STORE.** You can spray-paint it white or leave the wood a natural color. Decorate it with vines, flowers, or battery-powered twinkling lights. Exchange vows in front of the trellis or while standing under the pergola. After the wedding, either can be used in a home garden.

■ **ASK FOR PLANTS AS WEDDING GIFTS AND REGISTER FOR THEM AT A PLANT STORE.** This tip comes from Beverly Ann Bonner of The Wedding Beautiful, Inc., in Norwood, Massachusetts. "Bring the plants to the reception. It is amazing how a ficus tree or group of plants together add a lot of ambiance. Put little white lights on them and place them in a corner of the reception hall or tent."

INEXPENSIVE FLOWERS

Alstromeria
This graceful yet hardy flower comes in many colors and is used as filler in arrangements and bouquets.

Aster
Dainty, daisylike flowers with heads the size of quarters, nickels, or dimes. Long-lasting, they have yellow centers and come in many colors: white, pink, lavender, purple, and yellow. Asters often are used as filler flowers.

Baby's breath
An airy filler flower with tiny white or pale pink buds. Baby's breath is very hardy and dries well, making it a popular choice for children's headpieces and bouquets. It looks fragile but stands up to any punishment a kid can dish out.

Carnation
Everybody's favorite for corsages, and perfect for centerpieces and altar arrangements, too. Carnations come in a wide variety of pastel and bright colors, and head sizes range from miniature to large. Many have frilly-edged blossoms. Don't let the florist talk you into dyed varieties—they nearly always look fake.

Eucalyptus
A native of Australia, this landscape foliage ranges in color from gray to blue. It has a slightly spicy fragrance and comes in a wide variety of leaf shapes and sizes—the leaves may be round, oval, narrow, or shaped like silver dollars. Eucalyptus is a great filler, and its branched foliage can be used as long sprays in a bouquet.

Geranium
Most people know geraniums as the perfect "container" plant for patios and window boxes, but they are also lovely in bouquets or centerpieces. Geraniums have thick stems, and the blossoms come in all shades of ivory, pink, red, or peachy red.

Gerbera daisy
Big, bold, and beautiful, this variety of daisy has a large head and comes in both pale pastels and bright, almost neon colors. It's great for arrangements because it comes in many colors and can be matched to almost anything.

225

Ivy
A great filler, ivy is hardy and comes in many leaf sizes. It's perfect for children's headpieces and wreaths, and looks beautiful spilling majestically out of the bridal bouquet.

Queen Anne's lace
In the Northeast, Queen Anne's lace grows wild along the roadside. This pretty filler flower is ivory colored and has a large, flat head with lacy edges.

Statice
A hardy filler flower that dries well and comes in yellow, white, and purple.

Zinnia
Popular in home gardens, the zinnia is an easy-to-grow cut flower with sturdy stems. It has colorful heads that range in size from small to large. Zinnias come in a staggering range of colors from neon pink to tropical orange.

INTERNET RESOURCES FOR INFORMATION ON FLOWERS

About Flowers
http://www.aboutflowers.com

A consumer information site maintained by the Society of American Florists. Designed mainly for the news media and consumers, it includes information on floral facts, holiday stats, weddings, flower varieties, color trends, and more.

California Cut Flowers Commission
http://www.ccfc.org

A nonprofit consumer information site with a veritable garden of
information on wedding flowers, design tips for arrangements, gar-
lands, tabletop bouquets, and care tips. Offers a free brochure,
"Easy Steps to Flower Arranging." Features links to more than a
dozen other floral-related sites.

Flower Link
http:///www.flowerlink.com

An on-line flower shop that allows you to order from local florists
across the United States and Canada. Users can view local styles as
well as FTD and Teleflora selections.

Flower Stop
http://www.flowerstop.com

An "on-line fresh flower market." View color photos and order
flowers, bouquets, and centerpieces on-line.

Proflowers
http://www.proflowers.com

A discount floral service that offers floral bouquets and centerpieces shipped directly from the grower, priced at 30 to 40 percent
below comparable retail. Includes tips on flower care and information on popular wedding flowers.

DO IT YOURSELF

If you've got the time and the talent, consider making your own
bouquets or centerpieces. This isn't for the faint of heart, however.
Flowers are fragile and require proper storage and refrigeration—

and you'll need plenty of time and plenty of work space. I wouldn't advise taking on anything as formidable as floral design for a formal or very large wedding. If the wedding is informal or at home, however, you can create a wonderful, natural look for next to nothing.

Friends or relatives may be willing to contribute cut flowers from their gardens. Or shop for flowers by the bunch or basketful at a wholesale flower market; many cities have them (though you'll

probably need to be up before the sun rises to catch the flower vendors). Explain your situation to a local garden club, and the members may be willing to volunteer their time or use your wedding flowers as a community project. Everybody loves weddings, and chances are they'll be thrilled to help.

Ask your local florist to show you how to make an easy centerpiece or a simple bouquet (see directions below). A do-it-yourselfer is wise to stick to simple designs with hardy flowers that are easy to arrange. If you are all thumbs, try a quick-to-make hand-tied bouquet or an arrangement of loose, cut flowers in a vase.

A good place to start is by calling the California Cut Flower Commission and asking for its free "Easy Steps to Flower Arranging" brochure. Call (831) 728-7333 or visit www.ccfc.org. The brochure includes easy-to-follow instructions for making several bouquets and arrangements, basic flower care and handling advice, and ideas for unique vases.

Floral Terms

Filler flowers

Usually refers to green foliage and floral stems with many little flowers. Filler flowers include baby's breath, Queen Anne's lace, ferns, eucalyptus, heather, aster, ivy, and statice and stock.

Floral tape

Narrow, slightly sticky tape used to wrap stems around floral wire and sticks so that they are easily manipulated into bouquets. In arrangements, floral tape is used to build a grid across the top of the container; the grid helps the flowers stand up straight.

Glamelia

A composite flower made when a florist wires together clusters of individual petals or blooms to a create a fuller blossom on a single stem. For example, a florist might split the individual florets from a tall gladiolus to create one camellia-like blossom.

Line flowers

Tall flowers that give an arrangement height and width. Branches and tall foliage are examples of line flowers. According to the California Cut Flower Commission, most line flowers have buds growing up a center stalk. Examples include snapdragon, gladiolus, delphinium, stock, veronica, iris, lily, and tuberose.

Mass flowers

Also called "face" flowers, these blooms are the focal points of arrangements or bouquets and have one round flower on the end of a stem. They add mass or fullness to a floral design. Examples include tulip, zinnia, rose, peony, chrysanthemum, gerbera daisy, daffodil, and carnation.

Oasis

A type of floral foam that holds flowers in place when soaked in water.

Create Your Own Pew Decorations

- ❖ Ask the cake baker to make oversized gingerbread cookie "brides" and "grooms," leaving a hole at the top of the head for threading a ribbon. Tie the bride cookies on the bride's side (left) of the church, and the groom cookies on the groom's side (right) of the church. After the ceremony, give them to children at the wedding.
- ❖ Place a store-purchased flowering plant at the ends of the pews.
- ❖ Make bows from yard-long lengths of ivory or pastel tulle and use a hot-glue gun to attach seed pearls or silk flowers. (If you thread the tulle through a large, heavy rubber band before tying it into a bow, you can use the rubber band to attach the bow to the pew.)
- ❖ Hang holiday ornaments on the pews.
- ❖ Hang wedding portraits of the guests on the pews.
- ❖ "Create elaborate pew bows with floor-length streamers," says floral designer W. Donnie Brown. "Move them to the reception and tie them to the backs of the head-table chairs. A little extra touch, no extra charge!"

Create a Simple Hand-Tied Bouquet

1 yard (3-inch-wide) silk, French-wired ribbon, or raffia

8 long-stemmed flowers such as tulip or calla lily

5 stems foliage, such as fern or eucalyptus

Pick up one flower and place a foliage stem on top of it at a 45-degree angle. Continue adding the other flowers and greenery at an angle, building up the bouquet so that it looks balanced and even. Place a rubber band or tie a piece of string around the stems to keep them in place. Trim the stems so that they are even. Hold the bouquet in your hands to determine the best place to tie the ribbon. After the ribbon is tied, cut off the rubber band or string.

Create a Rose Bowl Centerpiece for Your Wedding Reception

Loretta Stagen, a professional floral designer and floral design instructor from Stamford, Connecticut, provides the following directions for making your own elegant but easy centerpiece. For more information, visit her Web site at http://www.lstagendesigns.com.

This centerpiece fits a 60-inch round table. Be sure to keep the centerpiece height at no more than 12 inches. "The rose bowl is an attractive and easy-to-use container," Stagen says. All materials for this project are available at floral supply and craft shops or at your local florist shop.

1	6-inch clear glass rose bowl
3	cups clear marbles
5	stems stock
5	stems larkspur or delphinium
20	roses (with large heads)
6	stems tree fern
	Clippers
3	votive candles

After you have selected your colors and purchased your supplies and plant materials, you are ready to create your centerpiece.

1. Fill the rose bowl with water. Gently pour the marbles into the container.
2. Cut the stock and larkspur or delphinium at an angle to a length of 12 inches, measuring from the tip of the flower to the end of the stem.
3. Arrange the flowers in the container by pushing them into the marbles. Place three flowers in the center of the bowl, standing upward, and seven flowers near the sides of the bowl.
4. Cut the roses at an angle to a length of 10½ inches, measuring from the tip of the flower.
5. Arrange the roses by pushing them into the marbles. Fill in all of the spaces.
6. Cut the tree ferns to a length of 10 inches. Arrange the ferns along the edges of the bowl.
7. Place your centerpiece on the table, surrounded by three votive candles. Sprinkle petals from one rose around the arrangement.

One Final Great Idea

What will you do with your floral arrangements after the ceremony and reception? Drop them off at a local nursing home or children's hospital, where your joy will be shared with others.

CHAPTER FIFTEEN

THE WEDDING CAKE

At every wedding celebration, the cake holds a place of honor. It symbolizes happiness, good fortune, and a shared life together.

Here's good news about the tastiest bridal tradition of all: it's a piece of cake to find a beautiful wedding cake that won't take a huge bite out of the budget. If your budget is especially tight, consider trimming the wines, exotic flowers, and other pricey items in favor of a simple champagne reception with a show-stopping cake. Guests will never forget a cake that tastes wonderful and looks marvelous—and they won't forgive one that's bland or dry.

A wedding cake may blow a diet, but it needn't break the bank. Wedding cakes are like wedding flowers: the cost of the finished product depends entirely on the quality and/or rarity of the ingredients and the amount of labor that goes into creating it. Just as a Biedermeier bouquet with hand-wired roses will cost more than a loose bouquet tied with a ribbon, a columned wedding cake that keeps the baker toiling for days will cost more than one with simple stacked tiers and piping.

Spun sugar flowers that look amazingly like the real thing, and gum paste decorations that are veritable works of art, take lots of time and skill to produce, and therefore are expensive. Some bakers charge by the piece ($2 to $80 each) for these artistic decorations. Specialty ingredients like imported Vahlrona chocolate, real gold leaf, fruit liqueurs, and specialty flavorings will add to the price tag.

Tasty fillings are as important as the layer flavors. Ask the baker to suggest a delicious cream, custard, mousse, or fresh fruit filling.

FLAT, TIERED, OR STACKED?

After choosing the flavors, the filling, and the frosting, decide whether you want a tiered cake or a flat cake in the shape of a heart, square, oval, or rectangle. You'll want to tell the baker how many guests are attending and whether the cake will be served as the only dessert.

Three-tiered cakes are the traditional standard, but a talented baker can make cakes with six or even eight tiers. Don't be surprised if the baker asks you about the size of the reception room. If it's a huge ballroom with high ceilings, a taller cake is more appropriate. That's because the cake is considered a wedding showpiece and something to be displayed during the reception. (Which means, don't let the caterer or banquet manager talk you into cutting the cake early in the reception. This is often a ploy to rush the couple along and make it easier for the serving staff.)

The average wedding cake consists of three tiers—12, 9, and 6 inches each—and serves about 125 to 150 people. Wedding cake layers can be stacked on top of each other or separated by sturdy columns and discs designed to keep the cake balanced and stable. Wooden dowels (or even plastic drinking straws) are inserted into each tier to distribute the weight. A stacked cake takes less work to assemble than one with columns separating the layers, and therefore costs less.

Costs usually are calculated by the serving. Expect to spend between $1.50 and $18 per slice. Most couples end up spending somewhere in the middle, or between $200 and $600 for the cake.

Always insist on a taste test. You may have to schedule it for a day when they are baking for another special event, but sampling the wedding cake is as important as trying on the wedding gown. Try to sample a few combinations of cakes, frostings, and fillings to get the full effect.

EASY WAYS TO SLICE THE COST

On the Wedding Cake

■ **ORDER YOUR CAKE THROUGH THE BAKERY YOU VISIT MOST OFTEN.** You'll already be assured of the bakery's freshness, quality, and artistry, and you may even get a discount. Some bakeries offer special prices on wedding cakes to their best customers (especially if you have many brothers or sisters to be married down the line!).

■ **COMPARISON SHOP.** A large, well-known bakery may not be any better or less expensive than a small neighborhood shop. Taste the cakes at several shops and compare prices. It's amazing how widely they vary, especially in large cities and regionally throughout the country. In major cities in the Northeast, for example, a three-tiered wedding cake can easily run more than $800. In other parts of the country, the same cake might cost $300. (Obviously, a bride who lives in New York City isn't going to have a cake shipped from Ohio just to save money, but you get the picture.)

■ **ASK THE BAKER TO MAKE A BASIC STACKED THREE-LAYER CAKE WITH PIPED BUTTERCREAM FROSTING.** This style is quick and easy to prepare, and you'll avoid the extra cost of buying or renting the discs, separators, and columns that keep the cake balanced and stable.

■ **ORDER A STACKED, THREE- OR FOUR-LAYER CAKE AND ADD THE DECORATIONS YOURSELF!** Ask the baker to just slather it with frosting or pipe a simple edging or dotted Swiss design. Then gild the lily yourself.

- Place fresh flowers or greenery around each layer.
- Press silver or gold dragée candies into the sides of the frosting in a geometric or free-form design.
- Purchase faux pearl necklaces and wrap one around the base of each layer.
- Wrap the base of each layer with a pastel silk ribbon. Secure the ends of each ribbon with a tiny dab of frosting.

■ **ORDER A SMALL "PRESENTATION" CAKE FOR DISPLAY AT THE RECEPTION AND SEVERAL SHEET CAKES FOR SLICING BEHIND THE SCENES.** A small, ornately decorated cake won't cost a fortune, and once the cake is displayed and cut, it's whisked back to the kitchen for slicing anyway. Guests will assume that the little masterpiece cake fed all 200 people! (Who needs to know that the hidden sheet cakes were baked with the same flavor and frosting?)

■ **SOME BAKERS WILL PREPARE A DUMMY CAKE WITH LAYERS OF STYROFOAM COVERED WITH FROSTING.** The only real layer is the top one. Once the bride and groom make a ceremonial cut, the cake is taken behind the scenes, and inexpensive sheet cakes are sliced.

■ **FIND OUT *EXACTLY* WHAT THE CAKE COSTS WILL BE.** Does the per person price include delivery? Assembling the cake? All decorations? The discs and columns? An extra top layer for the couple to save and freeze as a first anniversary cake? How much of a deposit is expected? When is the balance due?

■ **"ORDER LESS WEDDING CAKE IF IT IS PART OF A DESSERT OR SWEETS TABLE,"** advises bridal consultant Lois Pearce of Beautiful Occasions in Hamden, Connecticut. Most people are very conscious of fat and calories these days, and the confections often follow a large wedding meal.

■ **SERVE THE WEDDING CAKE AS THE ONLY DESSERT.** Most guests *don't* eat both the cake and the dessert. If the menu includes a dessert, cancel it or negotiate for something else. It's a waste of money. By trimming this unnecessary extra, you'll save around $600 ($3 times 200 people). Just keep in mind that the size of an average wedding cake slice is smaller than the average dessert cake slice. The serving size is generally a 2-inch square or an angled slice 2 inches wide and 3 inches high.

■ **ORDER SEVERAL SQUARE, ROUND, OR HEART-SHAPED LAYERS AND DISPLAY THEM ON CAKE PEDESTALS OF VARYING HEIGHTS, OR ON A CAKE SEPARATOR WITH DISPLAY TIERS.** These accessories, made from plastic, metal, or porcelain, are available at cake decorating, candy, and culinary supply shops. Some have movable arms that rotate into place so you can arrange the cakes on see-through tiers that seemingly "float" in midair. Or order cake separator sets with interlocking plates and columns that snap into place. It's a piece of cake to turn three or more basic layers into a tiered masterpiece in seconds.

■ **IF YOU WANT A TRULY WHITE CAKE, FIND OUT WHAT KIND OF BUTTER THE BAKER WILL BE USING.** Butters range from sunny yellow to pale ivory. A buttercream frosting made with bright yellow butter may not produce the true white shade you'd hoped for.

■ **ORDER "CENTERPIECE" CAKES.** Instead of ordering floral center-pieces, ask the baker to create a centerpiece cake for each guest table. This doesn't necessarily cost a lot. A talented master baker can create faux flower cakes using terra-cotta pots topped by a round cake decorated to look like a blooming bouquet. The cost of ordering a cake for each guest table is offset by the fact that you won't need to order fresh flowers for each table.

■ **DON'T ORDER THE CAKE THROUGH A BRIDAL SALON.** The charges will be inflated because the salon will order it through a bakery or pastry chef and charge a markup.

■ **WAIVE THE DELIVERY CHARGE BY ARRANGING TO PICK UP THE CAKE YOURSELF.** Ask the baker to fill a pastry bag with icing for touch-ups. (It may not be needed but is reassuring to have.) Bring along a corrugated box slightly larger than the base of the cake; be sure the box is a few inches taller than the top tier. The flat base of a station wagon or the trunk of a car offers the best flat area for transporting the cake. Don't try to balance a cake precariously on the backseat of a car, since seats are generally tufted or curved. It's a good idea to place a damp towel or thin piece of foam rubber under the box to keep it from sliding around. *(Note: Before transporting a cake yourself, talk to the baker. If the weather is extremely hot or the cake is especially fragile, it may be wiser to have a professional transport it in a refrigerated truck.)*

■ **DON'T BE LIMITED TO WHITE CAKE, WHITE FILLING, AND WHITE FROSTING.** Just about any cake can be made into a wedding cake—sponge cake, butter cake, chocolate cake, carrot cake, cheesecake, pound cake, fruitcake, genoise, meringue layers, or even cream puffs arranged into a towered croquembouche shape and wrapped in spun sugar. Can't decide? Ask the baker to create each layer in a different type of cake. Guests won't notice the absence of expensive decorations if they have a choice of tasty layers!

■ **TALK TERMS.** The term *buttercream* means different things to different pastry chefs. Some make frosting from a mixture of confectioner's sugar, milk, and vegetable shortening and call it buttercream. Others insist the only real buttercream is the classic version made from egg yolks, corn syrup or sugar heated to a rolling boil, and loads of real butter. These two versions taste *nothing* alike, so know which one you're ordering. The buttercream made from a commercial mix or from confectioner's sugar is less expensive than the real thing.

■ **TASTE TELLS.** Don't sacrifice great taste to save a few dollars. The cake needn't be an architectural wonder to taste wonderful. Guests are pickier than you think. They'll remember a wedding cake that's dry, tastes fake, or is absolutely tasteless.

Save on the Cake Knife

Avoid purchasing a cake knife from a bridal salon or invitations/accessories catalog. You'll spend $25 to $150 for what's invariably a gussied-up knife with bows and a plastic or faux crystal handle. Instead, ask for one as a shower gift, or purchase an inexpensive long-handled knife (that you'll use later on in your home kitchen) and decorate it with silk or French-wired ribbon. Or shop in a consignment or antiques shop for a cake or pie server that will be a keepsake worth keeping. After all, the cake knife is used only ceremonially for cutting the first slice. Once the bride and groom make their cut into the cake, it's usually whisked behind the scenes.

Cut Out the Cake-Cutting Fee

Some catering establishments charge an extra fee for slicing and serving the wedding cake. (This fee can be up to a few dollars per slice!) Many wedding consultants feel this is an outrageous and unnecessary charge. After all, you'd never expect to be charged for cutting a birthday or anniversary cake, would you? Negotiate with the caterer or banquet manager to waive the fee or include it in the per person price. If he won't budge, tell him you'd be happy to cut the entire cake yourself, or ask a friend or relative to do the honors.

Save on the Cake Topper

Save $10 to $60 on a cake topper by borrowing the one your parents or grandparents used. The vintage topper will have great sentimental value for the newlyweds and for the person lending it. Or invest in a topper that can be handed down from one sister or brother to the next family member to marry.

Whatever you choose, be sure it's not too heavy or bulky, or it will topple off the cake or crush the top layer. Think twice about placing a priceless antique topper on the cake and risk having it broken or stolen.

Consider decorating the top with any of the following:

+ A craft store ornament or tiny figurine such as an angel, swan, or Hummel collectible
+ Fresh flowers or greenery picked from the garden or ordered from a florist (just be absolutely sure the flowers are edible and nontoxic)
+ Dolls from a family doll collection
+ Flags signifying the newlyweds' ethnic background(s)
+ A silver-framed picture of the bride and groom
+ A pouf of ribbon or fabric matching the wedding gown

- A small floral wreath (dry it and use it later as a Christmas ornament)
- Chocolate shavings or chocolate ribbons
- A colorful cloisonné egg or bell
- A goblet or antique teacup and saucer filled with flowers
- A tiny white basket filled with silk flowers
- Colorful silk butterflies or flowers
- A small cornucopia basket brimming with fruit or flowers

Save on the Groom's Cake

Trim $50 to $200 from the wedding budget by making the groom's cake yourself or asking a family member or friend to bake one. Traditionally, the groom's cake is a fruitcake topped with fondant or marzipan icing. The groom's cake is served during the reception along with the wedding cake or is sliced and packed into tiny boxes for guests to take home as favors.

This tradition dates back to the days when guests traveled far to attend a wedding. The groom's cake was meant to be eaten on the long ride home or placed by single guests under their pillows so that they may dream of a future spouse. Today, the groom's cake is often served at the rehearsal dinner. It may be baked in the bridegroom's favorite flavor or in a shape that reflects his interests or hobbies.

SOURCES OTHER THAN A BAKERY

Supermarkets

There may be a master baker hidden in your local supermarket. Many supermarket chains with bakeries produce wedding cakes. I was surprised to learn from several of my students that they were ordering delicious, inexpensive cakes from a supermarket bakery. As a former food writer for a daily newspaper, I was skeptical. The next time I taught the class, I called a Shop Rite Grade A market and asked if we could sample one in class. The bakery donated an amazingly moist, delicious, two-tiered cake with swirly piped frosting. At the end of class, I asked students to guess which bakery it came from. No one believed it was ordered at a grocery store. The moral is: Don't be a food snob. You may miss out on a tasty bargain.

Cooking Schools and Hotels

Look in the Yellow Pages under "Cooking Instruction" or "Higher Education" and find the listings for a local culinary academy, community college, vocational schools or high school home economics department. There may be instructors or pastry chefs in training who make wedding cakes on the side. Ask for referrals. You may get lucky and find an instructor who will make the cake with his or her class as a class project. Or call the pastry chef at a local inn or hotel and ask for a referral.

POPULAR WEDDING CAKE AND FILLING COMBINATIONS

- White cake with lemon curd filling and Italian meringue buttercream frosting
- Espresso genoise with mocha buttercream
- Pound cake with rolled marzipan frosting
- Traditional fruitcake with rolled fondant frosting
- Fresh carrot cake with cream cheese frosting
- Vanilla cake filled with dark chocolate mousse

- ❖ Chocolate cake filled with white chocolate mousse
- ❖ Yellow cake with caramel nut and cheesecake filling
- ❖ Lemon pound cake with buttercream, raspberry, or lemon mousse filling
- ❖ Cheesecake with apricot or lemon filling
- ❖ Strawberry shortcake with whipped cream
- ❖ Rum cake with vanilla mousse filling and rum glaze
- ❖ White chocolate cake with lemon mousse filling and white chocolate ganache glaze
- ❖ Chocolate cake with mocha frosting
- ❖ Lemon cake with lemon filling and vanilla buttercream frosting
- ❖ Cream puffs filled with pastry cream and arranged in a croquembouche pyramid shape
- ❖ Chocolate cake soaked in apricot glaze and covered with chocolate ganache
- ❖ Chocolate almond torte with bittersweet chocolate ganache frosting

BAKE IT YOURSELF

Baking your own wedding cake, or asking a friend or relative to do it, can save hundreds of dollars. You'll be paying only for the basic ingredients—butter, sugar, flour, eggs, flavorings, and so forth—and the purchase or rental of discs, columns, and dowels. The final cost will be even less than a supermarket cake, and the flavors will be limited only by the baker's imagination and skill. You could easily make a different flavor for each layer, freeze them, frost them a day or two before the wedding, and assemble the cake at the reception site to avoid the challenge of transporting it. Save even more by buying the ingredients in bulk from a wholesale "club" store.

But preparing your own wedding cake is a good idea *only* for the experienced baker, and only for those with enough time, equipment, and storage and refrigeration space. The challenge of making a wedding cake is assembling the layers and making sure the tiers are attractive and even. Don't be intimidated! Anyone with enough experience to bake cake layers can create a basic stacked wedding cake that's impressive. You can also bake sheet cake layers and display them flat or on pretty cake plates of varying heights.

Recipes and Inspiration

Lots of wedding recipe resources for the home baker are available.

- Log on to http://www.Allrecipes.com for the Recipe Network. This site features more than twenty-four categories of recipes, from holiday cakes to no-bake cakes to sheet cakes and wedding cakes. Listed among the wedding cakes are recipes for frostings, icings, groom's cakes, Mexican wedding cakes, layer cakes, and much more.

- Another great resource is *The Cake Bible* by Rose Levy Beranbaum. This cookbook is a treasure! It's the definitive resource for cake recipes of every kind imaginable. Beranbaum is a baker and cooking instructor whose cakes have been featured in many cooking and women's magazines. She includes step-by-step instructions for baking and decorating several wedding cakes, with detailed recipes that are easy to understand and follow.

- *Colette's Wedding Cakes* by Colette Peters features sumptuous color photographs of cakes created by Colette Peters, one of the foremost cake designers in the United States. Her remarkable cakes have been displayed at the Smithsonian Institution in Washington, D.C., and featured in many national magazines. The book includes recipes for more than three dozen wedding cakes, as well as techniques for making royal icing flowers, gum paste decorations, sugar molds, and quilted designs.

❧ *The Wedding Cake Book* by Dede Wilson is another gorgeous book with color photos of impossibly beautiful cakes. It includes thirty recipes and a comprehensive guide to the basics: cake sizing, baking techniques, storing and transporting, how to work with pastry bags and chocolate, and how to make crystallized flowers and marzipan decorations. There's even a recipe for a baked Alaska wedding cake.

❧ Visit the library for back issues of women's and cooking magazines. In honor of wedding "season," many magazines run an annual wedding cake recipe in the May or June issue. These are geared to the novice baker and easy to replicate. National magazines such as *Woman's Day*, *Gourmet*, and *Bon Appetit* are good sources for wedding cake recipes each year. Can't find a copy? Call the magazine's editorial office and ask for a back issue.

Tips for the Home Baker

Before cracking an egg, make sure your work space is conducive to baking a large, special-occasion cake. If the finished cake must be refrigerated or frozen, you must have adequate space. This may mean removing some freezer or refrigerator racks or borrowing room in a friend's freezer or refrigerator.

Keep in mind that you'll need one cake rack to cool each layer. Buy them or borrow them from a neighbor. Figure out the volume capacity of your mixer. Is it large enough? Will you need to make the batter in several batches? Is there enough room in the refrigerator to store unbaked batter?

Evaluate your equipment needs. Depending on the recipe, you'll need baking pans, spatulas, cake decorating supplies, a pastry bag and tips, a turntable or lazy Susan, measuring cups, an offset spatula or cake leveling knife, and mixing bowls. Parchment paper is handy for lining baking pans.

Consider oven space. How many layers can be baked at one time? It's important to leave enough space between the pans to allow air to circulate around them during baking.

Baking is an exact science—it's a form of kitchen chemistry. Ingredients must be measured or weighed accurately. Measure dry ingredients such as flour using the dip-and-sweep method. Dip the cup into the flour, then gently sweep a knife or spatula across the top of the cup to level off the excess. Don't shake the cup, or the flour will settle. Measure liquid ingredients in a liquid-measure cup or a bowl with a spout. (There is a difference in volume between measurement cups designed for measuring liquids and those for solids.)

If you've never made the recipe before, do a trial run by baking one small tier first.

How to Make Chocolate Leaves

With a little practice, anyone can make decorative chocolate leaves using real leaves as templates. White or dark chocolate will do, as long as it's of fine quality and tastes delicious. Slowly melt a pound of chocolate using a microwave or double boiler. Gently wash and dry eight to ten leaves. You can use rose, maple, lemon, or geranium leaves. Hold each leaf by its stem and gently coat with a thin layer of melted chocolate using an artist's brush or small spatula. Coat the leaf on one side only. If using white chocolate, you may need several thin coats.

Each leaf may be used several times. Place each coated leaf on a sheet of parchment paper or waxed paper. Refrigerate for a few minutes until the chocolate is no longer shiny. To remove the leaf from the chocolate, hold the stem end and gently peel it back. You'll get perfectly veined chocolate leaves for use in decorating the sides or top of the wedding cake.

Resources for Wedding Cake Decorating and Baking Equipment

Beryl's Cake Decorating
Equipment
P.O. Box 1584
North Springfield, VA 22151
1-800-488-2749

Bridge Kitchenware Co.
214 E. 52nd St.
New York, NY 10022
1-800-274-3435

Gloria's Cake and Candy
Supplies
3755 Sawtelle Blvd.
Los Angeles, CA 90066
(310) 391-4557

King Arthur Flour Baker's
Catalog
P.O. Box 876
U.S. Route 5 South
Norwich, VT 05055
1-800-827-6836

Williams-Sonoma
P.O. Box 7456
San Francisco, CA 94120
1-800-541-2233

Wilton Industries
2240 W. 75th St.
Woodbridge, IL 60517
1-800-772-7111

Call the Wilton Industries number, and an expert will answer your questions about recipes and decorating.

Wedding Cake Recipe

The following recipe for a traditional wedding cake was contributed by Lisa Maronian of Sweet Lisa's Exquisite Cakes in Cos Cob, Connecticut. Maronian is a graduate of the Culinary Institute of America and the International Pastry Arts Center. All of the cakes at Sweet Lisa's are made from the finest, freshest ingredients and are individually created for each couple. Maronian and her talented staff also make individually boxed groom's cakes, bridal cookie favors, edible place cards, and monogrammed cookies and petit fours. "This recipe will need to be made four times to make a three-tier cake to serve approximately forty people," Maronian notes. "Sizes for that would be 5", 8", and 11". The icing recipe will need to be made three times to fill and frost this size cake."

Golden Butter Layer Cake

2¼ cups cake flour, sifted	1¼ cups sugar
¾ teaspoon baking soda	1 tablespoon vanilla
¾ teaspoon baking powder	4 eggs
½ teaspoon salt	¾ cup sour cream
8 ounces butter, unsalted, at room temperature	

Note: This recipe must be made in four batches. Preheat oven to 350 degrees Fahrenheit. Line bottom of two 8-inch cake pans with baking parchment and grease sides. Combine cake flour, baking soda, baking powder, and salt. Cream butter and sugar. Add vanilla, then add eggs slowly. Mix in dry ingredients alternately with sour cream. Scrape down sides of bowl. Mix well for 1 minute. Remove and divide batter between pans. Divide batter among pans. Bake for 25 to 30 minutes.

Swiss Meringue Buttercream

½ cup egg whites	¼ teaspoon cream of tartar
¾ cup sugar	2 teaspoons vanilla
10 ounces butter, unsalted, softened	

Combine egg whites and sugar in mixer bowl and heat over boiling water, stirring constantly until sugar is melted and mixture is warm. Remove bowl from heat and place on (mixer) machine, add cream of tartar, and whip until doubled in volume. Let cool. Add butter slowly, then add vanilla and whip 2 to 3 minutes more. (Note: This recipe must be made in three batches.)

CHAPTER SIXTEEN

THE BRIDAL REGISTRY

A sk and ye shall receive. That's what a wedding registry is all about. This marvelous invention for recording the couple's gift preferences is the closest thing to having a fairy godmother who delivers the goods at the wave of a magic wand.

Give special consideration to registering what you really want and need for your new household through a bridal registry. A registry is a way for couples to record their choices for wedding gifts in a variety of categories, along with the wedding date, color and pattern choices, quantities, and where the gifts may be sent. The store keeps this information on file for guests to consult.

As a result, the couple receives gifts they love and really can use, and guests appreciate not having to guess about what to give them. Guests simply visit the store's local branch or ask for the couple's wish list by fax, mail, E-mail, or phone. As gifts are purchased, they're removed from the list.

It's a great system—and it's free.

At what other time in your life will you be *encouraged* to blatantly ask for things, and then stand back while the goblets, griddles, and water glasses just roll in? It may seem materialistic, but keep in mind that a registry really does make it easier for guests to choose thoughtful gifts and avoids the problem of duplications (who needs six toasters and four blenders?).

This free service was once limited to department stores with large china and crystal departments. A registry pretty much assured the bride she'd receive enough place settings in her china pattern. Generally, the bride made the choices and the groom stayed home.

But these days, the bride and groom tend to make the selections together, and they often register in more than one place. The options have expanded, too. Nowadays, couples may register at specialty emporiums, sporting goods stores, clothing stores, bed-and-bath shops, bookstores, spas, honeymoon resorts, discount retailers, gourmet shops, home improvement centers, landscape and garden nurseries, record shops, computer stores, and much more. You can even register for a honeymoon or a mortgage.

Cyber-savvy couples can register on-line. Most department stores have home pages that include bridal registry information. The Della and James Online Gift Registry (http://www.dellajames.com) features gift registries from several "premier" stores in one location. Couples may view and update their gift choices registered at Crate & Barrel, Neiman Marcus, Dillard's, Gump's, REI, and other stores. For information, call the site's gift consultant toll-free at 1-877-335-5252.

Take advantage of the free consulting services offered by bridal registries. Stores usually have a trained salesperson on staff who can offer practical, helpful advice on mixing and matching patterns, choosing crystal, and defining your own sense of style. This is a useful service. Most couples have a good idea of whether they'll host formal dinners on a regular basis but may not realize what kinds of basics they'll need or how many iced-tea spoons they'll ever use. If you are combining two households, a registry consultant will recommend items that complement pieces you already have.

WAYS TO SAVE ON THE REGISTRY

Consider registering for items that will set up a household and, at the same time, come in handy for wedding planning. For instance, if you register at a garden nursery for flowering plants, topiaries, or a trellis, you can use them to decorate the ceremony or reception site. (Yes, technically a couple shouldn't use wedding gifts until after the wedding, but friends will understand that they are helping you out and won't mind.) Planning an at-home wedding? Register for folding chairs, tablecloths, card tables, a tent, patio furniture, or a bar that can be used for the reception. If you register at more than one store, avoid overlapping items at both places or you may defeat the purpose. A thoughtful bride and groom will register gift selections in a wide range of prices, which gives guests more flexibility in making choices.

If you long for a big-ticket item like a canoe or a designer gas grill but don't have the budget for it, register for one and ask friends or the bridal party to give it as a joint wedding gift. People love knowing that their gift was loved. They'll appreciate knowing exactly what you wanted.

Can't afford a honeymoon? Again, ask friends and relatives to contribute to a honeymoon registry. If you trust your travel agent implicitly, ask her to set up a travel account to which gifts in your name may be sent. Or establish an account in your own name at a bank and ask the best man or maid of honor to coordinate deposits made into it. Register for a spa vacation, and then unwind at the spa on your honeymoon.

Let the bridal registry work for you even after the wedding. If a couple doesn't receive all the items they registered as gifts, many registries offer special discounts or bonuses if they decide to buy them for themselves. For example, if a minimum of ten place settings are purchased from the list, the store may give the couple one free, or let them buy more at 50 percent off the retail price. When registering, inquire about the store's policy.

After the wedding, ask for an updated printout of the registry list. It will come in handy during the first year of marriage, when loved ones ask what you'd like for birthday, holiday, or anniversary gifts.

Let guests know where you are registered. It's fine to include on a shower invitation where the bride is registered, but it's never appropriate on a wedding invitation.

If your favorite store doesn't have a registry, ask to establish one or at least keep a list of your preferences on hand.

Mortgage Registries

Buying a home is probably the biggest expense a couple will ever make. A small number of banks across the country have formal bridal mortgage registries in place. Basically, the couple sets up an account in their names to which wedding guests send contributions. If your bank doesn't offer this service, ask to set up a designated account for you and tell friends and relatives where you are "registered." For information on registering for a mortgage, contact your local bank or these sources:

BankAmerica Mortgage
Home Bridal Registry
1-800-272-6791

The Federal Housing Administration Hotline
1-800-CALL-FHA (225-5342)

The Federal Housing Administration offers its Bridal Program for first-time home buyers. Call for a free brochure.

UNUSUAL ITEMS TO REGISTER

- Musicians to play at the wedding
- A designer wedding cake made by a master baker
- A day at the local hair salon to prepare for the wedding
- A panoramic camera that can be used to create a group portrait at the wedding
- Silk or fresh flowers to decorate the reception
- A tent that can be used for the wedding and afterward for outdoor entertaining
- Potted plants and floral arrangements for decorating the ceremony
- Luggage to use on the honeymoon
- Cooking lessons
- Camping equipment
- Paint, tools, and lumber for fixing up a house
- Garden sculptures or patio furniture
- Wine for a wine cellar
- Opera tickets or theater subscription
- Hobbies and sporting goods
- Donations to a favorite charity or scholarship fund
- Tuition for higher education
- Personal computer and software
- Airline tickets or a Eurail pass for the honeymoon
- Landscaping and plant materials

BRIDAL REGISTRY RESOURCES

Contact the companies below for referrals to bridal registries in your area:

China, Crystal, and Household Accessories

Dansk	1-800-293-2675
Lenox	1-800-423-8946
Linens n' Things	1-800-568-8765
Michael C. Fina	1-800-288-FINA (288-3462)
Mikasa	1-800-833-4681
Noritake	1-800-562-1991
Pfaltzgraff	1-800-999-2811
Pier One Imports	1-800-PIER-101 (743-7101)
Ross-Simons	1-800-458-4545
Royal Worcester	1-800-257-7189
Swarovski Crystal	1-800-426-3088
Waterford Crystal	1-800-523-0009

Silver, Silver Plate, and Stainless Steel

Gorham	P.O. Box 906, Mount Kisco, NY 10549
Oneida Silversmith	1-800-877-6667
Reed & Barton	1-800-343-1383

Wallace Silversmiths	175 McClellan Hwy., P.O. Box 9114 East Boston, MA 02128
WMF Hutschenreuther	1-800-999-6347

Appliances and Cooking Utensils

All-Clad Metalcrafters	1-800-ALL-CLAD (255-2523)
Calphalon	1-800-809-7267
Farberware	(516) 794-3355
KitchenAid	1-800-541-6390
Krups	1-800-526-5377

Department Stores/Mail-Order Catalogs

Bloomingdale's	1-800-888-2WED (888-2933)
Bon-Ton	1-800-9-BON-TON (926-6866)
Burdine's	1-800-878-9783
Crate & Barrel	1-800-967-6696
Dillard's	1-800-626-6001
Eddie Bauer Home Collection	1-800-645-7467
Filene's	1-800-4-BRIDES (427-4337)
Fortunoff	1-800-937-4376
Home Depot	1-800-553-3199

HomePlace	1-800-456-7123
JC Penney	1-800-JCP-GIFT (527-4438)
L.L. Bean	1-800-341-4341, ext. 38020
Macy's	1-800-701-7112
Marshall Field's	1-800-243-6436
The May Bridal Registry National Network	1-800-9-SAY-I-DO (972-9436)
Robinson's	1-800-445-9959
Service Merchandise	1-800-892-4481
Target	1-800-888-WEDD (888-9333)
Tiffany & Co.	1-800-526-0649
Tower Records	1-800-648-4844
Williams-Sonoma	1-800-541-2233

CHAPTER SEVENTEEN

PHOTOGRAPHY AND VIDEOGRAPHY

Your wedding will take place over the course of several hours, but there are parts of it you won't even see. You'll be busy else-where—getting ready, greeting guests, or concentrating on the minister. Some couples are so nervous, they remember the whole day as one happy blur.

Once the day is over, it's over. That's why a visual record should be the highest priority, no matter what the budget. Photography is a luxury expense, but when it comes to wedding memories, it's a *necessary* luxury and an investment in the future.

After the gown has gone off to the cleaners and the last piece of wedding cake is in the freezer, couples cherish the wedding pic-tures. Trust your memories to a truly talented photographer. Even if the finances are down to pocket change, be sure you have at least a few portraits or candids taken by a professional. Sure, Uncle Fred or a cousin could do it, but what if the pictures come out grainy or with the guests' heads cut off? You'll never forgive yourself.

If the budget allows, book *both* a videographer and photographer, even if each is for a limited number of hours. There's nothing like a moment-by-moment video documentary of all the live action, people, sounds, and emotions at a wedding.

Most of the cost-conscious couples I've interviewed have said that if they can't afford both a photographer and videographer, they'd rather invest in professional photos and skip the video, or have a friend shoot a homemade video. Why? A video can't be displayed on the mantel or easily flipped through like a photo album—and everybody wants at least one perfect wedding portrait of the bride and groom that will be passed down through generations.

WAYS TO SAVE ON PHOTOGRAPHY

Photography is not an inexpensive proposition, but there are many ways to limit what you spend on a photographer to get pictures you can be proud of. Don't compromise on quality! One or two fabulous portraits are worth their weight in gold. You will value them more than a whole album full of mediocre pictures. Trust me.

"I don't think the couple should scrimp on quality photography. You want a style that you love, and you want to get somebody that really has a great reputation for producing what you expect," says Cele Lalli, former editor in chief of *Modern Bride*. "Don't buy by the package, buy the quality and style. You could make a mistake by just going for the best deal."

Lalli says economize by having some of the photographs taken before the wedding (it saves time, meaning coverage hours) and limiting the core shots at the ceremony. "Then, have a friend you know is a really good photographer do the candids," she adds. "It all depends on a couple's preferences. You don't want somebody there for four hours taking pictures of the guest tables if that is not important to you."

Hire someone who specializes in weddings. I've always been particularly impressed by wedding photographers. Weddings are especially challenging to shoot well. Most of the important moments are over in a flash—the bride walking down the aisle or the couple kissing for the first time as husband and wife. The photographer needs to remain unobtrusive and practically invisible, yet magically be in the right spot at the right time to capture all the major events. This takes skill, finesse, and timing.

The world is full of fashion photographers, commercial photographers, newspaper photographers, and corporate photographers. These are all specialized niches but vastly different from wedding photography. When my husband and I were married, we booked a corporate photographer and still regret that decision. In every picture, we look stiff and businesslike, as if waiting for a board meeting to begin.

Hire someone you feel comfortable with. The bride actually spends more time with the photographer on her wedding day than with the consultant, her mother, or the bridegroom. You don't have to fall in love with the photographer, but personality is important, and there should be a chemistry between the couple and the photographer. Most people hate getting their pictures taken, but on the wedding day they want their pictures to be the best ever.

The photographer should make the bride and groom smile and laugh and feel relaxed, because *that's* what makes for great photographs. Sure, the equipment is important, but a photographer who makes a couple feel at ease and helps them to actually *enjoy* the picture-taking process is guaranteed to deliver stunning photographs.

Ask to see samples of the photographer's work. When viewing a sample book or portfolio, find out whether the work was produced by the same photographer who'll shoot your wedding or whether it is a sample album purchased from a photo lab. Are the shots varied and original, and do they tell a personal story? Or does it seem like you've seen it all before, just with a different bride and groom?

If possible, ask to see an unedited proof book, with every proof taken from start to finish. This gives an idea of how many pictures the photographer takes of each pose and whether all of them are consistently great or just the random few. Most photographers shoot between 200 and 400 pictures, or at least ten to fifteen rolls of film.

Ask the photographer to discuss his "philosophy" of wedding photography. Photographers are both artists and skilled technicians. Some prefer to shoot in the classic portraiture style and are happiest composing shots and directing the bride, groom, and parents to stand in staged poses. Other photographers favor the photojournalism approach and "cover" the wedding in a documentary style the way a newspaper or magazine photographer covers a news event. The images captured for the album are unrehearsed, realistic, and faithful to the events that unfold throughout the day. The photojournalist quietly snaps candids and concentrates on on-the-spot shots. This style is the most expensive, since a larger number of photographs are taken. A photojournalist may snap up to 800 shots at the wedding! Some photographers use soft-focus techniques that create a soft, dreamy look. Everyone suddenly looks younger and wrinkle free, but, if done poorly, they also look fuzzier.

Ask the photographer to tell you about her equipment, but don't get too preoccupied with it. It doesn't matter what equipment she uses; the proof is in the finished product. Some photographers insist that 35-mm cameras are the only way to do it right, others swear by medium-format cameras, others use the latest digital cameras. It's a matter of personal preference and skill.

The medium-format camera produces larger negatives (2¼-inch square) than the 35-mm, which some argue makes it easier to crop and enlarge without grainy results. Other pros prefer the 35-mm because it's easier and faster to use, especially for candids, and they insist that enlargements look just fine.

The advantage of a digital camera is that the image is immediately visible on a screen on the reverse side of the camera. Much like a home video camera, the photographer sees the image in the camera window and instantly knows whether it's a keeper or needs to be reshot. Once the image is shot, the photographer can plug the digital camera into a computer and instantly see and print the photographs.

Thanks to the latest digital technology, it's a snap to improve someone's complexion in a photo, remove braces, smooth out crow's feet around the eyes, remove glare from eyeglasses, or even insert or delete people from a photo. (If you don't like Dad's new girlfriend, take her out of the wedding portrait!)

"This is the golden age of photography," says photographer David Bentley of Frontenac, Missouri. "Things are better and cheaper than they have ever been."

He notes that with digital cameras, it's easy to switch from black-and-white to color picture taking with the turn of a knob. It's also easy to tinker with a photograph to make it absolutely perfect. If the bride looks glum in one photo but is smiling in another, the photographer can swap her head from another picture. This technique is helpful in group shots, where it's nearly impossible to get everyone looking gorgeous and have their eyes wide open at the same time.

Ideally, you should meet with the photographer and the officiant at the ceremony site to discuss any restrictions on where or when the photographer can take pictures. Some churches and synagogues prohibit photography; others only allow the photographer to shoot from the back of the church or through a side door.

"I go to the rehearsal the night before to view the facility and find out what the rules and regulations are, and to make recommendations to the bride as far as the flow of the wedding," says photographer Christopher Semmes of Greenwich, Connecticut. "When the bridesmaids come down the aisle, they should be about twelve to fifteen pews apart to ensure they don't come down one on top of each other. You can space things out to get a decent picture of each."

■ **NEVER SHOP ON PRICE ALONE!** Crummy pictures are not a bargain, they're worthless.

■ **SHIFT THE WEDDING DATE OR TIME.** Photographers, like other vendors, charge a premium for Saturday night weddings. Others hate working on Sundays and charge extra for it. However, they may discount their prices for a Friday night or a Saturday afternoon, since the photographer is then free to book a second wedding for that evening. "Planning a Saturday wedding with a reception that ends before 4 P.M. will save you a lot of money. As a photographer, I am more flexible with my prices for these types of weddings," says Jay Jennings of Visual Image Productions in Addison, Texas. "A few times, I have photographed very nice weddings on a Friday night. The ceremony is usually close friends and family only, under a hundred people."

■ **LIMIT THE AMOUNT OF TIME THE PHOTOGRAPHER SPENDS AT THE WEDDING.** Perhaps have him just shoot the ceremony and the first half hour of the reception, with portraits taken of the couple near the wedding cake and at the head table. Or have the professional shoot the formal portraits and ceremony only. You can supplement with reception photos taken by relatives or a talented amateur.

■ **COMPARE PACKAGE PRICES VERSUS À LA CARTE PRICING.** If you don't want or need fifteen wallet-size portraits, thirty 8 × 10s, and twelve photo key rings, ask to swap them for items you do want— perhaps one larger portrait.

■ **PLACE DISPOSABLE "ONE-TIME USE" CAMERAS ON THE GUEST TABLES AND ASK SOMEONE AT EACH TABLE TO SHOOT THE GROUP THERE.** Disposables cost anywhere from $6 to $12 apiece, so buy them at a wholesale club store or order in bulk from a discount photography shop. (Expect about half of them to be totally unusable, but at least you'll have some great shots of friends taken by friends.) Leave a note at each guest table making it clear that the cameras are not favors and will be collected at the end of the evening. When shooting with disposables, make sure the subject is 6 to 12 feet away; any farther and the picture will come out too dark and fuzzy. Take the disposables to a warehouse store or national chain with inexpensive developing such as Wal-Mart, Sam's Club, BJ's Wholesale Club, or Costco.

■ **IF YOU AND YOUR FIANCÉ ARE PAYING FOR THE WEDDING, THINK TWICE ABOUT ORDERING SPECIAL ALBUMS FOR PARENTS AND BRIDAL PARTY MEMBERS.** The expense for these quickly adds up. Instead, order one or two photos for them as keepsakes, then hand them the photographer's phone number and reprint price list.

■ **HIRE A PROFESSIONAL WEDDING PHOTOGRAPHER FOR THE MOST IMPORTANT PORTRAITS ONLY.** At the very least, have a professional take three formal portraits: (1) the bride alone, (2) the bride and groom, and (3) the couple and the wedding party and parents.

These are the other core shots most couples want:

* The bride holding the bouquet
* The bride walking down the aisle
* The bride and groom staring into each other's eyes
* The couple exchanging vows
* The couple and each set of parents
* The couple and the wedding party
* The bride with her parents and siblings
* The groom with his parents and siblings

- The wedding cake
- The couple exchanging vows
- The newlyweds leaving the church

■ **NEGOTIATE TO BUY THE NEGATIVES OUTRIGHT.** You'll save a bundle on reprint costs and will have them for keeps. Not all photographers will agree to do this, because a big chunk of their business comes from reprints and special orders. However, many photographers discard wedding negatives anyway after a few years.

■ **ASK FOR CONTACT SHEETS INSTEAD OF PROOFS.** "If you wish to cut back on costs, instead of asking for previews, which are sometimes called proofs, ask your photographer to do a contact sheet with about twenty-five to thirty-six photos on a sheet. You have to look at it with a loupe, but it saves the extra step of the previews," says Joyce Scardina Becker of Events of Distinction in San Francisco, California.

■ **ASK THE PHOTOGRAPHER IF IT'S LESS EXPENSIVE TO VIEW THE PROOFS ON A VIDEOTAPE.** Some will load the photos on a tape that you can view at home. The downside is that the photo quality may be compromised by the quality of your television or videocassette recorder.

■ **HIRE THE PROFESSIONAL PHOTOGRAPHER FOR HIS OR HER TIME ONLY (A FLAT FEE OR BY THE HOUR) AND KEEP THE ROLLS OF FILM TO DEVELOP ON YOUR OWN AFTERWARD.** Take the film for discount processing and then arrange the photographs yourself in an album purchased at a photo or stationery shop. This route isn't for everyone, but if the bride or groom is artistic and knows something about cropping and matting, the result can be an attractive album.

■ **LOOK FOR DEALS.** Book a photography package that includes a free engagement portrait and bridal portrait.

■ **HAVE THE PHOTOS SHOT NOW AND DEVELOP THEM LATER WHEN THE BUDGET IS LESS EXHAUSTED.** Or purchase a smaller album now that has room for extra pages and add the extra pages later when you can afford it.

■ **HAVE EVERYONE IN PLACE AND ON TIME FOR THE FORMAL POR-TRAITS.** Time is money. The longer the photographer waits while the maid of honor hunts down stragglers, the higher the hourly fee rises.

■ **IF PICTURES OF CERTAIN RELATIVES AND FRIENDS ARE "MUST" SHOTS, ASSIGN SOMEONE IN THE FAMILY TO SHADOW THE PHOTOG-RAPHER AND POINT THEM OUT.** This is a good job for a reliable teenager who knows everyone at the wedding.

■ **ECONOMIZE ON THE ALBUM ITSELF.** "I don't think you *need* a leather wedding album," notes wedding photographer David Bentley of Bentley Studios Ltd. in St. Louis. "Some of the synthetic materials look and feel just like leather but don't cost as much. An expensive luxury car may have leather seating, but there are also beautiful alternatives for the seating material, and the car will still work just as well."

■ **LIMIT THE NUMBER OF ALBUM PAGES.** Do you really need fifty pages with nice but unnecessary shots of the family dog, the brides-maids in hair curlers, and four different views of the wedding cake? Cut the album back just a little and save a lot. "Spend all you can on hiring the best photographer your money will buy, then customize a package that will still give a wedding album but with fewer pages, perhaps only twenty-four 8 × 10s instead of thirty-six," advises wedding consultant Toni DeLisi of Memorable Events in Waldwick, New Jersey. "Or put the money into one knockout 11" × 14" portrait that will get more attention on your wall than in a drawer."

■ **CUT BACK ON RETOUCHING AND EXPENSIVE EXTRAS.** Special services—cropping, matting, hand-tinting of black-and-white pictures, special effects such as starbursts or multiple exposures—all cost more. Matting is adding one or more cardboard or special paper "frames" around the portraits. It's gorgeous, but do you really need to get artsy with double mats and special-ordered mats? Cropping is "editing" the picture before it is printed by cutting out certain parts. For instance, if the left half of the picture has an unsightly tripod in view, the photographer can crop it out.

■ **ARE ANY OF YOUR FRIENDS GOOD PHOTOGRAPHERS?** Find two or three who have decent cameras and provide them with dozens of rolls of film. Set them loose at the ceremony and reception and see what develops (no pun intended).

■ **AFTER THE WEDDING, RESIST THE TEMPTATION TO USE A ONE-HOUR DEVELOPING SERVICE.** The convenience will cost extra, up to double the regular processing price! Consider using a mail-order service that offers inexpensive processing and/or a free second set of prints. Mystic Color Lab in Mystic, Connecticut, sells film and does discounted developing. Mail the film to the lab and it comes back within a matter of days. The processing price is even cheaper (50 cents less per roll) if you've used Mystic brand film. For more information and film mailing packets, call Mystic Color Lab at 1-800-367-6061 or visit http://www.mysticcolorlab.com. The address is below.

> Mystic Color Lab
> Masons Island Rd.
> P.O. Box 144
> Mystic, CT 06355-9987

WAYS TO SAVE ON VIDEOGRAPHY

A video record of the wedding is a documentary of all the emotion and spontaneous action. If your budget has room for it, go for it! As the years roll by, a video becomes even more precious to a married couple because it's a record of both the wedding day and a historic family event. Twenty years from now, you'll be able to roll tape and see beloved friends and relatives chatting, laughing, and living as if time had stood still.

Videography fees depend on the number of cameras used, the quality of the equipment, the amount of postproduction editing, and the time spent by the videographer(s) at the wedding. The advantage of two cameras is that one videographer can be shooting events from the back while the other shoots from the altar or balcony. For example, you could have a view of your faces as you exchange vows, as a well as a view of the officiant reciting the vow prompts to you. The two views can later be merged for a complete perspective.

Expect to spend anywhere from $400 to $1,200 for videography. The average is around $500 to $600. Shop around for service and value. Prices vary a great deal. Your best test is to view a sample videotape. Look for bright, accurate color; clear image resolution; and smooth transitions from one scene to the next. Does the video look more like a high-quality, movie-style documentary or a cheesy home movie that a ten-year-old could have done better? Do the frames wobble (a sign the camera wasn't held steady)? Does the lighting look natural, or are guests bathed in blinding light? Are there too many zoom in/zoom out shots? Is the audio free of distortion and static, or do people sound like they're speaking inside tin cans? Trust your instincts; it doesn't take a technical genius or film director to detect these things.

When talking to the videographer's references, ask if the videographer uses clumsy carts for equipment or has dangling wires. This is sloppy and potentially dangerous for guests who might easily trip. Was the lighting system harsh or intrusive? Did guests practically reach for sunglasses every time the videographer came near? Were special effects used tastefully? Did the videographer use more than one camera?

Ask the videographer how he will work in tandem with the photographer. There are moments when the work of one might interfere with the other, such as both jockeying for position as you exchange rings.

Popular Video Shots

- Bride leaving her home
- Arrival of the bridal party
- Groom arriving at church
- Bride arriving at church
- Guests taking their seats for ceremony
- The entire ceremony including:
    Processional
    Service
    Vows
    Ring exchange
    Recessional
    Receiving line
- Outside activities at the church:
    Couple greeting guests
    Guests throwing rice or flower petals
    Group portrait of all guests and wedding party
- At the reception:
    Cocktail hour
    Candids of friends and family

■ **SKIP THE EDITING.** Ask the videographer if you can buy the raw footage of your wedding instead of an edited version, which takes more time to produce.

■ **ASK THE VIDEOGRAPHER TO SHOOT ONLY A 20-MINUTE "HIGH-LIGHTS" TAPE.** No one else besides the couple and their parents ever really sits through a three-hour wedding video more than a few times. The highlights are all you need.

■ **CALL THE LOCAL TELEVI-SION STATION AND ASK IF ANY OF THEIR CAMERA OPER-ATORS MOONLIGHT AS WED-DING VIDEOGRAPHERS.**

■ **ASK TWO OR THREE FRIENDS TO SHOOT VIDEO AT THE CEREMONY AND RECEPTION.** One can shoot the ceremony from the guests' perspective, another can record it facing the couple and capturing their expressions, and the third can shoot it from the balcony. At the reception, one videographer can shoot the guest tables, another can capture the action on the dance floor, and the last can follow the bride and groom around.

■ **LIMIT THE VIDEOGRAPHER'S TIME.** Hire the videographer to shoot the ceremony only, or the ceremony and the first 30 minutes of the reception.

■ **SKIP THE UNNECESSARY EXTRAS.** They're nice if you have money to burn, but nobody really needs a photo montage of the bride and groom's baby pictures, fancy fade-outs and dissolves, musical inter-ludes, or interviews with the couple's childhood teachers.

QUESTIONS TO ASK THE PHOTOGRAPHER
OR VIDEOGRAPHER

- Will the photographer/videographer I've chosen be the one who will shoot my wedding?
- How do you charge? Flat fee? By the hour? Package pricing?
- What does a package include? Are we allowed to make substitutions?
- Can you suggest creative ways to work within our budget?
- How will the photographer/videographer be attired?
- How long have you been shooting weddings on a professional basis?
- What kind of camera(s)/video camera(s) do you use?
- What backup equipment do you bring?
- Do you work alone, or do you bring an assistant to photograph or videotape the action from another perspective?
- Is the cost of the assistant included in the quoted price?
- Will you follow a list of suggested shots or scenes?
- Are you a member of a professional photography or videography association?
- Do you have a backup person in case of illness or emergency? Who will it be? May we see samples of his or her work?
- How long after the wedding can we expect to receive the finished album or video?

CHAPTER EIGHTEEN

Music and Entertainment

C hoosing music for a wedding can be challenging because it's really about making music for two separate events with totally different functions and atmospheres.

Music for the ceremony tends to be reflective, joyful, or inspirational. It provides fanfare and often includes religious and sacred selections rather than secular. Check with the officiant at the house of worship where you're holding the ceremony, because there may be restrictions on what you can play or even limitations on how much room the musicians will have. The band may be restricted to a small nook near the altar or chuppah, a perch in the balcony, or the space between the first row of seats and where the officiant stands.

Music for the reception is a whole different number. It puts guests in the mood for partying and provides music for dancing or for sheer entertainment. A reception is a festive celebration.

Whether the music is taped or live, it should loosen people up and get them in the mood for relaxing or dancing.

"Music sets the atmosphere at your wedding," says Gunnar Sahlin, a professional cellist from Greenwich, Connecticut. "You should spend quite some time thinking about what kind of music and what kind of musicians you want. You don't have to have a band of twenty musicians to accomplish this."

There are plenty of ways to stretch a music budget, beginning with the ceremony.

MUSIC FOR THE CEREMONY

At the ceremony site, ask the officiant or site manager what's available for free. Does the site have a house organist who is part of the package, or piped-in organ music or taped hymns from a sound system? If you're marrying in a church, ask what music is regularly used for the services there, and whether you can use it, too. Will the choir perform for free or for a nominal fee? Can you bring in the local high school choir, a gospel choir, or a community group to sing at your ceremony? Keep in mind that if a church has a house organist or vocalist and you choose instead to bring in your own musicians, you may still be charged for his services.

Consider a flute trio (flute, violin, and cello) or duo consisting of the church organist and a trumpet player. Another good combo is a harpist and vocalist. Or consider a string quartet (two violins, viola, and cello), flute duo, or harp and flute.

Once you've contacted a musical group, ask to hear them perform live or, at the very least, on a demo tape. Never hire musicians without listening to them first. "Contact a few musical groups to find out what they can do for you. The fee is often negotiable depending on how far the musicians will have to travel and the amount of equipment they use," Sahlin notes. "Usually there is a higher fee for the first hour and less for the second. You might say, 'This is my budget for music. What do you suggest?'"

Typically, instrumental groups such as string quartets are booked for two- or three-hour blocks of time, while disc jockeys and bands are hired for four hours. Overtime charges tend to be in 30-minute and hourly increments.

Consider music appropriate to the site and to the size of the crowd. "A bride came to me with the idea of have a string quartet to play during the cocktail hour at her reception of 400 people. After pointing out to her that it would be difficult to *hear* the quartet with that many people, she decided against it," says consultant Packy Boukis of Broadview Heights, Ohio. "However, in an appropriate situation, I have referred string quartets for playing at the ceremony. I checked at the local college for a referral. They were very talented and much less expensive than the established groups."

HIRING A DISC JOCKEY

Don't underestimate the value of a really good disc jockey. Sure, the music isn't "live," but if the disc jockey has a knack for sizing up a crowd and playing what they'll like, the results are unbeatable for the price. Relatives who have never gotten out of their seats at weddings will fight for space on the dance floor, and everyone will remember your wedding as the one where people truly celebrated and had a blast. A disc jockey can provide the music for the ceremony, too.

Remember this: A good disc jockey is always better than a lousy band. If all you can afford is a band of mediocre musicians, the fact that they are live won't mean a thing. No one will get out of their seats except to get their coats and go home early.

Besides, disc jockeys play well-known songs by the original artists, and the sound quality is good because most use compact discs or commercial tapes. And disc jockeys take fewer breaks than bands because the work is less physically demanding. (Band members need breaks to catch their breaths and give their lips or arms a rest. No kidding.)

"In terms of music and entertainment, a disc jockey is obviously the most economical route to go," notes Robbi Ernst III, a wedding consultant, lecturer, and author. "Here in Las Vegas, it can be as low as $450 for a good disc jockey because they are so competitive here. But the national average is around $650 to $700, and in major cities like San Francisco, it can be as high as $1,000 to $1,500."

Generally, the first two hours of the DJ's time are spent providing background music while the guests have cocktails, followed by dinner and dessert. The second two hours are for dance music. Rates can soar up to $3,500 for large events, or events where the DJ also entertains the crowd with pulsing lights, bubble shows, stand-up comedy routines, dance instruction, or audience participation "game" shows complete with light-up scoreboards.

Start your search for a disc jockey at least three to six months before the wedding—even earlier if the date is in June, in December (when companies hire them for holiday parties), or during graduation season when they are booked for school dances.

Friends or relatives who have recently gotten married are good sources of referrals to a dependable disc jockey who plays a nice mix of tunes and looks presentable. They can give you the inside scoop on whether the DJ showed up in a powder-blue tux and guzzled scotch, or came appropriately dressed in evening attire.

Consider attending a few bridal shows to meet and hear a variety of DJs and bands in action. Bridal fairs and shows tend to be three-ring circuses, but you'll walk away with a shopping bag full of free audiocassettes, videocassettes, price lists, and brochures. Read each brochure and compare hourly rates versus package deals. To enable potential customers to hear the DJs and bands firsthand, many bridal shows schedule a different DJ or musical group every hour or every thirty minutes. You'll get an idea of what they play, how they look, and how they act.

The disc jockey's personality and manner are important, especially if he will act as master of ceremonies or make announcements for you. Decide whether you would prefer a disc jockey who interacts with and entertains the crowd or someone who quietly fades into the background while playing music. The worst wedding nightmare is an obnoxious disc jockey who makes stupid or crass jokes and has an overbearing personality. Run the other way!

Hire a disc jockey who regularly works at weddings, as opposed to one who works nightclubs or on the radio. Radio DJs aren't used to picking songs specifically for a dance audience. And since they spend most of their time in a studio, they may not know how to "read" reactions from an audience and pick the type of song or tempo to accommodate that particular crowd. Nightclub DJs are skilled at responding to a dance crowd but cater mostly to a youngish, late-night audience. A wedding DJ has experience with all age groups, from teens to senior citizens, and knows how to get people away from the guest tables and onto the dance floor for line dances, classic ballroom numbers, ethnic dances, and group dances.

Ask what the disc jockey specializes in: rap music, Top 40, current hits, golden oldies, rhythm and blues, country music, ethnic music, world music, big band, swing, and so forth.

For a list of disc jockeys in your area, contact these industry associations:

The American Disc Jockey Association
10882 Demarr Rd.
White Plains, MD 20695
(301) 705-5150
http://www.adja.org

The National Association of Mobile Entertainers
Box 144
Willow Grove, PA 19090
(215) 658-1193 or 1-800-434-8274
http://www.djkj.com

Disc Jockey Terms to Know

Beat mixing
Blending two songs that have similar beats and tempos to create a seamless transition from one to the next.

Fade mixing
Starting the next song as the one being played is fading out.

Mobile disc jockey
A fancy term for a disc jockey who travels with equipment to your event.

Playback medium
Literally, the medium the disc jockey uses to play the songs. It might be compact discs, minidiscs, cassette tapes, records, or a combination.

Sound system
The equipment the disc jockey uses to relay the sound. The better the system, the better the sound reproduction. It's usually a good sign if the DJ is proud of how much he's invested in a quality sound system.

Subwoofers
Bass speakers that help achieve maximum sound reproduction.
(These are needed only for large crowds of 250 or more.)

HIRING A BAND

Book a band or musical group as early as possible, at least six
months to a year ahead. Like disc jockeys, the best bands are
snapped up early. Fees for a live band vary widely across the country and generally are higher in large cities. For four hours of live
entertainment, expect to spend anywhere from $900 to $2,000 for
a small, relatively unknown group to upward of $5,000 to $17,000
for an established multipiece orchestra.

A general rule of thumb in the industry is to hire a three-piece
band for small weddings (less than 75 guests); a five-piece band
for weddings of 100 guests or more; and a seven-piece band for
groups of 200 or more. Add another musician for each increment
of 50 guests. Some people choose band size on the basis of room
size, rather than on the number of guests. Ask the catering or
reception site manager what size musical group typically plays in
that room. Obviously, it takes more music power to project in a
cavernous ballroom than in a small room with low ceilings.

The bandleader will want to know the time and day of the
reception, the number of guests, their ages, and any musical preferences. It's important to find a band that regularly plays at weddings and includes musicians who regularly play together.

WAYS TO SAVE ON MUSIC

■ **HIRE A ROOKIE DJ—SOMEONE WHO HAS EXPERIENCE BUT HAS
JUST BEEN HIRED BY THE DISC JOCKEY COMPANY.** Some companies
are willing to give you a significantly reduced rate in exchange for

them listing you as a reference for these novice DJs, notes author Jeff Harrison in his book, *How to Avoid DJ Horror Stories: The Standard Reference Guide for Brides, Party Planners and Anyone Else in the Market for a Mobile Disc Jockey.*

Harrison, a professional disc jockey himself, writes that a rookie DJ may be new at that company but still have adequate experience to do a great job. Initially, many companies send their newest employees to informal events like birthday parties and cookouts. That's where they learn important basics such as "reading" an audience and responding with the right types of music. Once they've mastered the fundamentals, they "graduate" to more formal events like weddings.

For a copy of Harrison's book, write to the publisher at:

MegaWatt, Inc.
P.O. Box 60045
Washington, DC 20039

■ **DO WITHOUT MUSIC DURING THE COCKTAIL HOUR.** People really won't notice it. They're busy chatting, eating, and clinking glasses and plates—and the general noise level tends to get high.

■ **DON'T START THE MUSIC TOO EARLY AT THE RECEPTION.** Limit the playing hours to after dinner or after dessert; for example, from 8:30 P.M. to 11 P.M. only. Before and after that time window, play tapes you've made yourself or have music piped in through the reception site's sound system. Let guests know the schedule by announcing, "The band will begin playing music for dancing after dinner is served and before the cake is cut. Please join us on the dance floor then." The added advantage of postponing the musical entertainment is that people will have had time to relax and loosen up.

■ **SCHEDULE THE WEDDING FOR A FRIDAY NIGHT, SUNDAY AFTER-NOON, OR SUNDAY NIGHT.** Most DJs and bands charge a premium for Saturday nights, so the price is seldom negotiable. They may be willing to discount the rate for a Friday or Sunday, though.

■ **SKIP THE EXTRAS SUCH AS LIGHT SHOWS, BUBBLE SHOWS, DANCERS, OR A DJ ASSISTANT.** The added entertainment isn't necessary, and an experienced professional doesn't need an assistant. Chances are the assistant is someone in training.

■ **HIRE THE DISC JOCKEY FOR BOTH THE CEREMONY AND RECEPTION.** This usually means one additional hour of coverage, and it's just as easy for a DJ to provide classical or religious music for the ceremony as it is to provide Top 40 hits for the reception. Insist that continuous music is played even if the DJ or band takes a break.

■ **HIRE A VERSATILE BAND AND USE THE SAME MUSICIANS FOR THE CEREMONY AND RECEPTION.** If the band includes a trumpet player and pianist, they can play regal processional music at the ceremony (like Purcell's "Trumpet Voluntary"), then swing with big band music at the reception. You'll be paying for only an extra hour or so of coverage. If the band members include one or two vocalists, that's even better.

■ **TO FIND A GOOD DISC JOCKEY OR BAND, ASK CATERERS, WEDDING CONSULTANTS, AND RECEPTION SITE MANAGERS FOR RECOMMENDA- TIONS.** They are the people who'll know best, because they're *there* while the DJs or musicians are working. They can tell you who are the best, the worst, the most obnoxious, and the most professional. Ask these people for referrals in addition to asking your recently married friends.

■ **THINK CAREFULLY ABOUT WHEN THE DJ OR MUSICAL GROUP WILL SET UP THEIR EQUIPMENT OR BANDSTANDS.** Ask them how long this takes to do (10 minutes? 30 minutes?). Do you want the equipment ready and in place before guests arrive? (That may mean hiring the group to come earlier and stay later.) If not, are you comfortable with the disc jockey or musicians setting up while guests are eating dinner or sipping cocktails? This is a matter of personal preference.

■ **BOOK A GROUP WITH FEWER MUSICIANS.** Each extra musician will run an additional $150 to $350, so hiring a four-piece band instead of a six- or eight-piece band can save a bundle. If the musicians are good, four pieces will be powerful enough to entertain a crowd.

■ **FIND A GROUP TUNED IN TO TECHNOLOGY.** Today's computer and keyboard technology can make a four-piece group sound like a larger one. A drum machine can add the sound of extra percussion. Synthesizers and computer software can electronically add the sound of a string section, a horn section, or various extra instruments.

■ **FIND OUT IF THE RECEPTION SITE OR RESTAURANT HAS PIPED-IN MUSIC.** If it's decent and free, use it. If it's awful "elevator" or "dentist's office" music, skip it altogether.

■ **VISIT THE LIBRARY AND BORROW COMPACT DISCS OR CASSETTES TO MIX YOUR OWN LONG-RUNNING TAPE.** This may take a few evenings, but you'll have a keepsake from the wedding to play later.

■ **BUY PARTY MUSIC TAPES OR COMPACT DISCS AT A DISCOUNT MUSIC STORE.** There are many geared specifically to music for wedding ceremonies and receptions, including selections suitable for the procession and recession, choices for the cocktail hour, and selections for reception dancing. Ask a friend to give you a set of tapes as a shower present.

■ **IF A FRIEND IS A PROFESSIONAL SINGER OR MUSICIAN, ASK HER OR HIM TO PERFORM AT YOUR RECEPTION AS A WEDDING GIFT TO YOU.** Guests won't soon forget a talented violinist or opera singer entertaining them after dinner.

■ **CALL THE LOCAL RADIO STATION OR THE BROADCASTING OR MUSIC DEPARTMENT AT A NEARBY COLLEGE AND ASK FOR REFERRALS TO TALENTED DJS OR BANDS THAT FREELANCE.** Or visit a large music store and ask the manager if he or she can recommend a dependable group or DJ.

■ **CALL THE LOCAL SENIOR CENTER FOR A REFERRAL TO A BARBERSHOP QUARTET.**

■ **CALL A MUSIC CONSERVATORY OR THE MUSIC DEPARTMENT AT A COLLEGE OR UNIVERSITY AND ASK FOR REFERRALS TO TALENTED STUDENTS WHO MOONLIGHT.** Before hiring them, be sure they play well and will come dressed appropriately.

■ **CALL THE NEAREST MUSICIANS' UNION FOR A LIST OF MEMBERS WHO PLAY IN YOUR AREA.** The union is listed in the Yellow Pages under "Music" or "Entertainment."

■ **CALL THE LOCAL SYMPHONY ORCHESTRA.** Many musicians from these groups earn extra money by working at weddings and special events.

■ **LOOK IN THE SOCIAL PAGES OF THE LOCAL NEWSPAPER FOR ARTICLES ON FUND-RAISING AND CHARITY EVENTS.** These write-ups often include the names of the entertainers who performed.

■ **IF USING AMATEURS, BE SURE THE GROUP MEMBERS REGULARLY PLAY TOGETHER AND HAVE EXPERIENCE PERFORMING IN FRONT OF A LARGE GROUP.** Your neighbor's son and his classmates may make cool sounds together in the family garage, but are they used to working in front of a wedding crowd that includes people of all ages? The same goes for hiring amateur vocalists and close relatives. You don't want them getting stage fright or suddenly feeling so caught up in the emotion of the wedding that they can't sing well.

■ **HIRE A LOCAL DISC JOCKEY OR BAND TO AVOID ADDITIONAL TRAVEL FEES.** Understandably, many groups charge an extra fee for travel outside a certain radius—it may be for travel beyond 50 miles, 100 miles, and so forth.

QUESTIONS TO ASK THE MUSICIANS OR DISC JOCKEY

- When is the deadline to reserve the date?
- Do you have a demo audiotape or videotape?
- When will the band or group arrive?
- How long will it take to set up?
- What kind of music can you provide for a budget of approximately $_____?
- Do you offer any special package pricing or discounts?
- How can you work creatively within our budget? (Fewer musicians? More taped music? Shorter playing time?)
- If the reception starts at (give time), when do you typically begin playing (Before dinner? After dinner?)?
- Can we control the volume of the music?
- How large a band is typically needed for a wedding of our size? (The bandleader will want to know how many guests, whether the music will be primarily for dancing or for listening, and how large the reception site is.)
- How long will setting up take? Will it be done before the guests arrive?
- What is the cancellation or postponement policy?
- Has the band scheduled another wedding for the same day?
- Do you work from a predetermined playlist, or do you get a "feel" for the audience and tailor your playlist on site?

- Do you carry liability insurance (in case a guest trips over a wire or bandstand)?
- Where can I hear the band perform live (*not* at someone else's wedding!)?
- Will the band I've auditioned be the same band that will play at my wedding?
- How will the band members or entertainers be attired?
- How long have these particular musicians played together?
- Does the group have any special equipment or electrical needs (extension cords, extra outlets, podium, music stands, extra microphones)?
- What is the fee? Is it lower on certain days of the week or during certain seasons of the year?
- What is the surcharge for a Saturday night? For a major holiday?
- When is the deposit due? When is the balance due?
- Do you charge a flat fee or an hourly rate?
- Is a variety of music offered for selection?
- Do you charge a travel fee?
- How long do you play, and how many breaks do you take?
- How long are the breaks?
- Do you work with an assistant?
- What does your sound system include?
- Does the band take requests from guests?
- Do you encourage audience participation?
- What is the band's musical specialty?
- To what age group(s) do you usually cater?
- How many musicians and/or vocalists will perform? What instruments?
- How long has the group been performing at weddings?

- Is there an extra fee for the bandleader or disc jockey to act as master of ceremonies?
- Does the bandleader act as master of ceremonies and announce the special events throughout the reception (cake cutting, garter throw, bouquet toss)?
- What musical styles do you like to play most?
- What kind of food and beverages do you expect?
- What kind of microphones do you use?
- Will you provide continuous taped music during breaks?
- Can the length of time you play be extended? What are the overtime charges, and when do they kick in?

Additional Questions to Ask the Disc Jockey

- What kind of equipment do you use?
- What kind of playback medium do you use?
- Is serving as master of ceremonies included in the fee?
- Do you have a playlist of songs to choose from?
- Do you display signs with the name of the company? (Some couples regard signage as offensive advertising that mars the look of their reception. If you don't want it, insist they do without it.)
- Is the disc jockey willing to obtain songs I've requested?
- When viewing a live or videotaped performance:
  - Did the audience seem to respond positively to the DJ's selections?
  - Were people dancing?
  - Were people leaning forward to talk to each other (a sign the music is too loud!)?
  - Did the DJ play a variety of music styles, grouped in sets of three to five songs for consistency?
  - Were the song transitions smooth?

CHAPTER NINETEEN

TRANSPORTATION

Getting there in style is important on your wedding day, but keep in mind that fancy transportation carries a fancy price tag. If you long to make an entrance in a hot-air balloon, horse-drawn carriage, gondola, or stretch limousine, so be it. This is definitely a splurge category, but you can always save elsewhere.

WAYS TO SAVE
ON GETTING AROUND

The limousine is the vehicle of choice for most couples. Prices vary widely from company to company and also depend on the make and value of the vehicle. You may be quoted anywhere from $150 to $1,000 for a few hours of driving in style. Ask a recently married friend for a referral, or look in the Yellow Pages under "Automobile Rental," "Limousines," "Chauffeur Services," and "Wedding Services." Many limousine companies advertise in the back pages of regional wedding planner booklets found in local newspapers or regional monthly magazines. You also can ask for a referral from a high school student who recently attended a prom.

Use the Internet to begin your research. Many companies have Web pages where they post their complete packages and fees. Going on-line is a good way to view vehicles and get an idea of what a stretch limo looks like versus a luxury sedan. Many Web pages post pictures of the cars both inside and out. But don't be tempted to book one on the basis of a "cyber" photo! Always visit the company and inspect the vehicles in person before signing a contract.

If a company doesn't advertise a discounted rate, ask for one. Say something like, "What's your best possible price? Can you do better than that?" Or, "Is the rate lower if we book on a certain day of the week?" A discount may be available if more than one vehicle is hired or if one vehicle is hired for a long period.

For a referral to a licensed and insured transportation company in your area, contact the National Limousine Association, an organization of professional limousine company members. Based in Alexandria, Virginia, the association has a toll-free referral line at 1-800-652-7007 and a Web site (http://www.limo.com/) with great consumer tips on choosing a safe, dependable service provider.

When choosing a special-occasion limousine, give consideration to the color of car you favor and whether you'll want special extras such as chilled champagne or a sunroof. The more specific the requirements, the further in advance it should be reserved and paid for. Insist on a contract that states the details of the reservation: hours, vehicle make and model, features, color, and size.

Most companies require the limo service to be booked for a minimum of three hours. That time frame usually means round-trip from "garage to garage." The clock starts ticking from the minute the driver leaves the garage of the limo company to pick up the couple and stops when the driver returns to the garage.

(You can save by hiring a reputable *local* company.) Gratuities, tolls, and parking fees are usually extra. Expect to pay an additional rate if the car or limo is booked past 11 P.M, or if the driver is kept waiting a couple extra hours because the newlyweds can't bear to leave the reception.

You can save a bundle if the company is willing to hire the car and driver by the hour with no minimum number of hours. Consider booking a limo for the ride to the ceremony only. Arrange with a friend to transport you from the reception to the airport or hotel. (Savings: $60 an hour versus $150 or more for a standard three-hour package)

■ **HIRE A BLACK OR GRAY LIMOUSINE INSTEAD OF A WHITE ONE.** White limos tend to be requested for proms and weddings only, so a company will have fewer of them in its fleet and charge top dollar for them. In general, limousine companies cater more to business and corporate travel clients who don't want to be driven around in conspicuous white cars.

■ **ASK IF THE COMPANY PROVIDES PICKUP AND DROP-OFF SERVICE ONLY.** That way, you'll be charged only for the time needed.

■ **SAVE DOLLARS BY BOOKING A LUXURY CAR SUCH AS A CADILLAC OR LINCOLN CONTINENTAL INSTEAD OF A LIMOUSINE.** For even more savings, skip the chauffeured limo service altogether and hire a luxury car from a rental car agency for a day or weekend. Ask a friend or relative to be the driver and to return the car for you after you leave for the honeymoon. That way, you won't be limited to a two- or three-hour window and still can depart the reception in style.

■ **ON THE FLIP SIDE, HIRE THE DRIVER ONLY.** Many limo companies let customers book a chauffeur who comes to their location and drives them around town in their own car. (Total cost: $18 to $35 an hour)

■ **FIGURE OUT WHO HAS THE FLASHIEST CAR IN THE FAMILY AND ASK TO BORROW IT FOR THE DAY.** Ask a friend or relative to play chauffeur. (Total cost: Just refilling the gas tank and sending a thank-you note)

■ **IF THE CEREMONY IS WITHIN WALKING DISTANCE OF THE BRIDE'S HOUSE, CONSIDER HAVING A PROCESSION WITH FAMILY AND GUESTS WALKING BEHIND THE BRIDE AND HER DAD OR HONOR ESCORT.** The flower girl and ring bearer can lead the way, and your neighbors will love watching the romantic spectacle. Think of the great photo it will make! The groom could be waiting for them all on the steps of the church. (Total cost: $0)

■ **ASK FOR A REGULAR-LENGTH LIMOUSINE, NOT THE STRETCH VARIETY.** Stretch limos come in many lengths (from grand and imposing to Hollywood-style ridiculous) and seat six to twelve people. You'll pay a premium for a stretch limousine, which may come with pricey additional extras such as tinted windows, a privacy partition, fully stocked wet bar, television, fax, phone, videocassette recorder, sunroof, or even a Jacuzzi.

■ **FIND OUT EXACTLY WHAT MAKE AND MODEL VEHICLE YOU WILL BE HIRING.** Visit the company and inspect the vehicles. Are they clean and well maintained both inside and out? Does the interior smell fresh and clean?

■ **FIND OUT HOW THE DRIVER WILL BE ATTIRED.** Why go to the bother and expense of hiring a special-occasion car if the driver arrives in jeans and a T-shirt? Ask what kind of safety and customer-service training programs the drivers receive.

■ **THINK TWICE ABOUT SPRINGING FOR A BUCKET OF ICED CHAMPAGNE IN THE LIMO.** Chances are it won't be a fine vintage, and most couples say they had time for only a few sips before arriving

**Amy Connor, of An Affair to Remember in New York City, suggests:** "Save money on limousines by utilizing public transportation that has the character of where you're getting married; for example, a London-style double-decker bus, a San Francisco–style trolley, a taxi or bus, or even the subway. Not only will you save money, but think of the great photo opportunity it'll afford. There's nothing that shows off the white of a bride's wedding gown like the bright yellow of a New York taxicab!"

at the reception. Ask if you can bring your own, but liquor laws in your state may prohibit this.

■ **IF YOU NEED TO HIRE SEVERAL VEHICLES TO TRANSPORT A LARGE WEDDING PARTY OR MANY OUT-OF-TOWN GUESTS, CONSIDER BORROWING A MINIVAN.** Friends or relatives with children probably have one to lend.

■ **GET ON THE BUS.** Know someone who drives the local school bus? Ask if it's possible for her to drive your guests to the wedding reception. You may need permission from the local superintendent of schools or school board. Guests will get a kick out of riding in a bright yellow school bus festively decorated for a wedding excursion!

■ **IF YOU LONG TO ARRIVE IN A VINTAGE CAR, LOOK IN THE YELLOW PAGES FOR LISTINGS FOR ANTIQUE/HISTORIC CAR ASSOCIATIONS OR CALL THE LOCAL HISTORICAL SOCIETY.** Ask for referrals to car buffs who may be willing to rent you one. The local historical society may just have a Model T or elegant roadster for hire, and you'll feel like you just stepped out of a romance novel. Another good way to find a source is to attend an antique car show and chat with the collectors. Mention you'll be getting married in May and have your heart set on arriving in a vintage Packard or Rolls. Do they know anybody who hires out their car and driver?

SAMPLE HOURLY RATES

Chauffeured vehicles

Luxury sedan	$40 per hour (2-hour minimum)
6-passenger stretch limousine	$60 per hour (2-hour minimum)
8-passenger stretch limousine	$85 per hour (3-hour minimum)
10-passenger stretch limousine	$100 per hour (3-hour minimum)

Ready to splurge? These luxury forms of getting there are fabulous but expensive! And most require a three- to five-hour minimum.

Boat, gondola, or horse-drawn carriage	$200–$500 per hour
Antique trolley	$300–$500 per hour
Hot-air balloon	$100–$350 per hour

Remember, these prices vary widely nationwide.

QUESTIONS TO ASK
THE VEHICLE COMPANY

- What various limousine or car styles do you offer?
- How far in advance are reservations required?
- We are getting married on (date) at (time). Is our wedding date near a major holiday, convention, or prom time, when limousines may be scarce?
- Are your charges based on time or distance?
- Is a minimum number of hours required?
- Do you offer any special discounts, packages, or seasonal rates?
- Do you offer chauffeur services in case we want to use our own car and need a driver only?
- How can you work creatively within a budget of $_____?
- What does your wedding package include?
- How flexible is the company when it comes to negotiating the terms of the package?
- Can the "complimentary" champagne or decorations be skipped in exchange for an upgraded vehicle? Can a smaller vehicle be booked in exchange for longer driving time?
- When are the deposit and balance due?
- What is the cancellation or postponement policy?
- Can the vehicles be inspected before the wedding?
- Do you pick up several people in the same vehicle? Is there an extra charge for this?
- What kind of licensing and insurance do you carry?

CHAPTER TWENTY

THE HONEYMOON

A romantic honeymoon is the happy-ever after ending to the months of wedding planning. You deserve it!

Many couples leave honeymoon planning until the end, when their budget has dwindled down to pocket change. Don't even think of skipping the honeymoon! No matter how limited the time or resources, plan to take some sort of postwedding trip. You'll remember it for the rest of your life, even if the two of you joke about the "romantic view" of the hotel parking lot or the fact that it rained every day.

A honeymoon is a welcome respite after all the commotion of planning a wedding. Because marriage is a major life change, even a few days together will help you and your spouse begin to make the adjustment to a shared lifestyle. Besides, how often will you get the chance to be totally oblivious to the outside world?

Allow yourself a day to recuperate from the wedding before hopping on a plane or train. Some couples spend their first married night at a local hotel and then gather with out-of-town wedding guests the next day for a brunch or final farewell. Because many couples nowadays live together or host and pay for their weddings themselves, they don't feel pressured to formally "depart" the wedding before everyone else in order to make a grand getaway. Why not stay with your guests and enjoy wedding fun until the very end?

Nationwide, the average couple spends anywhere from four to nine days on honeymoon travel and plunks down anywhere from $2,000 to $5,000 for the trip. Resist the urge to say, "We're too busy to get away!" Postponing a honeymoon is a lousy idea, and if you ever do get around to taking that trip, it won't be the same. You deserve this special time as a newlywed couple.

Don't despair if you don't have the dollars to match your honeymoon dreams. A honeymoon is really a state of mind. Borrow a hideaway, ask friends to chip in for the airfare or daily expenses, or spend just one glorious night at a swanky hotel. You'll never regret it.

FINDING A KNOWLEDGEABLE TRAVEL AGENT

Ask friends to recommend a good travel agent. For travelers who've never planned a vacation before, sorting through the fares, deals, and destinations is complicated business. A travel professional will have glossy brochures to peruse and all the fares and schedules at the touch of a computer key. Best of all, the service is virtually free.

It sounds obvious, but think carefully about where you want to go, how long you'd like to be away, what kind of climate or special features you are looking for, and how much you want to spend. It's easier for a travel agent to find bargains if the client has several destinations or categories in mind. At the very least, think of one or two features you want—maybe a location with a beach and sailing, or historic ruins and walking trails.

Don't just announce, "Where should we go on our honeymoon?" The travel agent may try to sell you an expensive round-the-world cruise.

AVOIDING "HONEYMOON" SPOTS

Resorts and destinations geared specifically to honeymooning couples often are more expensive than other resorts. Who cares if the other guests just got married, too? Instead, check out something the two of you have always wanted to do, even if it isn't the "traditional" choice—camping, skiing, a music camp vacation where you brush up on your playing, a cooking class vacation, or a spa trip where the two of you get total pampering.

Popular Honeymoon Destinations

Following are some of the most popular honeymoon destinations (not in order of priority):

- Niagara Falls, Canada
- Maui, Hawaii
- Orlando, Florida
- The Florida Keys
- Las Vegas, Nevada
- New Orleans, Louisiana
- The Pocono Mountains, Pennsylvania
- The coast of Maine
- Southern Vermont

+ Lake Tahoe (California and Nevada sides)
+ The Grand Canyon, Arizona
+ Paris, France; Venice and Rome, Italy
+ Costa Rica

AIRFARE SAVVY

Being flexible about arrival and departure dates can save you a bundle. Flying on a Saturday is expensive. Fares tend to plummet for midweek flights (Tuesday through Thursday). If the wedding is on a Saturday night, you actually might enjoy hanging around for a few extra days to rest up and spend time with out-of-town guests before leaving on the honeymoon.

Depending on the destination, prices often are cheaper for midday flights and postmidnight flights. That's because most people want to leave early in the morning or late in the afternoon and not "waste" a day of travel. A midnight flight is actually a smart idea for foreign travel; passengers board the flight, fall asleep, and wake up at their destination.

Avoid flying during peak fare times—any major holiday, spring break week, or the high season for that destination. For example, airfares to warm locales are highest in the winter and lowest in the summer. The high season for European vacations is late spring and summer; the high season for cruises is December through March.

Ask the travel agent about seasonal weather issues. Will it be tornado, monsoon, or hurricane season when you visit that isolated, romantic spot? Sure, cruise fares are rock bottom to the Caribbean in late August and September, but that's because no one wants to go there in brutal summer weather—and it also happens to be hurricane season.

Do you or your future spouse travel often on business? Take advantage of frequent flier miles. Many hotels also offer discounts and perks to frequent customers. It may be a room upgrade or an extra night free with four nights' stay.

Ask your employer if you are eligible for special travel and hotel discounts. You may be able to book the trip through your corporation's travel department. Some airlines and hotels offer discounts to state and federal workers and military personnel. Find out if it's necessary to bring proof of identification, such as a union card, military ID, driver's license, or paycheck stub.

Consider applying for a credit card good for bonus points or free travel miles. Charge all household and wedding expenses on that card, then use those bonus miles to book your honeymoon trip. In addition to free trips, you may be eligible for discounts on hotel accommodations and car rentals. Some long-distance phone companies now offer bonus travel miles for switching to their phone service.

Aggressively research discount fares. Once you have a destination in mind, call the airline directly on its toll-free number and ask the reservations agent for information on "absolutely lowest possible" fares. Once a fare is suggested, don't settle for it immediately. Ask the agent if the airline can do better than that if you leave on another day or at another time. Being flexible pays off. Most airlines will hold a reservation for twenty-four hours if it's reserved with a credit card. You can easily cancel if you find something better. Shop around! Fares vary widely from airline to airline. You may save up to 80 percent simply by making a few phone calls and comparing prices.

Take advantage of fare wars. Even if you have already bought the ticket, call and see if the price has come down. If the fare difference is substantial, it may be worth it to pay a $35 to $75 reticketing fee.

Pay attention to advertisements in the travel section of the local newspaper. Fares change daily, and the ads often list the great deals before the travel agents even know about them. Be sure to read the restrictions and fine print—there may be "blackout" periods, meaning the fare is not valid on certain days or flights.

Find out if the city you're flying to is the hub for a particular airline, meaning it's the regional center for many of its flights. Often, the hub airline has the best fares to and from that destination.

Ask the airline if you'll need to bring a form of photo identification to board the plane. This is now common practice at many major airports that have heightened security. Are the honeymoon tickets in your married name but your photo ID still in your maiden name? Be sure to bring a copy of the marriage certificate to confirm your identity.

Name Your Own Price

Priceline.com, Inc., a company based in Connecticut (http://www. Priceline.com), operates a patented system allowing consumers to shop at a price they name for airline tickets, cars, and hotel rooms. When shopping for an airfare, consumers name the price they are willing to pay and the dates they wish to depart and return. The company then searches for a major airline willing to release seats on flights where there is unsold space. Of course, not every price is accepted. But if yours is, it's a win-win situation—the consumer can save hundreds of dollars, and the airline makes money on an otherwise empty seat.

WAYS TO SAVE ON ACCOMMODATIONS

■ **BORROW A HIDEAWAY.** Is money really tight? Ask a friend or relative with a seaside condo or vacation house to lend it to you for the honeymoon. They may be thrilled to make it their wedding gift. Let the maid of honor spread the word that a gift of airfare or contributions to travel expenses would be appreciated, too. Guests feel good when they give a gift that really is wanted and needed.

■ **BOOK AN ALL-INCLUSIVE VACATION.** While some travelers love the freedom of choosing their services à la carte (booking the airfare, hotel, and meals on their own), others prefer the ease of purchasing a honeymoon package. A travel package is usually paid for in advance and includes hotel accommodations, airfare, meals, and airport transfers. There are great bargains out there, so shop around. Some all-inclusive resorts also include sports instruction and equipment, tennis court fees, drinks, nightly entertainment, excursions, and tipping. The cruise is a popular example of the all-inclusive vacation—book the room, and everything else is included.

■ **CALL THE HOTEL DIRECTLY TO BOOK YOUR STAY.** Ask to speak to the manager or someone in charge and politely inquire about special discounts, a room upgrade, or their lowest rate. The reservations person at the front desk may not be able to authorize a special deal.

■ **CONSIDER STAYING ON THE OUTSKIRTS OF TOWN.** Hotels outside the city limits or a short drive from major attractions are always less expensive than those within walking distance of all the action. For travel to a major resort like Disneyland or Disney World, ask the travel agent about hotels just outside the park complex or within a short ride to the gates. Chances are the hotel offers a free shuttle to the site. In big cities, avoid downtown hotels that advertise being "in the heart" of things. (Proximity to main attractions translates into higher prices.) If you're willing to spend a few extra minutes each day in a cab or on public transportation, you could save up to $200 per night.

■ **DON'T BE SHY ABOUT ANNOUNCING YOU'RE BOOKING A HONEY-MOON.** The hotel or inn may have special perks for newlyweds, like a room upgrade or complimentary bottle of champagne.

■ **TRAVELING TO A MAJOR CITY? INQUIRE ABOUT WEEKEND HOTEL RATES.** In urban business centers—such as Washington, D.C., New York, Los Angeles, and Chicago—weekends (Friday through Sunday) usually are cheaper than midweek. That's because business travelers tend to stay Mondays through Thursdays only. Many luxurious city hotels offer bargain rates on weekends because they'd rather book a cheaper rate than have the rooms empty. The same room might be $300 on Monday through Thursday and only $135 on the weekend.

■ **IS YOUR HEART SET ON THE HONEYMOON SUITE?** Sure, it probably comes with a living room, wet bar, and fancy fireplace, but these amenities will double or even triple the cost of the room rate.

■ **INQUIRE ABOUT DISCOUNT COUPONS FOR LOCAL ATTRACTIONS.** Hotel guests may be entitled to free admission at a museum or discounted opera tickets.

■ **ASK IF THE ROOM RATE ALSO INCLUDES CONTINENTAL BREAKFAST, LUNCH, OR DINNER.** Continental breakfast usually means a light breakfast of coffee, juice, and sweet rolls or pastry. Take advantage of the free goodies. It's one less meal to pay for each day.

■ **CHECK OUT MEAL PLANS.** Resorts and hotels featuring several on-site restaurants sometimes offer the option of purchasing meals by the day or week. This can be an economical way to dine out and try all the restaurants in the resort complex. Ask if the property offers the American plan (breakfast and one other meal) or the

European plan (continental breakfast only). Compare plans and prices. If you intend to sleep until noon each day, a plan that includes breakfast will be a waste of money.

■ **DON'T MAKE IN-ROOM CALLS.** At the hotel, avoid using the phone in your room to place long-distance calls, or an extra service charge will end up on your bill. Some hotels even charge an access fee if you use your calling card. Beware.

■ **DON'T BE TEMPTED TO DRINK OR EAT ANYTHING FROM THE HOTEL MINIBAR IN YOUR ROOM.** You'll faint when you get the bill. Every time you open a soda or eat a bag of chips, expect anywhere from $3 to $8 to be added to your room tab. No kidding!

■ **INVEST $30 IN A COPY OF THE *ENTERTAINMENT BOOK*.** This publication offers steep discounts or 2-for-1 deals on airfares, accommodations, cruises, restaurant meals, car rentals, flowers, and hundreds of other goods and services.

The book is available nationwide, with regional editions geared to vendors in more than 150 major cities across the country and around the world. One version offers savings of up to 50 percent off room rates at various hotels, motels, and resorts. Proceeds from the book often benefit local charities.

For more information, call 1-800-374-4464 or visit http://www.entertainmentbooks.com. If you have questions about the Entertainment Book Hotel Program, call 1-800-926-0565 or write to the address below.

Entertainment Publications, Inc.
International Headquarters
2125 Butterfield Rd.
Troy, MI 48084

■ **GO WHOLESALE!** Join a wholesale savings club. Wholesale club members often are entitled to special discounts on hotels, cruises, vacation packages, and rental cars. By spending $35 to $50 on an annual membership, you can save on honeymoon travel and on shopping for household items all year long.

STAYING CLOSE TO HOME

Foreign travel is wonderful, but it's expensive and requires more time to make it really worthwhile. Between time differences, jet lag, and time spent coming and going, a honeymoon abroad isn't relaxing unless you have at least five days. According to *Bride's* magazine, the average amount spent on a honeymoon is $4,048 for a foreign trip and $3,266 for a domestic trip.

Consider traveling locally, maybe to a rustic inn just a few hours away or a ski or golf resort you've always wanted to visit. By planning a domestic getaway, you'll save hundreds, if not thousands, of dollars on airfare and won't have to deal with customs, passports, exchanging currency, and the fluctuating value of the American dollar abroad.

TRAIN AND AIRLINE PASSES

If traveling throughout Europe, ask a travel agent about purchasing a Eurail pass for discounted train travel in many countries. The Eurail pass is good for unlimited travel between certain time periods and certain destinations depending on which plan you buy. Travelers also may purchase train-pass packages that include hotels and rental cars. For information, call 1-800-4-EURAIL (438-7245) or visit the Rail Europe Web site at http://www.raileurope.com.

For information on rail passes for travel in the British Isles, call Rail Pass Express at 1-800-551-1977. If traveling across the

United States, call Amtrak at 1-800-872-7245 for details on train-pass deals.

Some airlines and rail services offer discounted youth passes for travelers aged twenty-six and under. Ask your travel agent or call the airlines for information on restrictions, rates, and age limits.

HONEYMOON CRUISES

Cruises rank among the most popular form of honeymoon travel because they are all-inclusive vacations. Once onboard, the fare includes a cabin, all daytime and evening entertainment, and all meals (which can consist of an astonishing ten to fourteen "meals" daily). Cruises last anywhere from three days to several months, and ships offer a remarkable range of onboard services from hair salons to spas, movie theaters, pools, nightclubs, casinos, golf driving, skeet shooting, and aerobics.

In the past, cruise ships generally were segregated into first-, second-, or third-class sections, with travelers restricted to only those areas of the ship for which they'd paid. Today's cruise ships are one class, which means everyone on board can use all of the ship's facilities. The price of a stateroom is based primarily on its size and location. Generally, the higher the deck is above the waterline, the pricier the cabin. "Outside" cabins with a window (porthole) are more expensive than "inside" rooms without windows.

Since most cruise travelers say they don't spend much time in their cabins anyway, consider booking an inside room on a lower deck. Depending on the length of the cruise, you could save thousands of dollars! This really isn't a hardship, because all the activities and amenities are the same whether you paid $1,000 or $10,000. Besides, the window usually is tiny on an "outside" cabin, and you'll want to spend most of your time wandering around the ship enjoying the round-the-clock activities.

Ways to Save Onboard

■ **BUY DRINKS ONSHORE.** Purchase soft drinks in port and drink them in your cabin. The steward will bring ice and glasses.

■ **BE SURE TO BRING THE BASICS.** Pack beauty items, shampoo, tampons, suntan lotion, film, batteries, Band-Aids, and over-the-counter medications (allergy medicines and decongestants, etc.) in your luggage. The same items may cost two to three times as much onboard ship.

■ **TRACK YOUR DAILY EXPENSES.** Visit the purser's office every day to find out what your shipboard charges were for the previous day. Or, better yet, pay for all drinks and services with cash.

■ **WHEN IN PORT, EAT MEALS ONBOARD.** They're already included in the package price.

■ **AVOID BUYING THINGS IN THE GIFT SHOPS ONBOARD.** You can make purchases on the last day of the cruise. That's when prices are deeply discounted to clear merchandise out before the next sail.

■ **FIND OUT ABOUT THE SHIP'S EXCURSION PACKAGES BEFORE SETTING SAIL.** You may be able to do some shore tours more cheaply on your own. For instance, you can rent mopeds or recreational watercraft yourself or share the cost of a cab or tour guide with other passengers. Long before the honeymoon, contact the local chamber of commerce or tourist office at your destination for brochures about sites of interest and rates for popular day excursions.

Extra Expenses to Keep in Mind

❖ How will you get to and from the airport?
❖ Are there extra fees for port charges? Are there departure taxes?

- Is it worthwhile to buy trip insurance or cancellation insurance?
- Do you need to buy or borrow luggage?
- What are the charges for buying traveler's checks?
- What are your expected costs for camera, film, and video?
- What will you spend on souvenirs and sundries?
- Does the package rate include meals, tips, and transfers?
- Is tipping expected onboard ship? What is the rate?
- What are the costs of obtaining or renewing a passport?
- Do you need to purchase suitable travel clothes?

BE A WARY CONSUMER

When booking a package, ask the travel agent or hotel representative to clarify terms like *deluxe*, *luxury*, or *four-star* accommodations. In some places, a "deluxe" hotel means a dumpy room with a shared bathroom—which may be down the hall or on another floor.

Don't accept vague descriptions such as "all major hotels" or "all major airlines." If the travel or hotel reservations are booked through another company, ask for the name, phone number, and address of that company.

Some resort vacation offers are made by companies trying to sell time-share options on condominiums. A time-share means a buyer purchases the use of the condominium or villa for a specific limited amount of time each year, say a week or two. Ask whether you will be required to attend a sales-pitch seminar and whether you will be charged a fee should you choose not to purchase the time-share.

Watch out for travel scams that are essentially credit card fraud. Some companies send a postcard or make a phone call to unsuspecting consumers, announcing they are the "lucky winner" of a free trip or cruise. These con artists say all you need to do to claim the prize is to give your credit card number. Don't fall for this! There likely is no travel prize at all, or you will be charged for an expensive trip that turns out to be the vacation from hell in a substandard hotel. Hang up if the company is unwilling to send you written information about the offer (including cost and specific terms and conditions) before you commit any money. If you suspect fraud, contact the local Better Business Bureau or the attorney general in your state.

Do Your Homework

Use the national toll-free directory (1-800-555-1212) to obtain free numbers for state and local tourism offices. Or call the local chamber of commerce or mayor's office for referrals to local information and tourist centers. Contact these resources directly and ask for any free maps, brochures on accommodations, travel guides, coupon books, vacation packages, or special offers.

Go to the library and check out the most current travel guides. It's a waste of money to buy a slew of travel books. By the time you get to the destination, many of the prices, addresses, and service hours listed may be out of date.

The Internet is a fabulous resource waiting to be tapped. You can search for exotic Hawaiian vacations; view photos of hotels, beaches, and points of interest; and check out car rentals. Use the Internet to find out about package prices, accommodations, and booking procedures. Save on long-distance phone bills by booking the trip on-line or sending an E-mail to the hotel.

CONCLUSION

By now, a wonderful thing should have happened to you.

After reading all the creative ideas from brides and consultants who've already "been there and done that," you should be ready to create an unforgettable wedding celebration that's delightful and debt free. What a wonderful way to launch into marriage! You'll have the satisfaction of knowing your wedding won't set you back a king's ransom, and you'll have found ways to personalize it all. (Why should your wedding be a cookie-cutter replica of everyone else's?)

Along the way, you will have learned ways to spend *carefully* (not frugally) and to make educated consumer choices—as a couple. Those skills will be invaluable to you both throughout the engagement and your entire life together. Bravo!

And who says you need to utilize every money-saving trick? Knowing when to splurge is as important as knowing when to save. Planning a wedding on a budget is all about finding balance and setting priorities and communicating to express what you really want. (It's like a happy marriage, see?)

So go ahead and order those orchids, or grow your own daisies. Splurge on a designer wedding dress or sew your own luxurious gown. Dance in diamond-studded shoes or discount store ballerina slippers. The choices are yours.

May you use this book to make choices that bring you beauty and joy and happiness. Enjoy the journey. Cherish each other. And may every day of your life together be as beautiful as your wedding day.

—Madeline Barillo

INDEX

date, shifting
  cancellations and double
    booking on same day, 182
  ideas, 182
day, shifting time of, 182–183
DeKay, Karen, 153, 190, 192
DeLisi, Toni, 219, 267
DeMille, Cecil B., *xix*
destination weddings
  cruise ships, 187
  popular destination wedding
    sites, 186
diamond, choosing
  caring for engagement ring,
    85
  four Cs, 82–84
  gemstones, 84
  right fit, 85
  what to spend, 85
disc jockey, additional questions
  to ask, 286
disc jockey, hiring
  advantages, 275–276
  fees, 276
  list of DJs in your area,
    277–278
  specialties, 277
  wedding DJs, 277
  when and where to start
    searching, 276–277
disc jockey terms to know,
  278–279
discount bridal service
  about, 104
  bridesmaids' dresses, 104
Dittler, Robert, 174
do it yourself
  bouquet, create simple hand-
    tied, 230–231
  floral terms, 229–230

pew decorations, create your
  own, 230
rose bowl centerpiece for
  wedding reception, create,
  231–232
when to do it yourself and
  where to find it, 228
dollars matching dreams
  early planning stages, 18
  geographical regions and
    wedding costs, 18–19

E

"Easy Steps to Flower
  Arranging" (California
  Cut Flower Commission),
  228
Entertainment Book, 303
Ernst, Robbi, *xix,* 212
expectations, clarifying
  expectations exercise, 3
  wedding expectations work-
    sheet, 5–8

F

Family Circle magazine, *xix*
favors and accessories
  about, 151–152
  do-it-yourself, ideas for, 155
  inexpensive favors, ideas for,
    154
  popular accessories, ways to
    save, 156–160
  resources for unique, 160–162
  wedding favors, ways to save,
    152–153

getting organized, about,
35–36
organization game plan,
36–39
planning it yourself or hiring
consultant, 36
top 50 shortcuts to savings,
45–53
gifts for attendants, ways to save
about, 125
female attendants, 126–127
male attendants, 127
Gourmet magazine, 200, 245
Great Wedding Tips (Ernst), 212
guest list, making his, hers, and
theirs, 135
guest tables, size needed, 196

H
Harrison, Jeff, 280
heirloom gown, wearing
cleaning or refurbishing,
108–109
cleaning or remaking
yourself, 110
common questions to ask
about restoring and
repairing gown, 111
common things you can do,
111
options for alterations or
makeover, 109
refreshing or remaking,
109–110
remaking or repairing, advice,
109–111

reputable person or company
to repair or restore gown,
finding and questions to
ask, 110–111
Hockin, Christine, 212
Hodges, Michelle, 218
home, staying close to, 304
honeymoon
accommodations, ways to
save, 301–304
airfare savvy, 298–304
cruises, 305–307
"honeymoon" spots, avoiding,
297–298
staying close to home, 304
train and airline passes,
304–305
travel agent, finding
knowledgeable, 296–297
wary consumer, 307–308
honeymoon cruises
extra expenses to keep in
mind, 306–307
ways to save onboard, 306
"honeymoon" spots, avoiding
about, 297
popular honeymoon
destinations, 297–298
*How to Avoid DJ Horror Stories:
The Standard Reference
Guide for Brides, Party
Planners and Anyone Else
in the Market for a Mobile
Disc Jockey* (Harrison), 280
How to Buy a Diamond
(Tiffany & Co.), 88

Y

Praise for Jesse Ball's

A CURE FOR SUICIDE

"Captivating. . . . Ball's lean, clinical prose puts us in mind of Samuel Beckett, and his heady concoction of unsettling atmosphere, sterile environments and authorial obfuscations and distortions is redolent of the potent brew that powered recent dark fables from Chang-rae Lee and Howard Jacobson. . . . Refreshingly unconventional, the novel sees a highly original writer take another left-field leap in a daring and rewarding direction."   —*Minneapolis Star Tribune*

"Ball deftly explores questions with the eye of a poet and the logic of a philosopher, revealing new facets with perfect timing and acuity."   —*The New York Times Book Review*

"A rich, tragic love story. . . . An enthralling thought experiment that considers the value of memory versus the pain of grief."
                                                —*The Huffington Post*

"The juxtaposition of the commonplace and the darkly bizarre has become something of a specialty of [Ball's], as has his books' skill at reflecting the ongoing struggle of the individual in a society based on conformity."   —*Chicago Tribune*

"Both a puzzle box and a haunting love story. . . . Whatever the source of this book's elusive magic, it should cement Ball's reputation as a technical innovator whose work delivers a powerful emotional impact."
                                    —*Publishers Weekly* (starred review)

"Profound. . . . Ball performs the remarkable task of pruning away layers of readerly skepticism in order to find the inherent beauty of small moments."   —*Flavorwire*

"A vision of a society that flees from hurt, numbing the tormented in order to save them." —*The Atlantic*

"Prompts a conversation about life—how we enter it, how we navigate its shoals, and how we exit it."
—*New York Journal of Books*

"A spare, spooky, muffled realm of continual surveillance and absolute control. . . . Ball slyly exposes the survival-focused aspects of human interactions, from small talk to shared meals." —*Booklist*

"Elegant and spooky, dystopian and poetic." —*The Millions*

"*A Cure for Suicide* ponders memory, identity, love, desire and choice. The question that remains is a heavy one indeed: Would you choose to start over?" —*Paste*